LETTERS HOME

REFLECTIONS OF A MARINE RIFLEMAN

GEORGE BERG

Publishing assistance by BookCrafters, Parker, Colorado.
www.bookcrafters.net

June 1968
76

July 1968
118

THE DREAM IS ALWAYS THE SAME.

The darkness closes in around me rapidly. The air temperature drops steadily, like a slow-moving theater curtain. The twilight catches a light grey mist rising gracefully from the warm, moist sand in loose billowing spirals. I lay there regulating my breathing, trying to keep my heart from pounding through my chest and rolling across the granular black volcanic sand. There, on the beach beside me, is a dead Marine, one of the hundreds who died there on that sand spit - the Japanese island of Iwo Jima. It was February 19, 1945. The dead Marine's hand still tightly clutches his carbine. His face, turned sideways to me, is partially buried in the sand. I slowly reach over, grab the dog tags from around his neck, and quietly read them out loud, "Berg, G.P., 2380364, 0, USMC, S, EPISCOPALIAN." I was looking at myself.

"Think of yourself as dead. You have lived your life. Now take what's left and live it properly."
— Aurelius

Jacksonville, Florida (circa 1950s)

PROLOGUE

Hello, I Love You – The Doors

I WAS VERY SUCCESSFUL IN MY WORK as a management consultant. Overall, except for the pain of divorce, I was content with how my life had turned out. I was comfortable, even happy, except for the occasional thoughts of the war that lingered – mostly at night.

Some of that changed on a rainy Saturday afternoon (1999) when the mail carrier delivered a package from my mother. I opened it slowly, carefully, so as not to damage the contents. I expected treats – cookies and candies. Instead I found, neatly bundled and tied with a narrow ribbon, all the letters I had written to my family while I was in the U.S. Marine Corps in Vietnam.

Sitting alone in an old comfortable chair in the back room of my home in Denver, Colorado, I read each of the letters over and over again – and remembered. In time I recognized how much I had either forgotten or suppressed about my tour of duty in Vietnam. I also realized that many of my memories collided with the words written on those pages of letters. This epiphany released, like water from a dammed stream, the realization that my war experience had been much different than I was allowing myself to remember. The striking differences between my memories and the letters prompted me to write to the Marine Corps Historical Center at the Washington Navy Yard and request declassified after-action reports for my unit. I obtained detailed maps (Universal Transverse Mercator Grid) of Vietnam from the U.S. Geological Survey at the Denver Federal Center; and my medical records, which helped me, remember the four months I spent in the hospitals in Vietnam, Japan, and at the Great Lakes Naval Hospital near Chicago, Illinois.

After reading the reports, it soon became apparent that each of my sources -- my memory, the letters and the reports – contained its own shade of truth. The Marine Corps records were bland, technical descriptions. My letters sugarcoated conditions in order to spare my parents grief and suffering. I had carefully guarded against telling them about my own abject fears and had definitely withheld information about my transformation from Boy to Marine to Warrior. Despite the problems of each of my resources, I was determined to patch together what had really happened to me and the Marines I fought with in the summer of 1968. Over time, the accuracy of my memories became doubtful, even to myself. I was either forgetting or unknowingly masking the realities of my war experience.

I realized that the way we remember evolves over time. Even memories of major, life-altering events erode over the years, influenced or even subconsciously altered, randomly, unpredictably, and how we want to remember. The memories I have of my experiences in the Vietnam war had been affected in this way. The memories had become twisted and turned, transformed into memories that I was no longer sure of.

We rely on memories to remind us who we are. They help define us and give us clues about our personalities and the choices we make. However, like a broken mirror, our memories can reflect distorted and fragmented images - some clear and others blurred. Memories are indispensable and yet notoriously untrustworthy. They can be inaccurate, misleading and sometimes completely false.

I had been resolutely struggling to put my memories to paper for some time, and when searching the internet, I stumbled onto a web site memorializing a Lance Corporal from the 27th Marines – my Regiment in Vietnam. The site had a link. On it I found an e-mail address for Lloyd Fernung, one of my squad leaders in Vietnam. Lloyd had been wounded and medically evacuated ("medevac") on June 5, 1968. I e-mailed him and he responded quickly. We were both outwardly delighted, although I was apprehensive; my uncertainty about the realities of the war tugged at me. Lloyd telephoned and we talked for an hour or so, trying to put faces, names, and places together. He said he heard I had died of my wounds in the hospital. He was only partially correct.

I found it oddly reassuring that our recollections did not always match. I felt somehow vindicated that my memories were as fallible as I believed them to be. We both had a lot of blanks to fill in. Lloyd sent me photographs of his squad. Mine was among the young faces peering out of the faded yellowing prints.

What follows is the story of the journey a platoon of Marines took in the summer of 1968 – a journey to a very intimate relationship with the ground. It is a story of innocence and conviction and a story of metamorphosis, doubt, redemption, grace and joy. There are many stories like it, to be sure but this one is mine. All of the anecdotes in this story are as true as my imperfect memory and reminiscences allow. Some of the vignettes may be out of order, but the sequence is not important to the telling of the story, which is essentially recapturing the flavor of the summer of 1968 in a Marine infantry unit in Vietnam. The dialogue portrays typical language and is paraphrased. The "f" word was deleted as much as possible, although it was an integral part of Marine Corps life. The language is reconstructed in the military vernacular of the day – the way Marines talk to each other. Some names are blurred to avoid embarrassment, however the people referenced, if they were to read them, would recognize the accounts, flattering or not. I traveled to Vietnam and retraced some of my wartime experiences by visiting Da Nang and Go Noi Island. I studied the climate, topography, and geology of that area from textbooks and reviewed some of the nonfiction literature of the Vietnam War. I read accounts from other books written about the 27th Marines and communicated with other members of *Charlie Company*. In addition, I attended reunions of *Charlie Company* in Gettysburg, Pennsylvania, Fort Worth, Texas, and Knoxville, Tennessee. We were older, wiser, but even after many years it was evident that we were all still Marines. It was also evident that we belonged to an unofficial brotherhood, the brotherhood of the survivors. We had done whatever it took to survive the brutalities and hostilities of the Vietnam War. We had also done whatever it took to survive the brutalities and hostilities of returning home, as we tried to assimilate back into a culture where we were often hated and reviled by our peers. Much of what follows was confirmed at those reunions.

I have put this story to paper for many reasons—to clear up unresolved memories but most importantly, so my daughters – Jennifer Anne and Kristen Anne Berg – might understand their father and why I raised them as I did, the best I could, from a distance as a divorced dad – as a Marine. Many of the values I wanted my daughters to believe in and hold dear were passed on to me from a Midwestern farm-raised Mother and a deep-South Father, rather than from my service in the U.S. Marine Corps and combat in Vietnam. However, some of my beliefs were certainly shaped there as well.

Honor, courage, and commitment are chief among the things I wanted my daughters to believe in and demonstrate. I also wanted them to be strong and brave in their daily lives. Through my parenting, albeit mostly part time, I tried to encourage perseverance—the idea of never, ever giving up, even in the face of the most difficult circumstances—and to always maintain their bearing in response to adversity—to keep their poise and maintain a positive attitude. Most of all, I hoped my daughters would be leaders. The most difficult of skills is to lead and to inspire people to want to follow. I wanted my daughters to develop that skill and have faith in their abilities, even when they were unclear about whether or not they were qualified to do so; to ignore gender and get people to want to follow either of them was the dream I held for my daughters.

When they were four and six years old, I would throw a stone to the bottom of the 10-foot deep end at the community swimming pool and make them dive in to retrieve it. They could swim and play only after they brought the stone to the surface. Later, that activity evolved into scuba school in a municipal water reservoir in Colorado which was both cold and muddy, and eventually into night diving in Kona, Hawaii at 60 feet to experience the giant manta rays feeding on plankton. I filled their lives with rigorous challenges, and with love and support; from long forced-marches in the rain and snow in Estes Park, Colorado, to repelling, rock climbing, and weekend camping trips on Colorado's 12,000 foot high mountains, along with the boisterous support I gave them at; baseball, track, basketball, tennis, and swim meets since they were four and six years old. I gave them equally boisterous demands of home schooling in the arts of boxing and tae-kwon-do—punching and kicking pillows and the open palms of my hands – *jab-jab-hook-cross!*

They were kissed, loved, and hugged but they were also driven by their father to excel in whatever they tried to do. They received measured amounts of kindness and affection, but were also pushed to the limit when skiing at Aspen, Snowmass, Crested Butte, Monarch, Winter Park and Breckenridge, and some of the smaller, obscure out-of-the-way places like Eldora, Chuchara, and Wolf Creek. *"Be like me-ski like me"* or *"Get off the brakes!"* and *"Yank 'em and crank 'em and twist 'em both ways!"* resounded across the mountains as I cajoled them to ski faster.

They unwittingly tolerated the recapitulation of my war experience through elk hunting. They endured hunter safety and the rifle range with "papa bear" - their hunter safety instructor. We shared books on tracking elk. The hunting trips damn near killed us all as we sat in long, cold, wet ambushes waiting for the elk. The endless walks back to camp in pitch darkness, or low crawling through dew, rain, lightning storms and blizzards, as well as through the sagebrush, scrub oak and aspen groves. We spent hours just listening in silence. They learned to tell the sex of the animal and the season from elk "poops." I also taught them hand signals: raised fist for *freeze*, point to the eye for *I see elk*, and raised forefinger and little fingers for *it's a bull.*

They experienced the unbelievable rush of adrenaline when an elk was spotted. They heard, at an early age, the eerie shrill of the bull elk bugling in the frosty fall mornings through the mountains of Estes Park, Aspen, and Steamboat, Colorado. They witnessed the ball of red and orange fire blasted from the end of a muzzle-loader, and the acrid smell of exploding black powder. They helped drag the bloody elk carcass for what seemed like endless miles with cold, wet feet and, finally, they assisted with the slow, meticulous dissection of the elk. The girls did all this because their dad said it was a good idea. They withstood it all, even sitting high up on some rocky escarpment, watching a storm roll in with their dad just because I wanted them to. We sat motionless as the autumn rain and sleet began to hit their small faces, but no one moved. "Cowboy up, girls – it's tough time. We're elk hunting."

No one ever moved or complained. The raindrops rinsed the sweat from our faces. They were Marines (albeit little ones), and we were special. We didn't move. We didn't flinch. And the storm wouldn't dare rain on our set. So we fixed bayonets and stood by in place. Our combat focus preserved. As the storms moved on, very often the elk remained unaware of our presence on a rocky ridge massif above them. Together, we could watch the elk for hours. I hope this account of my journey through warfare helps my daughters understand the childhood they experienced with their father – their own U.S. Marine Corps-style boot camp and what I've come to call my war in Vietnam. These two beautiful and strong women are my heart and soul – I hope this helps them understand their dad.

BEGINNINGS

Jumpin' Jack Flash - Mick Jagger/Keith Richards

~ DIXON, ILLINOIS ~

I WAS BORN GEORGE PHILIP BERG on November 8, 1947 in the small Midwestern town of Dixon, Illinois, situated on the willful but relentlessly slow, muddy Rock River. In certain ways, that river would become the river of my heart. Dixon is a city of merchants, light manufacturing, and farming—one of those towns where everybody knows everybody. Dixon is also well-known as the boyhood home of President Ronald Reagan. The Rock River divides the 16,000 people of the town into "south-siders" and "north-siders," with the absolute "cruds" and the "elite" coming from only a few families. Financially, Dixon was made up of a few rich families and a few families who were poor, but the vast majority fell comfortably somewhere in the middle. My family was one of those in the comfortable middle.

My father, a U.S. Air Force enlisted man, was born and raised in Jacksonville, Florida until he was fourteen, when he ran away from his abusive father and joined the shrimp fleet that fished off the southern coast of Florida, near Cuba. At age seventeen he enlisted in the United States Army and was assigned to the Air Corps. My mother was originally from a small town in northern Illinois called Lee Center. It consists of a grain elevator and a few houses and is located near the towns of Amboy and Dixon. Early in life I had the good fortune of being exposed to certain saving, powerful influences. Those influences included Midwestern, self-reliant, farm values and the ease and grace of the South.

When I was young, we traveled a lot like all military families tend to do. We were blessed with the opportunity to see the world, but were also burdened with the necessity of being uprooted every three or four years in order to do it. We experienced our fair share of inconsistency and push-pull in our young lives but, with few exceptions, we all enjoyed moving. It gave us the sense that nothing was ever over. Our experiences, friends, games, and childhoods were constantly expanding. Everything was refreshed and new, but conclusions were hard to come by. Our lives were built in layers, one lamination on another. We all gained strengths and weaknesses as a result, in different places and in different ways. The prime constant in my childhood was playing Army or *Cowboys and Indians* – still politically correct in the 1950s. Play guns and miniature plastic army men filled my toy chest.

Arguably, I received the best qualities of both my father and mother. My special gift was the enjoyment and exuberance for life. Life was, and continues to be, exciting and I understood fun. What I wasn't blessed with was academic prowess. I was an academic underachiever – to be merciful. A grade of "C" on any report card was a relief for me and was gratefully accepted by my parents because of its familiarity. We all just got used to it.

I played basketball with passion and planned on playing my way through college as a point guard, but was told I was too old to play my senior year of high school because I had repeated the eighth grade more than once. The joke at our house was that the only reason I got out of the eighth grade at all was because I was shaving, had a driver's license and was getting ready to vote. With basketball and the chance of earning a scholarship to college out of the realm of possibility, my new focus became football, which I was still eligible to play my senior year. I had played quarterback my freshman year in an all-white segregated high school in Smyrna, Georgia in 1963. We moved to Dixon, Illinois in 1964, the summer after the end of my freshman year, and I played quarterback on the high school football team for the next three years with various degrees of success.

My father decided to end his military career with one last tour of duty in Europe, so my parents separated. My mother, brothers, sister, and I would miss his quiet influence, steady hand and easy-does-it attitude at a time when, for me at least, they were needed the most. My father was an enigma, like so many dads. He served the purpose of a place holder, like an old dog warming by the fireplace. He returned to be a strong, loving influence on my younger brother and sister – something I missed.

Off and on throughout high school I kept the same beautiful and bright girlfriend. She was one school year younger than I. Like most adolescent males, I had no clue about how to treat a girl and she suffered from my being stupid, inconsiderate and self-centered – the archetype American high school male in the mid '60s. I ran for senior class president and won, was voted best dancer in my senior class, was an understudy cast member in *West Side Story*, and was a runner-up for funniest and best personality. Out of necessity I attended summer school and, to the relief of everyone, was able to graduate in May of 1967. My only goal at graduation was to maintain my sense of adventure. The vagabond seed, planted in my youth, had taken root. The war in Vietnam was intensifying, and I wanted to be a Marine. After all, what better way to escape my small town, validate my developing manhood, and become part of the grand adventure, the last great anti-

communist war – or so many of us thought at the time. As many of my better prepared classmates went off to primarily Midwestern colleges and universities,

I attended a brand-new junior college, Sauk Valley Community College. As luck would have it, it wasn't a rewarding experience. School, once again, was just plain boring, especially compared to the rapidly polarizing cultural and political situations occurring in the summer of 1967 – juicers, freaks, heads, frats, geeks, and jocks. The existing social norms were fracturing and we were all choosing sides. Rock and Roll music and drugs were both becoming harder. The most popular bands of the era— Jimi Hendrix, The Byrd's, The Stones, The Beatles, and Cream, were all inviting us to try pot, hallucinogenic drugs (LSD), to drop out and rail against the oppressive, lifeless middleclass values of our parents. We were all playing bumper cars with our lives.

In Vietnam the war was rapidly escalating, with the toughest, most brutal fighting occurring in the Northern provinces of South Vietnam. The war was ramping up in 1967. By December 485,600 troops would be in country and by 1968 more than 100,000 U.S. Marines were engaged with the North Vietnamese Army (NVA) that was heavily armed and well trained. Every day young American Marines were fighting for their very lives, and many were being seriously wounded or were dying at rates four times that of World War II Marines. Newspapers and, for the first time, television were sending stories back home delayed by only a few hours. The lure of joining a highly publicized televised war, coupled with patriotism, family tradition and a ready escape from a small Midwestern town, became irresistible.

I thought going to war would help me connect the dots from my past to my future. My great great-great-grandfather fought with Parmelle's Rangers in Vermont in the Revolutionary War. My great-great-grandfathers fought in the Civil War for both the north and the south. In 1917, thirty years before I was born, my grandfather, a University of Wisconsin student, was also tempted by the seductive call to arms. He served as a fighter pilot in World War I first in the Canadian infantry and then in the U.S. Army Air Corps and will forever be the standard in our family of a war hero. He had two sons who entered the military during World War II. Uncle Gordon joined the Navy Seabees (CB - construction battalion) and built military structures, mainly landing strips, while fighting alongside Marines in the islands of the South Pacific during World War II. He became another family idol for his exploits of island-hopping after the Marines to places like Okinawa, New Caledonia supporting the famous battle for Guadalcanal. My namesake, Uncle George and my father both joined the Army Air Corps. My father was a tail gunner on a B-17, but because of a crash landing in training, his good looks, charm, and considerable verbal skills he was spared the messy inconvenience of combat and was assigned to recruiting and public relations duty - work he never regretted. My forefathers were full of fervid democracy, its inventiveness, its resourcefulness, enterprise, and good sense.

Members of my mother's well-to-do northern Republican family, however resented that my southern Democratic father did not fully participate in a combat role in World War II, and they labeled him a lazy Southern slacker, among other things. As a very small boy, I sat on my father's lazy lap, listened to his lazy sea stories, and lazily watched hours of *Victory at*

Sea and *The Story of Iwo Jima* – reel after reel with my slow-talking, southern drawl father. I thought he was fun, and intelligent and enjoyed his reserve.

But my decision to join the Marine Corps was not an easy one. For months, I mulled over the consequences. I would listen to The Byrd's greatest hits album and the song *Eight Miles High* over and over again, thinking about the possibility of going to war. Then, on one clear fall day, while driving to class at Sauk Valley College, with the *Dixon Evening Telegraph* newspaper resting on the seat next to me, I became mesmerized by the large, grainy black and white photograph on the front page. It showed beleaguered Marines in torn uniforms, with dirty faces partially hidden under tilted helmets at an artillery firebase in Vietnam.

There in the grainy photograph they were, frozen in time, captured and preserved forever by the journalist's camera, surrounded by dust hanging in the air as they lugged massive artillery rounds toward the breach of a 155-millimeter howitzer. They had squinting eyes, the fixed gaze of snarling pit bulls. They appeared too tired to stand, too fatigued to care.

I pulled over onto the shoulder of Illinois Route 2 and fell vividly into the details of the photograph. The image of those Marines reverberated around and around in my mind. I saw myself with perfect clarity as one of them. After a few moments I jerked the car back onto the highway, made an abrupt U-turn, both on the road and in my life, went to see with the Marine Corps recruiter, and enlisted the next day.

I felt an excitement well up inside me as my capacity for violence seemed imminent. Soon I would be certified to go to the edge of the human experience, to the remote margins that maniacs and infantry Marines inhabit. The dusty cobwebs of childhood war games became one of the cables that pulled me toward Vietnam. The other was the possibility of defining new dimensions for my life – the bliss of sheer becoming.

That evening, I was riding on the north side of town. As I rounded a corner, the driver in an old convertible cut me off and forced me into a ditch. I wheeled around and caught up with him at a stop sign. I pulled up behind him, jumped out of my car, ran up to the driver's side window and sucker-punched him on the side of the head. His head slumped to the steering wheel. Satisfied, I calmly walked back to my car and drove off. I was intoxicated with the promise of invincibility that enlisting in the Marines provided. I was changing; part of me was leaving for an audacious journey. I did not know how I would change in the following months or what I'd see or do. I had no idea. I was activated in the Marines with a buddy, Dave Baux (who became a decorated Marine scout/ sniper), on my birthday, November 8, 1967. Within a few days I would be in San Diego, California, and Marine Corps boot camp.

United States Marine Corps

Certificate of Acceptance

This is to certify that _____ GEORGE PHILLIP BERG _____ has successfully passed the required mental, moral and physical examinations and has been accepted for enlistment in the United States Marine Corps.

The defense of our country and our freedoms is the duty and privilege of every citizen. The Marine Corps has a proud tradition of outstanding service to our country in peace and war. Voluntary enlistment in this elite military organization is a clear demonstration of those American qualities of patriotism and loyalty to God and country.

Presented this _____ 8th _____ day of _____ November _____ ,19 _ 67 _.

By the Officer In Charge
Marine Corps Recruiting Station

NAVMC 6648 (Rev.)

BASIC TRAINING

Bend Me, Shape Me - The American Breed

~ U.S. Marine Corps Boot Camp ~

After a short, uncomfortable bus ride from Dixon to Des Moines, Iowa, a not so short but slightly more comfortable plane ride to San Diego, and a perfectly calculated and timed midnight bus ride from the San Diego Airport to the gates of the recruit depot, I was there: Marine Corps Recruit Depot, San Diego, California.

Marine Corps boot camp begins with a brief, screaming orientation aboard the bus that drops you off at the receiving barracks. A series of incomprehensible instructions, the only one of which we understood was the shout of "GO," sent us scurrying from the bus into a mad dash to occupy the yellow footprints painted on the asphalt in the dimly lit courtyard in front of the receiving barracks. The footprints were stenciled on the ground, heels locked together in the correct position of attention – a position we would all come to understand.

The perfectly planned and orchestrated indoctrinations into the Marine Corps are precise, immediate, and fierce. Drill Instructors (DIs) yell to intimidate, their voices cracking like snapping whips, their eyes flashing, riveting into you with a fixed glare. They twist their heads into your face and burn holes in your eyes at point blank range, bulging veins popping out of their necks. There is no escape from their will or their wrath; you are snared in a trap you volunteered to be in. DIs are in the business of traumatically amputating part of your soul and replacing it over time with a new reconstituted being – you, reinvented as a Marine.

If there's even a second's hesitation in any movement you are immediately set upon, the DI's rage overwhelming your every sense. The sometimes erratic gait and jerky motions of the DIs imply they are unpredictable and volatile, and will go off at the slightest provocation. At Drill Instructor school they are taught to use these fractious, darting movements to make recruits feel insecure, very insecure. We quickly learned to pay attention and respond to everything, every detail, every sound, and every smell. The DIs were getting us ready to survive war. We were just trying to survive boot camp.

The distinctive voice of a U.S. Marine Drill Instructor penetrates beneath your skin, lodges between your muscle and bone, where it resonates. This distinctive voice is learned and cultivated at DI School. It is a training aid – a tool. The voice is also somewhat homogeneous

– all Marine Corps Drill Instructors sound like inbred cousins from the same family in southwestern Arkansas.

Our heads were shaved, and our civilian clothes were traded in for military issue. We were given a briefing about our duties and obligations as recruits and were lined up to wait for the DIs assigned to our platoon. Then they appeared – rigid and impressive – the archetypal Marine. They were introduced, gave a small speech about our responsibilities, and then they dispersed into the crowd of slack-jawed civilian scum – us.

Thinking for a moment that I could outsmart and beat this madness, I slipped the strap of my large canvas sea bag full of my newly issued gear – clothes, toothbrush, and a soap dish – off my shoulder and onto the floor to rest. The DIs were all busy ravaging some poor slob down the line who had screwed up in some minuscule way. I thought, momentarily, that I had this Marine Corps stuff wired – *hell, this ain't so hard*. No sooner had the thought entered my mind than I was beset by the Senior Drill Instructor. He was up close and in my face, screaming something about pulling some cheap-ass shit and then instantaneously, his clenched fist slammed into the space halfway between my eyes and the center of my forehead with a loud smacking thud.

"Pick that gear up, you fucking maggot," he screamed and punched his right forefinger at me, jabbing me in the upper chest. The gesture punctuated and drove home the true meaning of Marine Corps boot camp – Dante's Inferno, a literal hell on earth – and I'd only been there two hours. There were thirteen long, grueling weeks to go. The change in us that the Marine Corps had promised had begun. Change or be damned. We were being reduced to the meat our parents made.

"God," I asked, "What have I got myself into?" Maybe this time I had swam too far from shore. There was no escape. Boot Camp is a factory – basic Marines the product. I quickly decided to surrender to the processing and allow myself to become a highly disciplined instrument of U.S. national and foreign policy – a gung ho Marine. Would this transformation free me of the consequences of my actions? Would I then be able to commit acts of violence without the usual sanctions visited by society? How would I deal with the absence of feeling and perform without responding emotionally as I might have before? Could I escape, irresponsibly, into the extreme experience of the Marine Corps?

Person for person, possibly the most dangerous group on the planet is the United States Marine Corps; heavily armed, well trained, motivated, psychotic teenagers. The Marine Corps is the perfect amalgam of vicious street gang and college fraternity. I would gradually learn that Marines are a unique warrior

NOU. 10

UNITED STATES MARINE CORPS
"Semper Fidelis"

Dear JOANNE,

I AM Hear IN San Diego
I AM fine, I will have
more time to write IN 1
day (Later) I LIKE IT.

Please do not send anything
in your Letter Please gum
Candy Nothing

Please do not write anything
on outside of envelope but address.

you must have a return
address on all letters

THis is my mailing address write
it LIKE it is

Everything IN this Letter is important

PVT. Berg, George P. 2380364
PLT. 3309
"K" Co. 3rd BN.
R.T.R. M.C.R.D
San Diego, California
              92140

"semper fidelis"
always faithful

George

P.S. Say hi To mom
         give here This Letter

cult, with loyalty being the cohesive thread that stitches the Marine Corps together. What sets Marines apart from other branches of the U.S. military are their ethos, spirit, character, history and values. All Marine officers and enlisted folks must pass the same test, basic training – boot camp – which creates a very specific lore, and legend has it, a common bond. I was to learn later the absoluteness and truth of this axiom.

My experience in boot camp was as fearful as anyone else's had been in the storied history of the Corps, but I was ready physically and absorbed the emotional and psychological battering well enough. I did not want to fail; it was a fear I had at the molecular level. I could not have withstood the shame of returning home to hear, *couldn't make it, couldn't hack it.*

After a few weeks, I could see I would be OK but was surprised that I could actually learn the academic subjects in a classroom – maybe I wasn't stupid after all. That is what I had really been learning in civilian schools—that I was dumb, based on the types of intelligence being measured and emphasized by standardized testing, administered in standardized educational institutions.

I did well in basic training, but others were not so lucky. A few went crazy and tried to jump the tall chain link fence, crowned with coiled, razor-sharp barbed wire that surrounded the training depot. The escapees usually "ran" at night, only to get caught and be sent to motivational or correctional custody training platoons. A few got injured or could not keep up academically. One chubby Hispanic, who decided he did not want to be a Marine and who desperately wanted to go home, said he was homosexual, and he may have been, who knows. For his confession he was placed in the middle of a circle formed by the entire platoon in the sand outside the Quonset hut area, and was beaten to a pulp by anyone in the training platoon who wanted to take a few shots at the helpless "f-----," as he begged for mercy on his knees. Not many recruits put on the black leather gloves to take their turn, but nevertheless, the *"queer"* recruit was beaten to the point of tears and submission. The sobbing, ruined boy was hauled away in an ambulance. This was a world of this - not that. The American ideals of freedom and choice were now suspended, distant, unattainable concepts.

I learned fast, a new experience for someone who was most likely afflicted with Attention Deficit Hyperactivity Disorder and Dyslexia. Or maybe I was like many boys in school, just young, easily bored, and under-challenged in the care of mostly women, or men who acted like women? The Marine Corps fixes all that.

Contrary to official training doctrine, we were encouraged to study after lights out. We were issued pen light flashlights and ordered to commit to memory the history of the Marine Corp, our General Orders, all the nomenclature of the M-14 rifle, and anything else the DIs could cook up. These details and the focus on perfection were training us for the ultimate military experience, where failure would have dire and immediate consequences. I excelled, learned quickly, and impressed the Drill Instructors.

Part of the secret to success at Marine Corps Boot Camp is that everyone volunteered to be there and actually *wanted* the transformation from civilian to Marine to occur. It's not magic, it's just terribly uncomfortable. Because I had some college (60 days or so) and had scored well on the military aptitude tests, I was asked to consider officer candidate school in Quantico, Virginia. I respectfully declined the offer, to the dismay of my senior Drill Instructor. I declined because of the extraordinary level of commitment required to be a Marine officer and to have the power of a God over the lives of other Marines. That was beyond my comprehension and imagination - to be in that much command of myself.

The training days started at 4:30 a.m. Each "T-day" was a new, more demanding challenge: hand-washing clothes, military history, rules and regulations, endless physical conditioning, shaving, bathing, learning how to clean yourself in the field and correctly use toilet paper, hand-to-hand combat, and relentless marching in close order drills on the parade deck called the "Grinder." The proper technique for securing and satisfying airline stewardesses – flight attendants now – was a special feature class. Yes, we received instruction on that too, the Marine Corps way – Gung Ho, *Oorah*! The berating never ceased, never let up. We would be converted or be damned. (The new *"Oorah"* and old Gung Ho are Marine Corps speak that adds emphasis or agreement and is a form of punctuation.)

~ MESS HALL ~

Like everything else in boot camp, eating was regulated. A violation of any procedure would result in our being forced to "get down" and march into the chow hall suspended on our knuckles and toes – a painful appetizer. Once inside the expansive chow hall, we were served the bill of fare *de jour*, as we slid sideways in a synchronized lockstep down the chow line. Then, we had to stand at attention, after putting our trays of food on the table, and wait until we were given the order to sit down - "Ready, seats!"

We would respond by sitting down in perfect unison, so vigorously that our knees would fly up and hit the underside of the table, sending silverware flying in every direction. Sitting at attention, forbidden to reach down and pick up our; knives, forks, and spoons, we were ordered to "Get that good Marine Corps chow in your skuzzy mouths – now!" We pounded the food into our mouths with both hands.

Early on in boot camp we had less than five minutes to eat. Kicking the bottoms of the table to knock off the silverware was a sport until the DIs grew bored with it and made us stop and eat with our utensils. In the first few days of boot camp a few of the candidate Marines made the unfortunate mistake of regurgitating their meals. To discourage the practice they were forced to their knees and made to study their waste of U.S. Government property. A few were made to put their faces into the globs of creamy, stinking bile and partially chewed meat and potatoes. Many would never vomit again.

~ FAST SHOWERS ~

On board ship fast showers are necessary to conserve water, save time, and allow a dense population of Sailors and Marines to be supplied with basic hygiene in a quick and efficient manner. Talking without permission is prohibited in Boot Camp, and no exceptions are made in the shower and head. Naturally, it was a rule we broke, and usually paid the price for doing it. Drill Instructors, students of human nature, understand the predictable behavioral patterns of Recruits and are ready, willing and able to provide consequences for any infraction. It is all very calculated.

One day, when we whispered in the showers, the immaculately dressed Drill Sergeant rushed through the various streams of water, throwing sand all over us and screaming, "Oh, so you filthy maggots want to talk do you? You fucking pukes!"

He made us wash each other's backs and arms with the gritty mixture of soap and sand. We were exfoliated and hushed all at the same time. We talked much less after that.

~ KING RAT ~

Four high school buddies from California, who all worked on a plum farm in the central valley of California, decided to join the Marine Corps on the *buddy system*. The four had been friends their entire lives, had done everything together and now would endure boot camp together. The smallest of the four was of Japanese descent, the son of the plum farm owner and the unofficial leader of the pack. Because he was small in stature the Drill Instructors had chosen him to be their house mouse – errand boy, servant, valet, pissing post, boy Friday, shoe shiner and the person expected to perform any number of demeaning chores.

Drill Instructors made a sport of ridiculing their diminutive house mice. To summon their serfs to perform some domestic task, they would yell, "House Mouse!"

"Sir, House Mouse, aye-aye sir!" the entire platoon was obligated to reply, and the House Mice would scramble to do the bidding of the DI, or face punishment.

One evening the DIs were bored and decided to wager on which House Mouse could whip the other Platoon's House Mouse – a sort of human cockfight. Being beaten in this no-holds-barred fight would just add to the humiliation already heaped upon these future Marines, so the stakes were high. The human cockfight was held in the privacy of the DIs duty hut after "lights out." He knew judo and some karate and was able to quickly take out all the opponents, first one, then the other and then the third. Without rest he was forced to fight two at a time. He was finally beaten when, already exhausted, he was forced to fight all three of the other House Mice at the same time.

After that night, in honor of his fighting skill and courage, he was knighted King Rat. He was never called House Mouse again and received an escort of a jeep and machine gunner whenever he reported to the Drill Instructor. The jeep, in actuality, was another Private who had to run in front of King Rat, making horn-honking, beep-beep sounds to clear the way. The machine gunner was another Private who had to run in circles around the King Rat, imitating the rat-a-tat-tat sounds of a machine gun. The rest of us were forbidden from laughing, even though it was a hilarious sight. Squirming, we held back our laughter.

~ TRAIN, TRAIN NEVER STOP — TOUGH AS NAILS — HARD AS ROCK ~

The pace of Boot Camp is unremitting. Training, conscience-altering, and exercise are packed into our everyday routine nonstop. If someone fell asleep in an indoor training class, the entire platoon would be ordered to the floor, beneath their desks or worktables, where we had to bang our heads on the underside of the work surface. It sounded like buffaloes stampeding. It proved to be another efficient training technique, as we tended to stay awake after a head pounding.

~ CLEAR THE HEAD ~

We were also required to go to the toilet – which is called the head in the Navy and Marine Corps – in less than five minutes. That is more than sixty men, using only ten toilets, and all of us having to be finished in less than five minutes. The order was shouted, "Platoon 3309, clear the head."

"Sir Platoon 3309 clear the head, aye, aye sir!" we would bellow in reply, knowing the order meant that we had ten seconds to finish our business and be on the street in formation, or suffer, which usually consisted of being exercised into exhaustion. On one particular day, when the clear the head order was given, sixty some eager, excited bodies hit the 6'8" X 8' exit at the same time, lodging ourselves in the door opening, totally stuck. The human wedge was packed tight, recruits crushed by other recruits, all trying blindly to comply with the order. The pressure was so great that the doorjamb splintered on both sides of the frame. It bowed, allowing a few recruits, including me, to slip out of the side of the pile. The next time the clear the head order was given, we were a lot more organized and a little less enthusiastic.

~Edson Range ~

The rifle range at Camp Pendleton, up the California coast from San Diego, is one of the defining moments in the transition from civilian to U.S. Marine. It is at Edson Range where we were to learn the science of marksmanship – the Marine Corps way.

For this specialized training we moved all our gear, in trucks, from San Diego to Oceanside and Camp Pendleton where we spent hours on the range practicing, cleaning, and shooting our M-14 rifles. We were told that the rifle was our best girlfriend. Each person had a Personal Marksmanship Instructor (PMI) who helped us with our shooting skills. These instructors wore pith helmets on the range. They were a group of more relaxed specialists who served a different role than the immaculately dressed Drill Instructors, who wore their signature, wide-brimmed campaign hats, called Smokey the Bear hats. The range instructors wanted us to be great marksmen. The Drill Instructors wanted us to be Marines, I think. The concepts were closely related and similar, but not the same.

At the range we occupied a large dormitory with grey steel bunk beds, well worn wooden footlockers and nothing more. There was an office/sleeping room for the DIs and right next to them was the head, complete with showers and wash basins.

UNITED STATES MARINE CORPS
"Semper Fidelis"

Dear family,
   Things here are good!
  Today we fired M-14 rifle, slow
rapid, fire 200 meters. and 45cal. pistol
at 25 meters. It felt good - sense of
power. They are PUSHING here
for Viet-Nam. every (honestly) minute
is learning something new. after Lites
Out, on signal (against regulations)
we have secret meetings with fire
team leaders. when we are in formation
we reciet (sp) from Lectures. We run
alot but I LOVE it because of
cadence calls _ _ _ (filth) NOT reAlly!

MusT Go!
  HAPPY New Year!

P.S.
Mal - 1
study work
Push yourself
 NOTHING
  IS
 FREE

Love
George

" 1-2-3-4 I Love The "
   MARINE CORPS

MAL
~~CALL TELL~~
~~JOANNE TO SAY~~
Hi I LOVE you

KILL
KILL
KILL

The concrete floor was kept spotless, polished to a high, slippery sheen. Even here, though, the harassment and the enforcement of discipline never let up, in fact, it was while we were at the range that Boot Camp took on its most sadistic edge. During training, I fantasized about shooting people, live enemies. They would clutch themselves, bend at the waist and fall over slowly. I wasn't sure how I would feel after shooting another human being, so it might be better if they weren't human – if they were Gooks or Chinks, just like the Germans had been Krauts and the Japanese had been Zips and North Koreans Slopes.

It was the Christmas season of 1967. Anyone who received holiday packages was forced to open them in front of the assembled platoon sitting on the floor. If there was candy, cakes, or anything edible, it was mixed with hot water and loose tobacco from a few cigarettes in a galvanized pail. The recruit who received the goodies was forced to drink the sickening mixture until they threw up. On one occasion, a DI forced the recruit to put his head in the pail and then held the recruit's head underwater with his foot until the recruit gagged, either from no longer being able to hold his breath, or from ingesting the gedunk (what Marines called candy or treats) into his lungs.

The recruits were then forced to clean up their vomit while the DIs ridiculed them. This was child abuse with a capital "A." It was pitiful, the initiation process was compromised and it eroded the stature of the DIs and the Marine Corps. I remember thinking how I'd shoot that Drill Instructor in the face if I got the chance in Vietnam.

~ THIS IS MY RIFLE ~

Marines shoot rifles, not guns. We were all riflemen and ultimately, most Marines become very proficient marksmen. We are renowned for that ability. Physical fitness, ceremonies, drill, tenacity, and marksmanship are all characteristics identified with the United States Marine Corps. But we don't shoot guns. To ensure that the proper nomenclature is used, a Private who makes the mistake of calling his rifle a gun is badgered and berated. One Private, who consistently made that mistake, was forced to stand on a raised physical training (PT) platform in front of the entire platoon, holding his exposed penis in one hand and his rifle in the other.

"*This is my rifle*," he had to shout, lifting his M-14 rifle into the air. Then, shaking his penis he continued, "*This is my gun*."

"*This is for fighting*." The nine-pound rifle was lifted into the air again and the penis shook again. "*This is for fun*."

"*This is my rifle, this is my gun, this is for fighting, this is for fun*."

Frowned on years later, however, during our time in boot camp, it was used as a highly effective form of training, much to the embarrassment of the mortified Private degrading himself on the PT platform in front of us. We all stared at him in disbelief, trying to contain our nervous laughter (thank God that wasn't me) and feeling sorry for the humiliated recruit at the same time. But one thing we all learned – Marines shoot rifles, not guns.

~ HUNG ~

One afternoon we were all laying prone in a large semicircle, practicing our sight alignment and the placement of our cheek on the stock of rifles. We had an empty magazine inserted in the rifle and just dry-fired, slowly pulling the triggers of our rifles over and over. The idea was to be very controlled and meticulous about it. We memorized the process and sight/alignment rules. "When the tip of the front sight blade is halfway up and centered in the rear sight aperture breathe, relax, aim, slack, squeeze."

The Drill Instructors gathered, training their sharp eyes on us like hawks from a tree as the PMIs supervised our training. When the exercise was complete, we were ordered to stand up and fall-in formation. As I stood up, I heard my name called, "Berg! Get over here on the double!"

Wanting to avoid trouble, and hoping to possibly impress and gain the approval of the DI, I raced to the waiting DIs and presented myself, over-achieving as it was, to them at port arms, a ready position of attention. In my rush, I did not take the magazine out of my rifle and arrived in front of the DIs with a *loaded* weapon.

"Are you trying to kill me, you fucking maggot?" one DI asked.

"Sir, no, sir," I barked back. There wasn't an actual live round within two miles of where we were training.

A caper was afoot.

Without any further berating, the senior DI said, "Report to the duty hut at 24:00 midnight, let no one see you and bring your cartridge belt."

"Sir, aye-aye, sir!" I replied, standing frozen in place "Get back with the herd, maggot. Go!"

I didn't sleep at all that night. I just watched the large clock on the wall of the dimly lit squad bay. At a few minutes before midnight I slipped quietly out of my bed and combat low-crawled on my stomach toward the duty hut. As I got closer, I could see other privates doing the same, and I was somewhat comforted by the fact that at least I wasn't alone. I was the first to arrive. I quickly counted the other "lizards" on the floor. There were nine others. I recovered from the low-crawl position, stood up, knocked on the door and announced in a muffled voice, "Sir, Private Berg and nine other privates reporting as ordered, sir."

"Enter!" came the bellowed response.

We walked into the candlelight room and stood at attention, staring straight ahead as the flickering light danced off the grim DIs, their faces partially hidden by the sinister shadows cast by their wide-brimmed campaign hats. They were still dressed in their perfectly pressed and starched uniforms. The DIs hastily arranged us into two lines, five in front, five in the back, and ordered us to hold our webbed cartridge belts at our sides. The senior DI was positioned in front of us, seated at a table covered with a green wool blanket. With an unusually loud, but relaxed conversational tone, he explained what accidentally killing someone would feel like and how we would live with the guilt and shame all our lives if we weren't more careful with our rifles.

DEC. 24
Sun.
warm clear skies
breeze of the pacific
600 m. away

UNITED STATES MARINE CORPS
"Semper Fidelis"

Dear Family,

ITS ABOUT 0730, AND I've JUST done my WASH. THis week of firing IS QUALIFICATION week we must mAke a certain score with the rifle. I've set my goal at 221. To get an expert medal you have to fire 220. Yesterday I fired about 200 and I have 4 days to improve I Think I'll do iT.

We went on a Forced March Last night it was fun.. You wouldn't believe the hills out here. We are right in the middle of a lot of different training battalions 27th marines, and Amtract. and the much respected Force recon. Force recon. are the ~~~~~~~~~ toughest outfit in the corps. Our DI use to be one. He infiltrated in to N. Viet-Nam alot. Every night we get bedtime stories about Viet-nam. Great!..?. I THINK I'm Going to be a "Grunt" (no Liz iT means go into the infantry)

Mal. sorry I can't write much or couldn't answer your letter but there is no time. We exercise alot. I've found The Corps is just like everything else. you get out what you put into it. It sounds like am always giving advice with out any meaning or just giving it to do the right thing but I'm not. I' really believe what I say. Here when I feel myself sliping, slimeing or you know – I say: "George It's for your own good "aye aye sir" "do it" the quoation mark are wrong and so is the spelling but that doesn't matter now. If you have trouble with Vail or maybe with Bio, or anything else (or anyone) get mad ... and do it. don't slime on anything. OH! by the way there's no such thing as a dirty fighter you wouldn't believe what we are taught. I'll Tell ya when I get home about 38 days with luck!

What we had done today was inexcusable, careless and now we were going to experience death.

I was in the front row, standing braced at attention when the DI told the recruits in the back row to put their belts around our necks, tighten the belt, and roll their hips into a judo throw. I was yanked off my feet. Instinctively I grabbed the belt around my neck. No way was I going to be gagged to death! I put up a fight. I kicked, twisted, head-butted and struggled every way I could. Then, suddenly and inexplicably, I was home in bed, dreaming about breakfast and hearing my mom's voice trying to wake me. I had blacked out from the constriction of the blood flow in the carotid artery, and was being revived by the boot of the DI kicking me awake. "Get up you puke."

I was amazed how fast it happened. I was also angry by how enthusiastically I had been killed by the recruit behind me. Now it was my turn. I cinched the cartridge belt around his neck and pulled tight. I almost snapped his head off. I understood the leverage of judo. As a kid I had worked out a little in martial arts on the Military bases where I had lived and knew about the benefits of fulcrums. The poor guy was flopping helplessly for seconds on my hip until I dropped him in a heap on the floor. We each had to repeat the lynching one more time. The second time I relaxed, because I recognized the contrived game the DIs were playing and the futility of resisting. My neck and throat hurt for days, and I never spoke about the incident to any other recruit. The lesson in that training, though valuable, was not worth transferring.

~ IMMORTALITY ~

Some nights the DIs would assemble us as a group, make us sit on the floor of the squad bay at attention with our legs crossed, while they told bedtime stories about Marine history. The Marine ethos was reinforced with the exploits of our heroes. Individual initiative, resourcefulness and courage were celebrated and honored. We were told over and over again how special becoming an 0311-infantry Marine would be, if we were so lucky as to be blessed by God and actually graduate. My favorite story was the legend of the immortality of the Marines. Since, according to the Marine Corps Hymn, Marines are ordained by the Almighty to guard the streets of heaven and the reward would be that Marines live forever. The story goes something like this:

The warrior spirit transcends death and occupies the soul of Marines. When the body of a Marine dies, his soul ascends to heaven. At death, the warrior spirit is set free to drift aloft until it locates a new host. That new person then gets to become a Marine, as the warrior spirit enters his body. Thus, the unbroken cycle continues through eternity and life ever after for the Marines.

The promise of spiritual salvation was a powerful motivator; we were all stunned into silence when the story was told to us in the darkened squad bay at the rifle range. I fell asleep that cold December night wondering if it was true.

Our time spent on the rifle range was soon over. I was disappointed in my final score, but I had qualified. Recruits who didn't qualify had to carry a large rock around with them everywhere. They had their trigger fingers crushed in the bolt of their M-14s and were kicked in the shoulder until they were bruised, to correct their bucking and jerking.

We moved back to San Diego, where we drilled on the Grinder endlessly. My nose was broken by a punch thrown by a junior DI because I turned right when I should have turned left (dyslexia I suppose) as we practiced close-order drill. While we originally had 30 seconds to go to the head, we were now given more time. We no longer had to march into the chow hall on our knuckles and we could eat with our utensils instead of our fingers. We were now enjoying the finer things in life. We were almost – almost U.S. Marines.

~ GRADUATION ~

We worked intensely right up to graduation day. The brief graduation ceremony was seriously cool and a wonderful experience. To finally have someone, anyone, call you a *MARINE* was everything they had promised. Soaring and uplifted in spirit, I was now a very happy, gung ho, confident, mentally tough, physically fit, 6'1," 180 lb. (I weighed 148 lbs. when I enlisted), newly minted basic U.S. Marine.

In our final weeks in San Diego, we were assembled in platoon formation on the street in front of the Quonset huts and given our Military Occupational Specialties (MOS) and our advanced training orders. One at a time, the orders were read aloud; "Smith, motor pool, Jones, aviation mechanic," and so on. Those who got rear echelon specialties were booed. Then I heard my name called by the Senior DI; "Berg, 0311 grunt! ITR-BITS, Camp Pendleton."

In that moment it was confirmed. I was going to Vietnam. I would be in the infantry, a combat rifleman, and I would need to use everything I had been taught in boot camp to survive. I was not destined for; *"no rear echelon embassy duty, no sissified cook school, not even a door gunner on a helicopter."* Nope! I was destined to be on the ground with a rifle – 0311 grunt! I smiled and nodded to myself, satisfied, accepting my destiny. I was a Marine. I was going to Vietnam. The saying in the Marine Corps at the time was "Vietnam was not much of a war but it was all we had." For many Marines it would be the last thing they ever had, 13,067 would die in Vietnam, as though they had been randomly extinguished. One in four names on the Vietnam War Memorial Wall in Washington D.C. is that of a Marine. Vietnam would not be contested because it was important. It was important because it was contested. The communists were truly interested in world domination and Vietnam, like Korea had been, was a proxy for the Cold War. No country wanted to risk an all-out nuclear war, so small proxy wars were how the struggle between the Soviet Union and the west were fought.

The proportions of that war would soon grow, and be bigger than any of us anticipated, although none of us could have realized it on our last day in basic training as we waited for the bus to arrive and transport us to Camp Pendleton from the Marine Corps Recruit Depot in San Diego. The Drill Instructors were still our number one concern, as they had most of us newly turned-out Marines in the platoon down on the ground, doing push-ups. I had been spared group punishment several times because of the effort I had made in training. I had given it my all and tried very hard to learn how to be a Marine. Today, the last day, was no exception. I watched, held out of the punishment as the "*shit birds*" did push-ups, and listened to the DIs berate them one last time.

As my name was called to board the bus north to Camp Pendleton, the senior DI, the platoon commander, stopped me. He got very close to my face, stared directly into my eyes and said, "Private Berg, you are going to be an outstanding Marine."

I smiled and answered, "Sir, aye, aye, sir! The private thanks the platoon commander, sir," still referring to myself, at least to the Senior DI, in the mandatory, self-effacing third-person singular.

We boarded the green bus and it slowly pulled away, bound north up the California coast for Camp Pendleton and more training. Boot camp was over. I had survived the first level of *Dante's Inferno*.

ADVANCED INFANTRY TRAINING

Chain of Fools - Aretha Franklin

~ INFANTRY TRAINING REGIMENT ~

WE LEFT SAN DIEGO AND THE MARINE CORPS RECRUIT DEPOT on January 18, 1968 as new basic Marines, ready to be turned out to the fleet and our new training assignments. The ride in the green school bus to Oceanside, California and Camp Pendleton was uneventful and relaxing. Part of the enjoyment was reveling in the glory and relief of graduating from boot camp.

We rolled through the gates of the sprawling Camp Pendleton, past the sentries and to our distribution point, where we all somehow got assimilated into our new training companies. The barracks looked like the original structures from 1942, with white painted wooden clapboard siding. The squad bay had the ever present and now familiar U.S. Marine Corps steel bunk beds and wooden footlockers. We received our combat training gear in an orderly fashion, this time without the mind-bending haranguing of Drill Instructors.

Our war fighting training started early and was intense. We exercised and marched, double time, in formation everywhere we went, and usually arrived at the mess hall before sunrise. The chow was excellent and with a limitless supply – the-Military variant of the all-you-can-eat buffet. We ran ("humped") up and down the rolling, grass covered, southern California hills, from one training venue to the next.

The training schedule was daunting and relentless. It was exciting to get hands-on experience with the infantry weapons – machine guns, grenades and explosives. Camp Pendleton was alive with activity day and night. The training never stopped – land

JAN. 19

UNITED STATES MARINE CORPS
"Semper Fidelis"

DEAR MOM, FAMILY
    WELL BOOT IS OVER — DAMN
AND NOW THEY SAY "MARINE,"
HERE ITS HARDER, BUT EASIER
IF YOU KNOW WHAT I MEAN. I JUST
GOT MY NEW M-14 AND COMBAT GEAR
TONIGHT. WE START TRAINING TOMARROW.
WE'RE IN THE BOON-DOCKS. ACTION GOING
ON AII THE TIME, NIGHT FIRE OF THE
BIG GUNS WHAT KIND I don't KNOW YET
BUT I'II SNOOP and POOP TIL I DO. THE
GUYS HERE ARE GOIN NUTZ. CANDY GUM,
RADIO'S AII KIND'S OF GE-DUNK. ID LIKE
TO WRITE ABOUT SOME OF THE FIORID
CONVERSATIONS BUT LIZ might WANT
TO READ THE LETTER. THIS PIACE
IS GREAT! CHOW IS OK! BUT AT 1600
WE GET OFF! BUT SOMETIMES WE'LL
SLEEP IN THE FIELD ON A PROBIEM
AND IT'S COID IN THE NIGHT AND HOT
IN THE DAY. I'M GOING TO VOIUNTEER
FOR THE RECON. (RECONASSIENCESCES-- SP)
I, HOPE I'M QUALIFIED!
I'm EITHER GOING TO BE 0311 (BASIC
RIFIEMAN) 0321 AUTOMATIC RIFMAN.)
0331 MOTARMAN) 0341 MOTARMAN BIGGER)
0351 FIAMETHROWER OR 3.5 ROCKET
LAUCHERS

26

IT DEPENDS ON WHAT I'M BEST AT.
I'll BE HOME AFTER 25 DAYS HERE
20 DAYS AT B.I.T.S THEN HOME
THEN VIET-NAM - THEN TO SCHOOL
AT THE GOVERNMENTS EXPENSE

    HUMP THE HILLS! UGH WE'RE
IN THE MOUNTAINS AND IT LOOKS LIKE
IT'S NEVER BEEN TOUCHED! WILD!
HELICOPTERS LANDING All OVER HERE
AND THERE.

    LAST NIGHT I HAD GUARD DUTY
BUT TONIGHT I SLEEP!

        WELL GOOD BYE
        FOR NOW.

          LOVE,

P.S.
JUST GOT THE
WORD
[INSPECTION]
TOMARROW
OUR LIBERTY DEPENDS
ON IT'S OUT COME
I'll SEND SOME
PICTURES of me DRESS
for WAR SOON!

Ben

DAVE BAUX will BE HERE AT
THE SAME I'M HERE AND
WE CAN SKATE (~LOAF) TOGETHER
on SUNDAYS.

I'M TOO TIRED
TO WRITE SENSE INTO
MY LETTERS

navigation, escape and evasion, jungle survival and all things associated with making war. The noise of helicopters and artillery echoed across the hills. At night, illumination flares and brilliant yellow flashes from the booming artillery rounds filled the dark sky like stuttering neon signs.

After particularly long days or nights of training exercises, tempers would erupt and there would be fights in the squad bay. The challenges and duels would be fought with all the classic elements of drama; small Marines throttling eager more aggressive Marines to the raucous cheers of the more sane onlookers -- the original Friday night fight fans. During training I had two brawls. In one, I shoved a 30" horsehair sweeping broom at a Black Marine and told him to do his part to clean the floor so we could all go on liberty (weekend freedom). As I turned my back, he broke the long handle of the broom over my shoulder. Race relations being what they were in the late sixties, I kept moving and nursed the wound in private. The other fight was with a tall blonde Nordic Marine from Minnesota, who claimed I had stepped on his heels running down Old Smokey, one of the larger mountains we routinely conquered. I didn't, and I think he just wanted to have a fight just to have a fight. I obliged but I was a whole lot more than he had bargained for. I had boxed in grade school and knew a little judo. The fight was over nearly as soon as it started. We became spectators after that, and the Friday Night Fights became comic relief: a side show. None of us could have stopped the fights so we all decided to enjoy them at a distance, mocking the ridiculousness even as it occurred.

~ Recon ~

Running in formation to and from training stations, we often passed the Force Reconnaissance (Recon) billeting area. When we did, we were ordered to quicken our pace and get out of their area as fast as possible. Recon is the extreme warrior cult the Marine Corps used for infiltrating enemy territory and silently observing and reporting troop strength and movement. Recon units work in small teams. They are extremely physically fit and very skilled in their deadly trade craft. They attend parachute jump school, some Army Ranger type schools and can take on the equivalent of Navy's toughest combat diver schools. They are the ultimate alpha warriors ("bad ass motherfuckers"). I decided I wanted to be one.

A few days after deciding to enlist in Recon, as luck would have it while waiting in a long line to use the pay phone, I met up with Dave Baux, who I had known in Dixon, my hometown. Actually, I had convinced Dave to join the Marines with me on the buddy plan, but his entry into the Corps had been delayed due to anomalies in his blood work, nevertheless, we were still friends and were glad to see each other. He had graduated Boot Camp after I had but now quite by accident our paths crossed again. We spent the time in line catching up on what each of us had been through - trading basic training war stories. Later, over a few illegally acquired beers, I began to explain how exciting it would be if we signed up for Recon school - the baddest of the bad. It didn't take long to convince both of us that this was a spectacular idea and that we were both perfect candidates to become apex predators – Recon Marines. As

UNITED STATES MARINE CORPS
"Semper Fidelis"

JAN 30 1968
14 30
T-8 (TRAINING DAY OUT OF 20)
TUESDAY

HELLO GROUP,
    JUST A LINE TO SAY I'VE STILL
GOT THE CORPS INTACT. yuck!

        HOW'S THINGS- I'm WORKING
HARD TO LEARN WHAT I'm TAUGHT
SO AS TO SAVE MY YOUNG _____ IN
THE LAND ACROSS THE POND. YESTERDAY
WE HAD A 14 miles OUTING AT 0300 - oh no!
TO THE RANGE. THE BEST THING ABOUT
THIS PLACE IS THE WILDLIFE. EAGIES
ARE MY FAVORITE SUBJECT. I SPIED A
DOE ON THE WAY TO THE RANGE. SNAKES
ARE NOT COMMON but I'VE SEEN ONE.
MOST ARE UNDERGROUND. IN THE SUMMER
I TOLD THIS PLACE CRAWLS WITH EVERYTHING
IMAGINABLE. WE'RE UP IN THE HILLS
AWAY FROM EVERYTHING HERE'S AN EXAMPLE
OF A HILL
Hump!
Hump!

YESTERDAY WE FIRED M-60 MACHINE
GUNS. 3.5 ROCKET LAUNCHERS (BAZOKA'S ARE 2.6)
ON FOOL GOT HIS HEAD? CAUGHT IN BACK
BLAST POOR FELLOW.

→

I REALLY DON'T KNOW WHY I DREW THOSE
PICTURES. - OH WELL

LOVE,
George

Hi, LIZARD - BREATH
BE GOOD GAL
READY.....DO IT!
NOW!

MAL,
YOU'VE GOT
ABOUT 40 dAYS
TO GET INTO
Supper SHAPE
BEFORE I GET
HOME! READY - DO IT!

READY ... GOOD NIGHT

I AWAKEN AT 0330 MOST
MORNINGS AND IT'S AIMOST TIME
TO HIT THE RACK

READY GOOD . NIGHT

luck would have it, the pre-qualifications and interviews of volunteers were set for the next week. We agreed this was our destiny, and we would volunteer.

Sure enough, that next week rolled around and we met and joined the lines in front of the advanced specialty schools. I don't really know how it happened, but Dave ended up in a parallel line, which turned out to be for Scout Snipers. Oddly, the Recon line was shorter than the rest and the few that were in the line looked Paleolithic. Undaunted, I filed forward as the rejected interviewees staggered or were physically thrown out of the tent. The loud screaming and successive rejection of Marines suggested that the first phase of the screening process was going to be highly selective. I stopped one big Marine who had been bounced out and asked him the scoop. He told me that the Recon Marines were assholes and besides, to get into Recon you had to sign a six-year commitment, and the chance of finishing the entire course of instruction and becoming a fleet Recon Marine was about one in ten. Recon school had a very high attrition rate.

I decided then and there that being an infantry Marine was good enough for me. Besides, the Sergeant in charge of our training had told me that being a 0311- Marine rifleman was where all the action was anyway. Convinced that I was now making the correct decision, I relinquished my place in line (while Dave dutifully stood fast in his) and headed for the beach and a cold beer, neglecting to tell Dave about my decision.

I was enjoying myself comfortably lounging on the beach, resting on one elbow, watching waves break in the surf, humming Otis Redding's *Sitting On The Dock Of The Bay* to myself, when I heard an approaching voice yelling, "We're in, we're in. We are in. Scout Snipers! Gung Ho!"

Dave was overjoyed. He had dutifully committed to the six-year requirement for advanced specialty schools and had signed up for Scout/Snipers – stealth warriors, snake eaters, slip and slide behind enemy lines to snoop and poop. When I told Dave of my decision, he was incredulous. I was in fact, as he repeatedly pointed out, an asshole.

Dave soon left Camp Pendleton for Vietnamese language school in Monterey, California, and then on to Scout school to learn highly specialized infiltration techniques, escape and evasion and how to stay awake for an extraordinary number of hours and still function efficiently, despite the lack of sleep. Dave later used his skills to infiltrate into North Vietnam on very dangerous scouting missions and as an interrogator of enemy prisoners of war – both grizzly, nasty occupations. For his courage and resourcefulness in Vietnam, Dave was awarded the Bronze Star with the V device for valor.

After the war, Dave and I attended the same junior college, and then were roommates at Southern Illinois University. Dave studied for accounting finals in 48-hour, uninterrupted, sleepless marathons. A few times, after a couple of beers, we would slip into the swamp next to our trailer in pitch black and capture Viet Cong (VC) bullfrogs, which we would keep in our shower as prisoners of war (POWs). The only sounds that could be heard on those nights, as we slunk through the swamp were the crickets chirping and frogs croaking. Dave had learned his silent craft well. At times Dave and I would cook some of our meals in a hole in the ground over hot charcoal. We would get quart bottles of beer in town and drink them as we cooked our meat. Our standard assumption was that the food, mostly chicken, was done when the beer was gone, regardless of its actual readiness for human consumption – it became the one quart rule. So, I guess he forgave me for being an asshole after all.

I tried very hard to do well in ITR-BITS, primarily to earn liberty. Although it was very lonely during training, our days were full. At the graduation ceremony, we were assembled in company formation and a senior training officer announced that the top 10 percent of the class would be meritoriously promoted to Private First Class. Of the 250 Marines in our cycle, I graduated around number 12. I was stunned. The pride rose in me like a surging tide.

~ HOST FAMILY ~

The political climate in 1968 was becoming decidedly anti-war/military. Protestors had grown in number and were now more than just a few small dogs barking at a passing car. The war would now be fought on two fronts, in Vietnam against the Viet Cong/North Vietnamese Army, and at home against strangers, neighbors and sometimes family members. There were some civilians, however, who still supported the men in uniform and still possessed what remained of nationalism, patriotism, and Americanism. The Marine Corps had instituted a program that matched Marines with civilian families during holidays. A great couple in Brea, California hosted me. We went to Knotts Berry Farm, had a barbecue and made homemade ice cream. I had been influenced by both of my parents to be polite and have good manners, and the Marine Corps taught me to say "yes sir" and "thank you, ma'am," so at first I was stiff and formal around my host family.

UNITED STATES MARINE CORPS
Semper Fidelis

FEB. 15, 1968
2100
I T R (is now finished)
THURSDAY

DEAR DAD,
WE ARE NOW IN THE PROCESS OF OUTPOST-
ING. TOMARROW I REPORT TO BASIC INFANTRY
TRAING SCHOOL (BITS). I WILL RECIEVE
13 DAYS OF TRAINING, 10 ACTUAL DAYS AND
3 PROCESSING AND INFORMATION DAYS. EX.
HOW TO GET CIVILIAN TRANSPORTATION HOME
AND HOW AND WHEN TO REPORT TO THE NEXT
DUTY STATION.
TODAY WE HAD A CERMONY ON THE
PARADE DECK. (THE "GRINDER").
OUT OF A CLASS OF 250 MARINES THEY MERITORIOULS
PROMOTED 10% TO PFC. AN INTERESTING
CERMONY.
SOME MARINES OF THE 27TH REG. 5TH MAR. DIV
JUST GOT PUllED OUT TO GO TO VIET-NAM.
AS YOU KNOW THE 1ST MAR. DIV. AND THE 3RD
REINFORCED ARE THE 2 MAR. DIVS. IN "NAM".
BUT SOON MOST OF THE 5TH WILL BE THERE
TOO. THE 3500 MEN CAME FROM (MOSTIY)
THE SCHOOL (BITS) I'M GOING TO. THEY WE
GIVEN 1 HOURS NOTICE AND AII LEAVES
CANCEALED. MOST OF THEM ARE JUST LIKE
ME. THEY HAVEN'T BEEN HOME ON LEAVE
AND WON'T BE HOME FOR 13 MONTHS.
I DON'T KNOW MY ORDERS YET AFTER
BITS BUT I'M "SNOOPING AND POOPING"
WHEN I'M ACTING DUTY NCO (PHONE WATCH)
I GO TO NAM ON OR BEFORE APRIL 12
I HOPE NO SOONER.

I THINK I will COME HOME (50%) CHANCE MY WEAPON IN VIET-NAM WILL BE AN M-16 I WILL GET COMBAT TRAINING (EXTENSIVE) AT BITS.

THE USMC IS A "TIGHT" OUT FIT. WE HAVE "JUNK ON THE BUNK" SOMETIMES WITH ONLY AN HOURS NOTICE, WE FIELD DAY ALMOST EVERY NIGHT. OUR C.O. USES A PEN LIGHT DURING RIFLE INSPECTION. AND "IF YOUR RACK IS NOT "TIGHT OR RIGHT" STAND BY" BECAUSE IT WILL BE ALL OVER THE AREA PIECE BY PIECE. BUT I LIKE THAT SHIT, IT MAKE THE CORPS WHAT IT IS. SOMETIMES I GET PISSED OR TIRED BUT THAT'S WHEN I SAY "READY DO IT" AND BUST A BUN. THERE IS ALOT OF SPIT AND POLISH, STARCH AND SOWING AND UP KEEP TO DO. BUT IF YOU STAY AHEAD OF IT. YOU STAY "SQUARED AWAY." TRADITION AND SPIRT AND COMPETITION PLAY A BIG PART, ESPECIALLY COMPETITION. REG. VS REG BN. VS BN. CO. VS CO AND SO ON DOWN TO MAN TO MAN. HOPEFULLY I WILL BE HOME IN THREE WEEKS

YOUR SON.

P.F.C. George P.

I WAS ABOUT 10TH IN THE CLASS I NOW HAVE 4 MONTHS TIME AND GRADE OVER THE MEN HERE WITH MY MERITORIOUS PROMOTION. LANCE CORPORAL NEXT. THEN CORPORAL (NCO)

My mother died, at age 84, of cancer. When her children collectively recognized her true condition, we moved her from Florida, where she had lived for 15 years. We moved her back to Dixon, her hometown, to stay in my sister's home as the disease laid siege to her body. Her dying was the struggle between the ruthlessness of a self-ravaging body and her keen supple wit. Back and forth for a month her internal battle was fought. Her only concern was the potential of losing the mind she had so dearly cultivated to the duplicitous pain medications. Never a thought given to her soul – it was her mind she cherished as she lay dying. I obeyed her instructions, our pact, to the end, "Don't you dare cry – stand up straight like a man."

"Yes, Mom," I replied, as the four-year-old, trapped inside me choked back tears. *Don't worry, Mom*. I thought to myself, *I won't disappoint you*.

She alternately laughed and grimaced in her final hours and agreed on her death bed that she had a good life. My mother's sometime prickly and fractious personality actually helped her as she passed on to the other side as she had wanted. She had died a lady. She had made peace with her perceived shortcomings and her cold distant father. With a single heaving breath she passed into her long night. With that last breath, the center pillar of our family was gone.

Sorting through her artifacts and treasures, trawling for missing fragments of our experience and memories, I was again amazed to find a trove of the bits and pieces of our lives that she had saved. Everything that she could put in a box and that was relevant to my experiences from birth to Marine and beyond she had saved. Every piece of paper – cards, notes, and letters – all of it gently stowed in dusty boxes.

I reread the letter sent to my parents in early 1968 by my Host Family. I reread this particular letter because of its sweetness and because it was the last written words of the person I had been before Vietnam.

My Dear Mr. and Mrs. Berg,

Our family had the pleasure of the company of your fine son this weekend. We have two small children, Maurice Jr., just five years old, and Molly, who is 1-1/2. Both of our children loved George. He is very good with children, gentle and they understand that very quickly. My daughter did quite a bit of 'flirting' with our Marine. My wife and I found George to be very polite, a real joy to have in our home.

Mr. and Mrs. Berg, we are one family that really believes in what your son is doing for our country. Without men like George, we would soon be lost. It is our hope that his visit with us will help keep his faith in what he is fighting for. We took George to the Marine busses this evening. I told George "Via con Dios." We were sorry to see him go, but know God will protect him in the coming days and years. We can tell you he is as strong as an ox and looks and acts very happy. We are sure he will be a good Marine and make you very proud. We will be proud just for having known George for two days.

Our prayers will be with your boy, and with you for raising such a fine son. Faithfully, Maurice and Mary
Maurice Jr. and Molly

This was the last time in many years I'd be referred to as "happy." After my war, my faith and conviction about governments was doubtful. In trying to help our nation to not become lost, I became lost and without a sense of any real direction for years afterward. At that time though, these wonderful, terrific people encouraged me to relax and have fun. One afternoon, sitting on their patio, eating and laughing, I slipped and asked the Mrs. Clifton to "pass the fucking potato salad, please."

A tense silence blanketed the party until they looked each other in the eyes and burst out laughing. She said, "We wondered when that would happen. We've been around Marines before." She chuckled to herself for some time. They were truly very nice, giving people.

~ FIRST LEAVE ~

I was intensely proud of my accomplishments in training, my decision to be a Marine, the 35 pounds of sinew and muscle I had gained, my highly aggressive attitude, and even my uniform. After graduating from ITR at the top of my class I received a 30-day leave. When I arrived home it was February, the late winter was cold and gray and so was my reception. My high school girlfriend was distant. She had found other things to do and other people to do them with. My other friends were enjoying college, and my immediate family was all busy with their lives. So I ran, worked out and caught up with the few friends that were here and there. When the time came to leave, I was ready. I had no reservations with respect to my decision to serve my country and help stem the tide of Communism.

It was now, March 1968 and my thirty days of leave were almost over. My parents drove the ninety miles to O'Hare Airport in Chicago, and stayed with me until it was time to board the plane. By then, more than 485,600 American military personnel were in Vietnam. Of that number, 16,021 had been killed.

Meanwhile, back in January 1968, the North Vietnamese had initiated the single largest battle of the Vietnam War when they attacked the Marines dug in at fire base Khe Sanh in what was actually part of a massive diversion for the surprise widespread Tet Offensive into the south on January 31, the start of their lunar New Year. The massive Tet Offensive was launched by Viet Cong forces in over 100 cities and towns, including Saigon, and was intended to spur a popular uprising by civilians in the South and massive desertions by the Army of the Republic of Vietnam (ARVN) military.

Neither of these happened nor were the VC able to hold onto any military gains they had made in the cities or towns for more than a few days other than Hue which they held for 25 days. Causalities included about 1,000 Marines and 2,000 ARVN military, 32,000 VC and 165,000 civilian. In the battle of Khe Sanh 500 American and about 10,000 North Vietnamese troops were killed.

The 27th Marines fought in and around the ancient and historic city of Hue. Although it was not known at the time, during the occupation of the city of Hue, Communist cadre searched door to door to locate "uncooperative elements." Using lists of names they had spent months meticulously preparing, the Communists apprehended approximately 3,000 people – merchants, Buddhist monks, Catholic priests, intellectuals and people with ties to the South Vietnamese government – who they summarily executed, shot, clubbed to death or buried alive. Their shallow graves would be discovered around the city for several years to come. It would be a largely untold story. I would soon join the 27th Marines after the fighting at Hue, when they moved to the south, west of Da Nang.

Suffering from their devastating military defeat, the VC retreated back to the jungles. According to their own admissions later, the VC never recovered from the high casualties they suffered during Tet. While it had been a military fiasco, Tet became the decisive spark that would guarantee victory. After years of having generals tell the American public that the Vietnam War was being won, Tet displayed on the nightly newscasts that the enemy was far from defeated. Public tolerance reached the breaking point, and the high cost, both in dollars and casualties, became unbearable, but it would take many more years and lives to resolve the war. Ultimately, the war was won on the ground (the enemy was close to exhaustion by 1968) in spite of the U.S. Army's overall strategy (devised by the then President Lyndon Johnson, the Secretary of Defense Robert McNamara and the Joint Chiefs of Staff). However, it was lost on television and in the living rooms and college campuses across the U.S.

After Tet, General Westmoreland (the general responsible for carrying out the overall strategy of the war in Vietnam) requested an additional 206,000 troops. The odds were increasing daily that this would be the last time I would ever see my parents again.

When my flight was announced over the public address system, I hugged and kissed my mom and shook hands with my dad, smiled a brave smile and turned toward the ramp that led to the waiting jet. Coming down the ramp, walking with a limp and a cane, was a Marine, dressed in his tan tropical uniform, unusually out of season, as it was winter here in the United States. His hat was crumpled and pulled down past the eyebrow line, in a scowl. His open collar shirt was wrinkled but tucked neatly into his trousers. On the shoulder of his short sleeve shirt were corporal stripes. Three rows of campaign ribbons, including the Silver Star, Bronze Star with V-device, two Purple Hearts, indicated by a miniature gold star, and more were mounted over his breast pocket. He was a warrior – no doubt. There was an air of nobility about him, a regal quality. This was an authentic and genuine war fighter just back from Vietnam. His forearms were tanned dark brown and the skin in the crook of this arm around to his elbow joints was peeling away from what looked like chemical burns. His face was weathered and deeply sunburned around the eyes, and highlighted by the raccoon line college kids covet from snow skiing in the Rocky Mountains over spring break. He had not acquired his from skiing – that much was very clear. His muted expressionless stare was riveting as his piercing eyes locked on to mine.

As we passed, his head turned toward me with his icy deadpan gaze. He was trying to tell me something, to warn me. I felt it. Cold and distant, his focus was a thousand yards away, but he was looking directly at me. Then he turned his head slowly forward, as if to say "How copy?" (Military speak for do/did you understand) and just like that he limped away fading into the crowd of people milling around the airport. In those brief seconds he had told me, with his hardened, piercing eyes, about the real war in Vietnam, and what was to become of me. In a momentary flash encounter, I had seen my future. He had given me a sobering, encoded account of what was to come. I was going to be tried and put to the test. This was not going to be a high school football practice or a camping trip. This was going to be a horrific, long, hard, deadly experience, and I would look like the Marine on the concourse when I made it home—if in fact I got home at all.

I turned around and took one final look back at my smiling, waving parents. I was stunned by how simple and uncomplicated the two of them appeared to be in that moment. *Oh Christ*, I thought, and boarded the waiting plane for the flight back to California. The inevitability of finally going to Vietnam was never far from my mind during the flight. I tried not to think about it much, or dwell upon the bone chilling feelings of apprehension and loneliness that were building with each passing hour. I just steeled myself for whatever would come.

APRIL 1968

I Feel Like I'm Fixin' To Die - Country Joe and the Fish

"...Next Stop Vietnam" ~

I CHECKED BACK IN AT CAMP PENDLETON and started the mind numbing, asphyxiating Military process again. We continued training at the new Counter Guerilla Warfare School set up at the Las Pulgas area of Camp Pendleton. The jungle warfare training was exciting, and the unconventional nature reminded me of the Cowboys and Indians games I had played during my childhood. I've always excelled at free form and improvisation, and this type of low intensity warfare would be right up my alley – a brawl with no rules. We learned about mines, snares, trip wires, booby-traps, and tactics used by the Viet Cong – "Victor Charley, i.e., the VC, the Gooks" - our new enemy. They were the absolute enemy, yet I had never even seen a Vietnamese. I couldn't even point out Vietnam on a map.

The finale of "jungle school" was a simulated battle between conventional forces and guerilla fighters. Because I was infantry, I was chosen to be the enemy – a VC guerilla. Our mission was to harass the holed-up Marines and probe their lines all night, throwing rocks into the perimeter and otherwise deprive them of both sleep and self-respect. They were helpless in their compound, and we mercilessly attacked their routine, textbook, standard operating procedure patrols. The desk clerks, aviation specialists, cooks and office "pogues" ("people other than Grunts") - in the rear with the gear Marines - were bewildered, sitting ducks. The lessons of vulnerability were learned by only a few of us. At the time, the American military was incapable of fashioning a response to the challenges of wars of national liberation. The harassment was scheduled to last all night, but we aggressors grew tired of the fun and found a rocky outcropping dug into the nearby hills where we could put up for the night. I fell asleep, delighted to have successfully played out and recaptured the Cowboy and Indian games of my childhood.

The Marine Corps had considerable success with guerilla warfare. It brought that institutional memory of its "small wars" in the Caribbean and Central America to Vietnam. The Marines employed combined action patrols in and around villages and assisted local

Vietnamese Army units in rooting out insurgents. Pacification, as it was called - was effective. However, most of the military wanted to fight in Vietnam in the conventional way – to get out in the jungles and chase guerillas and bomb them from high altitude. The Pentagon was dominated by the Army and Air Force (both lacking in memory and experience of guerilla warfare) and they would shape the American experience in Vietnam. Early on, the Marine Corps and the U.S. Army's Special Forces (The Green Berets) had it right.

We slept soundly until dawn, when we were awakened by the noise of about 200 very pissed-off, tired, hungry Marines, walking on line up the valley toward our encampment. They may have been in-the-rear-with-the- gear Marines, but they were still Marines and right now their goal was to catch up to us, put a Mesmer (Prisoner of War) bag over our heads, and beat the living hell out of anyone they caught who was part of humiliating them. Luckily, the exercise was stopped just as they were closing in. The game had become very personal by then and a little unruly.

Finally, it was time to go. Our group flew on a commercial airline from California to Hawaii. We were allowed to get off in Hawaii as the plane was refueled, but were caged on the tarmac by a chain link fence. I thought to myself that you'd have to be a complete idiot to go UA (Unauthorized Absence) here. I marveled at how little confidence the Marine Corps must have in its troops if they felt they had to put up a barrier to keep its people from running away. My thoughts darted back to the face of the Marine I had encountered on the concourse at O'Hare Airport. I shifted my gaze to the naive, untested, overly confident brash Marines I was traveling with and suddenly the chain link fence made perfect sense. Somebody knew a whole lot more than we did. Everybody, it would seem, knew a whole lot more than we did. Many of us would become road-kill — slaughtered and left on the shoulder of a political highway, and we were laughing about it.

The Hawaiian air was warm, moist and fragrant. The smell of tropical flora wafted on the gentle breeze, mixing with the odor of spent jet fuel and the exhausts of other aircraft coming and going to and from Hawaii. Added to this was the background noise of the active airfield and in the distance a gray mist hung like a chain of pearls around the mysterious dark green volcanic mountains that are Hawaii. When summoned we reluctantly clamored back on board the airliner, found our original seats and settled in for the next long leg of our journey. I fell asleep almost immediately and dreamed of the future. I wondered if I would be brave when the time came. I was sure I would be. I had a long family history of military service to uphold.

Our next stop was Okinawa, the southern most islands in the Japanese Archipelago, a group of islands that have hosted Marines since the end of World War II. It is home to a Marine base turned staging and training area for troops going to Vietnam. We thought Okinawa would be more relaxed but instead it was a series of long lines; getting probed and perforated one final time with tropical disease vaccinations and more jungle warfare training.

We received a shot to thicken our blood, inoculations for exotic diseases and we were given a physical, a last test to be certain that we were sound enough in body and mind to go into combat.

While in Okinawa we passed some of our time in the lines laughing at the new tattoos that many of the Marines were getting on just about any part of their bodies. My favorite was a scrawny turkey vulture whose long thin neck disappeared between the butt cheeks of one Marine. Tattooed on the guy's lower back were the words *Gobble-Gobble*. This guy's naked ass was a big hit as he walked, with his skivvies proudly pulled down, slowly toward the wary Corpsman who was waiting to inject the next inoculation into his bare butt cheeks. As each Marine approached the Corpsman would yell, "Stop your grin'n and drop your linen." Smiling and playing the fool, the Marine stayed in character the entire time, thus the tattoo. Like the chain link fence, it all made perfect sense now.

Our time in Okinawa, which was intended to get our bodies prepared for a tropical climate as well as provide for any extra training, could be captured in one word: confused. Marines were in transit everywhere, going in all directions, arriving, departing, coming, going, or just moving around. We were scheduled to receive additional jungle warfare training, but that was cut short, after all it was now spring of 1968, and the war was at its apogee. Consequently, our butts, even the tattooed ones, were hustled onto a civilian Boeing 707 for the last segment of the journey to Vietnam sooner than we had expected.

~ Welcome to Vietnam ~

The flight attendants on the plane were cordial and businesslike, serving soft drinks to the ocean of green Marines who sat dutifully and a little apprehensively in their seats during the long flight. Some of the Marines slept, others read magazines and some of us just idled away the time, talking about cars, family and girlfriends. I donned stereo headphones and daydreamed, my thoughts wandering to everything conceivably associated with my life before, during, and after Vietnam.

I woke up when the sound of the engines changed and the plane dropped altitude, preparing to land in the city of Da Nang, located in the northern portion of the Republic of South Vietnam. It was April 25, 1968. The landing pattern took the plane into a long circling figure eight, gradually decreasing its altitude but never really preparing to land. It was as though we were suspended in the air. I was now ten time zones and 12,000 miles from Dixon, Illinois, sitting by the window and staring out at an alien landscape and turquoise sea. Just beneath us were the sharp, tree covered spires of the coastal range, and the dusty, ramshackle, dry Military Base in Quang Nam province of Republic of South Vietnam. The Beatles' Eleanor Rigby played softly in my headphones as I stared down, watching puffs of gray smoke mushroom and tumble across the runway as VC 122mm rockets exploded in rapid succession. The plane pitched steeply to the right.

Welcome to Vietnam. The *Fasten Seat Belt/No Smoking* lights flashed on as we left the holding pattern and rapidly descended to the runway. The hydraulic system opened the wheel well doors, tires clunked into place and locked into position. The wheels touched down, bouncing against the concrete runway. The pilot reversed the thrust of the engines to brake, pushing us against the seat belts. We rolled to a stop. As the doors swung open and we walked down the portable stairs into the airport, several overpowering sensations blasted me at the same time, the horrendous smell coming from the raw sewage flowing beside the roads near the airport, and the extreme heat and humidity. The combination made me waffle and I almost went down to one knee. I shook my head like a stunned boxer brushing off a hook shot to the temple. A neatly-painted, red and yellow plywood sign directed us to a large open-air pole barn where we, the inbound *replacement* Marines, were dispatched to our specific units.

Gagging and figuring out how to breathe, I wandered around in the barn until I determined that I was on my own. Apparently, I would have to get to my assigned unit, the 27th Marines of World War II Iwo Jima fame, anyway I could. I saw some other new arrivals scrambling up the tires and tailgate of a duce-and-a-half truck and decided to join them. Luckily, the vehicle was going to the Headquarters of the 1st Battalion 27th Marine Regiment aka - 1/27. I climbed on board and soon the truck stopped and started its way through the clamoring mass of people and vehicles, and headed south, down the main highway of Vietnam. The ride was bumpy and dusty. The potholed road was cluttered with Vietnamese in pointed conical straw hats and baggy silk pants tending to the daily affairs of their lives. The culture struck me as primitive, almost primordial. Off in the background, never far away, were the lush, forested mountains looming through the gray mist. It looked like Hawaii, but I knew it wasn't. The grand adventure was beginning, and I felt anxious, apprehensive. I withdrew inside and wondered what forces had compelled me into this situation.

~ THE FORTRESS ~

The jarring 7.3 Km ride (which seemed like 20 miles) lasted an hour or so and finally, up ahead, I spied our fortress, Duong Son. The Headquarters of the 1/27 was a giant hodgepodge of sandbags, barbed wire, large green tents, and guard towers made from telephone poles topped with rickety, rusting corrugated metal roofs and sandbags. The road, Highway 1, ("Street Without Joy") for a short distance became Liberty road that ran right through the middle of the encampment. The truck stopped and we all jumped off with our sea bags. I looked around at what struck me as a western frontier landscape. White, granular sand was the predominate feature. It was everywhere, blinding you as it reflected the bright sun back skyward.

The road and open areas were all covered with loose, dry, dusty, hot sand. Offices throughout the compound had hard wooden sides half-way up covered by sandbags, then screens with corrugate metal roofs. Wooden shipping pallets covered with plywood served as sidewalks. Hitching posts for nonexistent horses had been made by lashing long poles together. The entire compound had a Wild West frontier feel about it. In fact, that area had been nicknamed *The Arizona Territory* by the officers. Music, broadcast from the Armed Forces Radio - Vietnam was playing on the stereo sets that a few of the more hip Marines had acquired, drifted through the air. Across the street were rows of green tents and beyond them a large trench, with sandbags lining the outbound edge. Tanks were parked every so often, with their fronts sandbagged for additional protection against mortar rounds and rocket propelled grenades (RPG's).

There were amenities, primitive streetlights and a shower area with hot and cold running water coming from a large, black rubberized plastic tank mounted on a wooden platform with shipping pallets for a shower floor. I would soon learn that there were bush Marines (grunts) and not so bush Marines. I would soon become a bush Marine.

There was a mess hall with screens on the windows. Nearby was a small stage for the occasional USO show that made it this far into the boonies. Various other buildings and areas bore signs labeling them as Officer Country, or Off Limits. I had no business in any of those places. I checked in, was assigned to Charlie Company, and headed for the tents across the street that neatly divided the base in two. I was still dressed in my starched *stateside* solid green utilities and had no rifle or weapon of any kind, and I was starting to get anxious as I made my way to my home away from home.

There were only a few Marines in the tent when I walked in. To nobody in particular, I asked, "Hey, where can I bunk?"

"Almost anywhere." Came a mumbled, disinterested reply. "The Company is up north, at Hue City – on the Pipeline."

"Oh yeah? Cool." I stated, naively, "When do we get to go north, to where – Hue?"

The reply was bothersome. "Man, you don't want to go there, not north, never north. Enjoy hiding and skating here as long as you can."

I found a rack (bed) and stashed my sea bag beneath it after brushing off the road dust. Then I just rested awhile in the baking heat. I had arrived; I thought I enjoyed the relative comfort of the rear area for a week or so, although we received 10-15 incoming mortar rounds almost every night. We would race to the nearest trench or bunker when we heard the first round explode or when someone in the perimeter trenches would shout, "Incoming!"

We'd stare out into the black night wondering where the rounds came from. The routine attacks served their purpose – harassment. The visceral jerking response to those first nights in camp got you prepared for what was to come. It also stayed with me for decades after I returned from the war. For years I was twitchy. Loud noises or sudden, unexpected movements kept me ducking and flinching.

Artillery was located inside the perimeter along with mortar crews. Those artillerymen and the heavy mortar crews could work all night, cramming shell after shell into the breeches of their guns or down their tubes. I remember wondering, how could they do it hour after hour like that? They did though, for days, weeks, and months on end. When their tour of duty was up after thirteen months they went home. That was their war, fought from a distance dueling with NVA gunners and rocketeers they would never see.

While the Company was up North, the other replacements and I basically just hung out. We were issued jungle boots and fatigues and finally our M-16 rifles which we sighted in on a small rifle range. We also learned how to clean the new finicky firearm. As the boring days crept by, I started to get excited about the prospect of getting in the mix and making history. I was ready to get it on to make this the last war in Indochina so that Vietnam could finally be free of the pesky Communists – or so I thought.

~ 1ST BATTALION, 27TH MARINES ~

The history of the 1st Battalion, 27th Marines began on January 19, 1944, when the unit came into existence as part of the newly organized 5th Marine division at Camp Pendleton, California. Upon activation the battalion immediately began combat training and then sailed to Pearl Harbor in August to participate in maneuvers and training exercises with the rest of the 27th Marines. In January 1945, after one year of training, the 1/27 received its combat orders and sailed to the island of Iwo Jima, arriving on February 19, 1945, where they became part of the assault wave assigned to land on Red Beach, on the southern part of the island. The first commander of the 1/27, Lieutenant Colonel John A. Butler, was killed when an enemy shell hit his jeep. Butler was replaced by the regimental operations officer, Lieutenant Colonel Justin C. Duryea who was seriously wounded five days later, along with several other officers, by a land mine. The official capture and occupation of Iwo Jima were proclaimed on March 26, 1945. During the fighting for Iwo Jima the 1/27 suffered the loss of more than 230 of its men, including its first commander.

On March 27th the 1/27 boarded the SS Sea Sturgeon and returned to Pearl Harbor to train for the invasion of Japan, which became unnecessary when Japanese surrendered in August. After the surrender, the 1/27 was detached from its regiment and became part of the occupation forces, assigned to Sasebo, on the island of Kyushu. In December 1945, the 2nd Marine Division replaced the 5th and the 1/27 was transported back to the United States, arriving in San Diego, California and then returning to Camp Pendleton. On January 5, 1946, the 1st Battalion, 27th Marines was deactivated.

In 1965, due to increased fighting in and the commitment of American military force to the war in Vietnam, the 5th Marine Division was reactivated, with the 1/27th reactivated on June 1, 1966, as the ground component of the 1st Marine Brigade. Soon after its reactivation, 1/27 began training for eventual deployment.

~ THE STORK AND BUZZARD ~

While waiting to be transferred to Charlie company ("C Company") we replacements filled sandbags, learned about the M-16A1 semi-automatic rifle we would use in combat and otherwise got acclimated. Somehow, I found a new football somewhere. I tossed the football whenever I could – to anyone who ever had the sense to "go long," this for me was a maximum of 40-yards, maybe. There were some things the Marine Corps could not improve upon, like my throwing arm. Nevertheless, I threw passes to whoever would catch them. To kill time before we went to the bush, we decided to have a touch football game. We chose sides and began the game. I played quarterback. It was, after all, my football. During the loosely organized game I rolled out several times and continued to hit an open receiver. This same Marine just kept getting open. He reminded me of an athlete I knew in Dixon High School in 1966, his name was Buzzard, and he was one of the best players on our football team. He received a full-ride athletic scholarship to Southern Illinois University and played there for four years. We had played some together in high school, and I had practiced throwing bullet passes to him, as hard as I could. Buzzard never missed a pass. He caught anything that came near him, just the same as this Marine on the sandy parade field did. After the Marine caught my hardest bullet passes over and over again and held onto the ball as he was gang tackled by the defending Marines, I yelled, without thinking, "Great job, Buzzard!"

The Marine ran back to the huddle and got in my face, shouting, "Fuck you!" "Smell my shorts, asshole," I responded, "what's up with you?"

He thought I was making fun of his name, explaining that his name was Stork not Buzzard. I was stunned by the coincidence. "Wow! I wasn't fucking with you, man. I actually have a friend named Buzzard."

"No shit?" he replied, skeptically and then roared, "What a fucked up name. No one should have a friend named Buzzard."

To prove that I was telling the truth about Buzzard, Stork and I later wrote an obscene letter to Buzzard and the other members of his Tau Kappa Epsilon (TKE – "Teak") fraternity at Southern Illinois University. Bill Buzzard and the Teaks wrote back an equally obnoxious, bird-brained letter, making comparisons between Teak and Marine anatomies. In essence, the Teaks claimed that their pubic hair was thicker, the girth and length of their male members were larger, and their testicles weightier, their fluid discharge could be propelled farther and was less viscous and more adhesive. We knew better. The letter exchange between the Teaks and Marines would continue for some weeks. The letters were very funny (mostly disgusting) thus entertaining for all of us – Teaks and Marines alike. Stork and I would laugh for hours at the insults and embedded challenges. The letter war of words ended later on, however, when I heard Stork got shot by an NVA sniper. The last I saw of Stork was him sitting on top of a tank wrapped in bandages headed to the rear. He rumbled by in a dust storm and was gone.

~ First Listening Post ~

After a few days in the battalion rear area, the other replacements and I were taken out by helicopter to join Charlie Company. I was ready. My hair was cut high and tight, I had new jungle boots, the brand-new light fabric jungle utilities, and a clean, late model, although slightly used M-16. Yes, I was ready—ready to kick ass and take names - Gung Ho!

A bumpy helicopter ride delivered us to the field, dropping us off unceremoniously along with the other commodities: crates of ammunition, C-rations and the mail, those precious letters from home. When we had finished unloading the cargo, the helicopter lifted off, the down wash from its blades kicking up dust devils of dirt and debris that engulfed everything. As the dust settled and the deafening mechanical chopping sound faded, I found myself feeling very alone. It was like being in the middle of nowhere, surrounded by the expansive savannah of low coastal plains punctuated with a thick jungle of bamboo groves.

I walked up to a Marine and announced my presence, only to be summarily dismissed with a pointing finger, mutely directed toward a scruffy looking Lieutenant who was sitting down, leaning against a bamboo cluster with his shirt unbuttoned. The reception I received from him was cool and reserved. He stared into my eyes with disdain and snarled some orders in my direction. The only thing I heard was, "stow your shit and report to..." "Yes, sir," I replied, then I wandered away too stunned to ask for clarification – I'd never seen a filthy Marine officer before. Welcome to the war. I was shocked by what I saw. The Marines of Charlie Company were dirty, unshaven, and grim-faced with thin hollow cheeks, the result of two meals of C-rations a day for weeks on end.

The Marines busied themselves cleaning rifles and cooking C-rations over miniature tin can-sized stoves. Some stood around smoking cigarettes or cigars, and they were all dressed in a jumble of uniforms. Their clothes were ripped, ragged - a mixture of tiger-striped, standard camouflage issue and enemy uniform shirts. Their green canvas and leather jungle boots were unlaced and some were barefoot, their socks hanging on nearby tree limbs.

I thought I was in a hobo jungle full of maximum security prison inmates. Cold blooded snakes, they possessed a stridency and callousness developed from suffering the deprivations and indignities of a long, hot jungle war. Some had already been in country for thirteen long, brutal months and starting their second tour in combat.

All Marines new to combat units were ignored by the veterans. They were shunned. Nobody even wanted to know their names. I received the same treatment. I may have been "outstanding" in training, but here I was inexperienced and, therefore, dangerous to myself, which was acceptable, but I also brought a degree of danger to them, which was not. I was a *freshy*, a *cherry*, a *FNG* ("fuck'n new guy") - pond scum. I had no combat skills, therefore I was a liability; barely grist. To be accepted was going to take time and I would first have to pass the bloody shared experience of combat. Being a replacement meant being relegated to the lonely margins of the unit. I felt that I was a useless stranger and didn't belong there.

The air temperature grew cool and then cold as a gentle rain started to fall. I dug the rubberized cloth poncho out of my new backpack and put it on, pulling the hood over my helmet. The rain tapped out a message on my cowled head. I thought, *You're alone, you're stupid, and you are with the most dangerous group of assholes in the world – tired, hungry, pissed off, battle-hardened Marines out looking for stone-cold killers—the North Vietnamese regulars. Damn, what next?*

In answer to my unspoken question, my new fire team leader rolled up in my face and told me I was going out on a listening post (LP) tonight and I should saddle up and get ready. He told me I was going outside the wire just after dark which was quickly approaching.

When the time came, we walked, bent at the waist for some reason I wasn't aware of at that time, quietly into the wet, green, rapidly darkening, steaming bamboo jungle. The Corporal positioned me in front of a fallen log, and I sat down. He muttered some vague instructions and faded away. I sensed what to do and chambered a round in my rifle. I settled in and just waited in the light rain, as darkness closed in around me. My first day in the field was ending. My first night was just getting started.

The rain intensified after sundown and the drops hitting the leaves of the broad jungle foliage made it impossible to hear anything. It was dark, darker than I had expected out there in the bush. What little moonlight that did filter through the clouds was diffused by the mist rising up from the wet ground and impenetrable jungle canopy. Cold and very wet, I hunched my shoulders forward to conserve heat and make my silhouette as small as possible, settling in for what was going to be a long, uncomfortable night. The hardships were just beginning. This would be just a small sample.

An hour into my stupefying ordeal, staring into nothingness, mesmerized by my situation, I felt a hand grab the curved brim of my steel camouflage-covered helmet and jerk me back over the log. My entire body weight was raised and pulled over the dead tree in one horrendous motion. As I hit the ground, I sat up and felt the blade of a K-bar Marine combat knife pressed across my Adam's apple. I heard the angry voice, "If you ever fall asleep on an LP again, I'll slit your fucking throat."

"I wasn't asleep," I tried to explain.

"I'll kill you myself and save the enemy ("gooks") the trouble, you maggot." Then he disappeared back into the green, rainy darkness, moving ever so slowly to guarantee silence. The harshness of this new reality was setting in. I resumed my humiliating vigil, very aware of my vulnerability.

I was relieved by another Marine, who crawled out to get me about an hour later. I found my way back to the alien group to spend the rest of the night huddled in my poncho under a tree. I never fell asleep. The breaking sun the next morning was the most comforting sight and cause for joy in my young life. Sunrises would remain sacred to me forever after and for the rest of my born days. Every sunrise, every one of them, would be a cause for celebration.

~ PATROLLING ~

American military policy early in the Vietnam War had been the Strategic Hamlets Program. In 1966, however, that policy shifted to Pacification, which intended to build pro-government civilian infrastructures in each village. To protect these villages against attack and infiltration, American troops were tasked with search and destroy missions and endless patrols of the surrounding areas, to "show the flag" and to interdict enemy incursions. While U.S. forces generally controlled the countryside during the day, the guerilla VC usually controlled it by night. They were adept at infiltrating the villages and, even without heavy weapons or air power, managed to inflict heavy casualties on U.S. and Army of the Republic of Vietnam ("ARVN") troops through ambushes mines and booby-traps.

On one of my first night patrols we came across a large contingent of VC or North Vietnamese Army (NVA). As I lay on my stomach on a steady inclining embankment, probably a dry irrigation canal, I was surprised to discover that someone had inexplicably made the decision to not engage the enemy as they passed by. When I questioned what was going on, I was told to shut up and keep my head down. When I tried to crawl up the side of the ditch to see what was really going on, I was pulled back down and sternly told to stay put. I was totally confused. Weren't we here to zap commies or had this suddenly become a discretionary war? I never did get an exact answer, but eventually found out that it was wise to choose your battles. I think now that we were on a reconnaissance patrol and not supposed to engage the enemy.

Patrolling in Vietnam was supposed to be going out looking for trouble – a hunting trip. The strategy was that by walking in the rice paddies or jungle we would cross paths with a group of VC or NVA, get the jump on them and kill them ("dust their ass"). That almost never happened. The reality was the opposite. We would walk out and it seemed liked the VC would know everything about us, like where we were headed, and would go ahead of us to lay mines, booby traps, or just take pot shots. We became professional targets. The only questions were whose turn was it to get hit and how they'd get it – a bleak proposition that gradually embittered us, turning any remaining humor a dark black. Cynicism became an everyday part of our lives in the boonies. Fighting the VC and NVA was like boxing smoke.

~ CRISPY CRITTER ~

Patrols were a game of chance – human roulette – and I was getting eager for the kill. I thought about death and the process of dying but I had never even seen a dead human being. I felt almost eager to encounter my first dead man. Death had always been an abstraction. I was curious about the effect witnessing death would have on me. As I found out, it was a profoundly emotional experience.

On one patrol, a platoon-sized combat sweep, we walked on line through a large sandy clearing each man spaced apart, some looking ahead and alert, others lagging behind to sip water or otherwise listlessly sleepwalk in the heat and humidity of the day. As we walked through a sandy treeless clearing, I suddenly saw a crumpled mass just ahead. I approached it cautiously, anxious to identify the curled-up shape on the ground that I suspected would be human. My pace quickened until I pulled up short. In fact, it was a dead Vietnamese.

The barely recognizable human head hung awkwardly on the carcass's shoulder, not quite disembodied. The scalp was seared black, with only small patches of hair remaining. One eye had been scorched closed, the eyelid welded shut by some type of intense heat. The other eye had been half-burned, the eyeball still precariously laying on the remnants of skin on the scorched cheek, dangling from the remaining thin muscle. The toasted eye looked alive, searching for a way home, back to the security of the skull, back to where it belonged. It would never make it; its skyward focus would never change again. What a sad end for an eye. Seeing this burned remnant of a human being was making me dizzy. The lower jaw was agape and the corpses' bleached and brilliant white teeth permanently revealed. The lips were gone. The macabre expression, a sort of toothy smile, and the almost peaceful fetal position allowed this twisted, partially clothed body to almost seem alive, yet this man had probably been burned alive—barbequed by American Napalm or baked by the tropical sun. I would never know which.

As more Marines wandered over to stare at the body, I shook myself free of reflection and morbid fascination, and said, "Hey, it's a dead gook – a fuck'n crispy critter."

Pausing only a second or two longer, we moved on slowly, not talking, only walking straight ahead. Then we navigated carefully around other barriers: stumps, logs, and other stuff on the drifted sand with no soul – like my first dead man. My first dead man, but he would not be the last by far. The worst was yet to come; I felt it in the pit of my stomach. "God," I pleaded silently, then tapped the brakes on my emotional downward spiral and diverted my thoughts to the ordinary. I hadn't showered in four days.

As we moved on, a gentle South China Sea breeze pushed the scent of decaying human flesh up our noses. The dead man's own indigenous bacteria was against him now, busy finishing the grim task that perhaps an F-4 Phantom Jet had started, turning him first into liquefied mush, and then into dirt. The prospect of ending my life all alone like this V.C. soldier had was overwhelming. I puked through my nose, not wanting anyone to see me getting sick—my own stomach acid burned my nostrils. The putrid, pungent scent of death in Southeast Asia was gone for the time being, but that distinctive, sickening sweet odor would return many more times. We moved silently through the sand dunes to some point on our map, turned south, I think, and returned to our patrol base.

~ UNHINGED — UNFRIENDLY FIRE ~

Very early on, the war in Vietnam took on new unfamiliar dimensions. For some reason they developed a disdain for one another - two Marines with a visceral contempt that exceeded jealous rivalry. It was loathing. At the time there was a growing animosity between Black Marines and "whitey." Their rage was directed at the undefined establishment. It was old pale males that put them in the untenable unwinnable "conflict." While the rest of the "folks back in the world" were enjoying the tune on turnout hippie/civil rights movement, they the dark green Marines were warrior slaves in some of their minds disproportionately represented and persecuted. They believed they were bearing an extraordinary burden of the war. Disgruntled they walked out "en mass" from some of the battalion areas – and returned only when ordered faced with charges of mutiny – they surrendered.

But these two white Marines hated each other more. The reason is lost now.

Again, that is the nature of recollections. Memories are creatures of the moment; they evolve over time serving different purposes at different intervals in our lives. The lesser Marine desperately wanted to get out of Vietnam. The other more stout and resolute

Marine was willing to serve out his 13-month tour. Frustrated, the frightened Marine pressed his nemesis to shoot him in the leg. The comparative wound would get him out of the "boonies" and harm's way. I stood there and watched as they negotiated this oddest of pacts. Bartering only the distance and the other's willingness to take this thing all the way. Soaked in sweat, the angry, disillusioned Marine walked 20 paces or so away and set his leg away from his body doe-se-doe style heel down toes up in the sand. Then he instructed his enemy in a loud voice filled with conviction to "shoot me." Gladly, the other obliged taking careful aim while lowering to one knee where he could steady himself. He clicked off the safety and slowly pulled back on the trigger. My neurochemistry accelerated — intense emotions hung suspended. I knew this moment would get lodged in my brain in a remote cluster of neurons and be difficult to organize, this among the most unpleasant war time experiences would be difficult for a variety of reasons.

Fratricide: witnessing a conspiracy of an illegal act, the reversal of courage in the single splitting of a second. The bullet boring into the lesser Marines calf muscle would make him the most gallant if only for the moment and the stout Marine a villain. Then the shot rang out – he'd missed! Frustrated, the bullet recipient moved closer halving the distance – saying "now you dumb ass, see if you can hit this," providing the same pose and now easier target. Without any hesitation the Marine re-aimed, yanked back on the trigger and shot him.

~ 1ST BATTALION, 27TH MARINE'S DECLASSIFIED AFTER-ACTION NARRATIVE ~

On April 2, 1968, the 1/27, under the operational control (OPCON) of Task Force X-ray, moved to the area of Hue city. During fighting in that area 1/27 played a significant role in destroying the remaining North Vietnamese troops who had previously been part of the forces attacking Hue. During the month of April 1968 over 5,300 small unit activities were conducted by the 27th Marines. These activities resulted in over 350 contacts, of which 200 were initiated by VC/NTVA, and 150 initiated by friendly forces. Due to the deployment of the lst Battalion, 27th Marines on 31 March to Task Force X-Ray, the Command was required to make temporary TAOR (Tactical Area of Operation) adjustments in order to meet the assigned mission and still ensure that intensive small unit saturation patrolling of the rocket belt was accomplished. No named operations were conducted during the month of April. Numerous smaller un-named operations were conducted. A total of 29 Combat Sweep operations of company size and five Clearing Operations also of company size were among these un-named operations conducted. Small unit operations for this Command consisted of 3,835 patrols within the Regimental TAOR and the AO assigned the 1st Battalion working with Task Force X-Ray. Additionally 1,456 small unit ambushes were conducted.

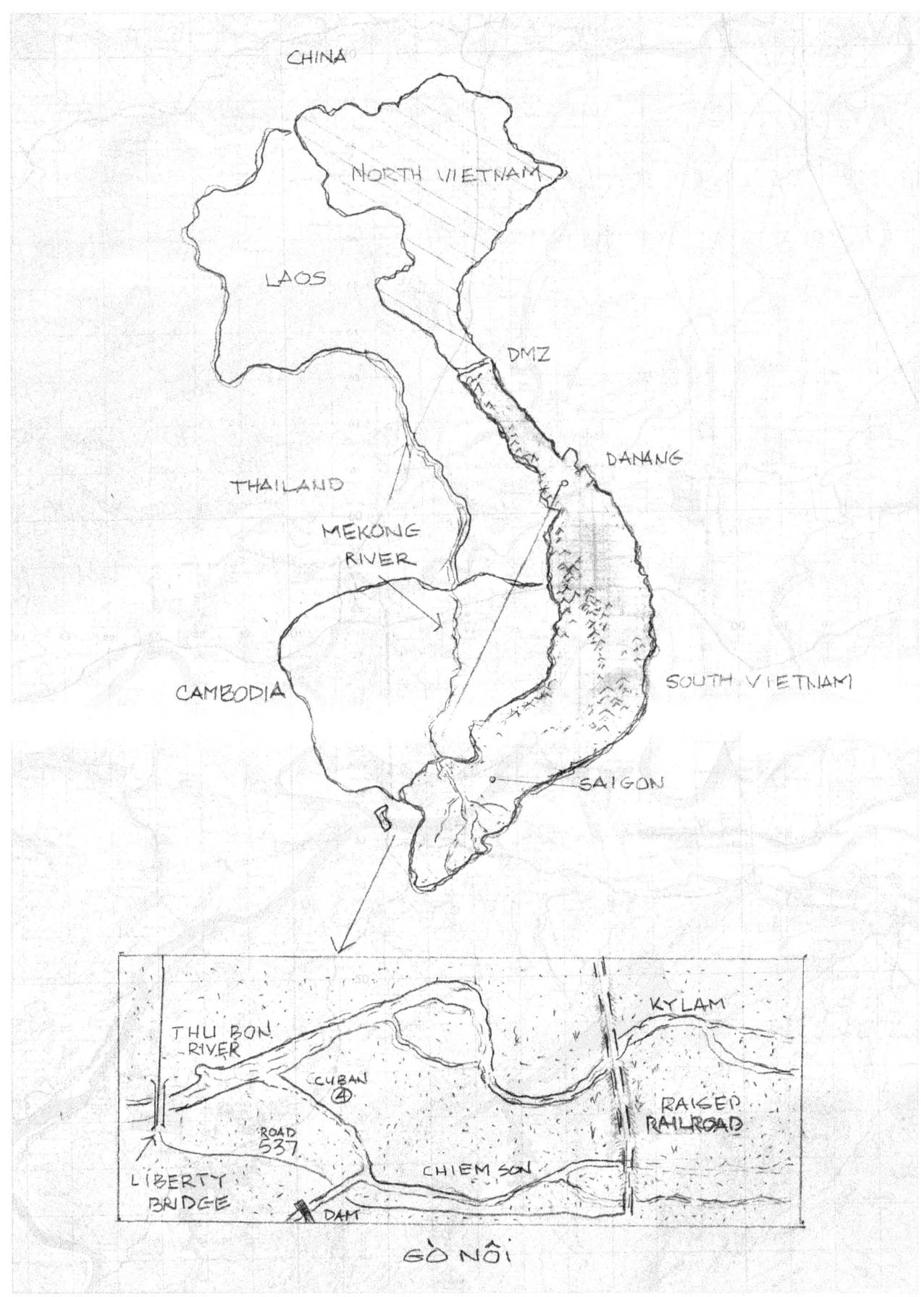

MAY 1968

Light My Fire - **The Doors**

~ Go Noi Island ~

Go Noi Island, located some 20 miles southwest of Da Nang, isn't really an island at all. It is a vast alluvial fan shaped delta, a transitory plain made up of a mixture of gravel, sands, and silt. The rivers are part of a great watershed that directs the monsoon rains to the South China Sea, building Go Noi Island over tens of thousands of years. The names of the rivers that built Go Noi Island vary and are taken from the region they flow through. The same channel can have a different name every other mile or so. The rivers that coursed through the tactical area of responsibility (TAOR) of the 27th Marines were Song Thu Bon and the Song Ky Lam.

We called Go Noi Island simply, *Gonad*. It was easier to say and reflected nicely how we felt about it.

The seasonal rains that began in late summer and lasted through October created torrential downpours and opaque feelings in the Marines, for a new treacherous element had been added to the mixture. These rains sucked the heat from the air and the ground and created a grim chill that rattled your teeth. The rains poured over the nearby mountains coaxing rock fragments from the nearly vertical cliffs. The weathering process is predictable. It occurs year after year, decade after decade. The rock is first broken physically then altered chemically — dissolved and mixed again by the monsoon rains in the swollen rivers into a mysterious brown-colored witch's brew that flows to the sea. The disintegration is a combination of the breaking and shattering of the rock which reduces it into smaller and smaller fragments. The impact of the water and its ability to penetrate even the smallest cracks finally weakens the rock and gravity forces it down the steep slopes. The abrasion of the rocks in the tumbling, churning water finishes the job. Eroded now, it isn't rock anymore; it has become something else.

The majestic mist-covered vertical faces of the peaks to the north and south of Go Noi are endlessly being transformed over time as the branches of the rivers and small tributaries strengthen their flow to the brackish Dai estuary and finally to the South China Sea. The process of disintegration of the rock starts as a trickle through the hills and rocky gorges of the mountain jungles above Go Noi. The rivers end, very often in a horrendous torrent that fans out and imperceptibly blends into the warm salty coastal sea. The rivers lace back and forth, diverted and rejoined countless times, always changing, each season producing a slightly altered flow. The flooding rivers scour the delta, and it is renewed showing a different face each year. The water course has masked and unmasked the truth of the river basin thousands of times.

Thick with foliage, the rough mountain slopes surrounding the sandy delta appear deceptively peaceful and safe. They are not. The wonderfully romantic-looking, green valley-walled pastoral landscapes are lethal. The NVA had dug into these hillsides, like their grandfather did years ago to fight the Chinese and then the French. When they fight, this is where they live. It is their warren. It is their home. Now, it is from here, this redoubt, that they will fight the Americans. A massive enemy military offensive was scheduled to begin in early May, and it would start here on the coastal lowlands.

Over eons, bit by bit, the mountains had become the horizontal plains of Go Noi. The solid rock eventually would become soil. Decomposed, the feldspars, ion oxides, and picas of the green mountains would, over time, become the substance of Go Noi. The destruction was not always gradual; it could happen in a single season, over a summer, in only months. The process of destruction was accelerated by the intense heat, the moisture, and the cataclysmic fall of the rock fragments to the valley floor. The droplets of monsoon rainwater, transformed into rivers, flowed to the sea, leaving the demolished rock as irregular mounds of sand. Piled in great white and tan heaps, the great sand bar became the medium for low-growing vines and mulberry trees cultivated for silk worms, peanuts, bananas, melons, and the delicate, small, red pineapple plants native to Vietnam.

The light-colored sands of Go Noi Island absorb heat and reflect light. Patrolling here was difficult. Walking was a tedious chore, and the glare of the reflected light forced your eyes into an almost permanent squint. Saturation patrolling on the sand spit was an all-day, all-night, full-time effort. Walking on the sand 16-18 hours a day took its toll. Like the mountain rock, the process of decomposition of the Marines had also begun. It was insidious, almost undetectable, but nonetheless unrelenting. The combination of heat, moisture, and the abrasion of this form of combat created a sort of gravity and warfare of its own. We were all being worn down, metamorphosing into something new. We would never again be carefree high school boys. We were now combat infantry Marines.

The use of counter guerilla warfare strategies, primarily by the Marine Corps, were not allowed to work over widespread areas of Vietnam. In the summer of 1968, the North Vietnamese switched tactics to more conventional and aggressive type combat. Unknown to us grunts, the island of Go Noi was becoming a strategic lightning rod. A safe haven for NVA and Viet Cong for years, intelligence reports showed three local Viet Cong units located on the island: T-3 Sapper Battalion, R-20 Battalion, and V-25 Battalion. Throughout the month of May however, Communist forces in Quang Nam were making preparations to launch an offense into Go Noi to capture full control of the area and use it as a staging area

4 MAY, 1968

DEAR BROTHER MALCOLM,

ITS MORNING NOW, AND THE SUN
IS ALREADY HOT.

I LIVE IN KIND OF A "FORT" ITS

REALLY A 360° PERIMETER AN IRREGULAR
CIRCLE. WE ARE GUARD BY SNIPER TOWERS
SAND BAGS, BUNKERS, LISTENING POSTS
4 FLAME TANKS, CONCERTINA WIRE, CLAYMORE
MINES. "HUEY" GUN SHIPS, HAWK MISSLES,
AIR SUPPORT. NAVAL GUNFIRE, "ARTY" (ARTILLERY)
GRUNT PATROLS, PUFF AND SPOOKY.
OH! by THE WAY "THEY" GOT TROUGH LAST
NIGHT AND INTO OUR CAMP. HOW? WHO
KNOWS NO DAMAGE NO CAUSALITIES

MY TENT-BUNKER IS ABOUT 60 ft.
AWAY FROM THE TRENCH (DEFENSE) WE
GOT SOME MOTARS THE OTHER NIGHT
WHAT A SCRAMBLE - I ENDED UP IN THE
TRENCH WITH MY BOOTS RIFLE TROUSERS
AND ALL MY AMMO & HELMENT. NO SHIRT
OR FLACK JACK JOHN WAYNE STYLE.

AT NIGHT IS WHEN ALL THE ACTION IS ~~DURING~~ THE DAY IT'S LIKE BOY-SCOUT CAMP.

HOW WAS TRACK A FRESHMAN REALLY HAS GOT MUCH OF A CHANCE BUT WHO CARES.

ME AND A LANCE CORP./POPE JUST KILLED A BIG LIZARD. I'LL SKIN IT AND SALT IN FROM THE MESS HALL. POPE PLAYED SEMI-PRO BASE BALL IN NEW ORLEANS.

I GOT A HAIR CUT FROM A VIET-BARBER A SHAMPOO.-MUSTACHE TRIM- TOTAL COST 60¢

NOW ↓ THIS HOW I WANT MY MUSTACHE

I DON'T THINK JOANNE AND I WILL LAST THROUGH THIS. BUT WHO KNOW GOT TO RUN.

GOING UP TO HUE NEXT WEEK MORE ACTION

LOVE, George

Have Fun This Summer be good

for future attacks on the major city of DaNang. They had begun re-infiltrating forces back into their old positions on Go Noi. U.S. Military Intelligence reported elements of the 2nd NVA Division and the 308th NVA Division were also infiltrating the area, apparently in an effort to connect with VC units already there. This information convinced Major General Don Robertson, Commander of the 1st Marine Division, that he needed to take action to deprive the Communists of the use of Go Noi Island.

In early May, company-sized operations were ordered into the area, originally using the 2nd Battalion 7th Marines. These operations would continue throughout May and June, with units from the 7th Marines, 5th Marines, 26th Marines and 27th Marines rotating in and out of the area of operation. The overall operations would become known as Operation Allenbrook. Charlie Company, 1st Battalion, 27th Marines would become directly involved in late May, fighting elements of the 24th NVA Battalion. Throughout the early part of May, however, we were running village sweeps and other functions in support of the main event, but the collision course was set. Soon the 308th NVA Division, with a stellar history of combat, and the 27th Marine Regiment, who had chiseled a place in history on Iwo Jima at the time more than twenty years previously would meet. The fighting that was about to occur in the river basin and the coastal lowlands would become some of the bloodiest of the entire war.

~ AN INSPIRED LEADER ~

The walk to our first rendezvous with the 308th NVA division on Go Noi started with a long march through the island toward the northwestern hills above the delta. We filed in around tanks, walking beside and behind them, sometimes dog trotting to keep up. At times, we even hitchhiked on them, scrambling on board when we heard the tanks at the head of the column gun their engines, or when we saw the black diesel smoke cloud as the engines lugged down by what appeared to be a change of gears. The unfortunate ones who didn't get on board had to lope behind breathlessly and run in the dust kicked up by the squeaking tank tracks. Then, gunfire would come from somewhere and the whole battalion would stop. We'd take cover along the side of the narrow dirt road or on the new path cut in the 8-foot high sharp-bladed elephant grass by the tanks if there was no road to follow. Combat seemed like a game to me. It wasn't real yet. It was as though I was watching myself from outside my body.

When we moved, some Marines were volunteered to flank the column by walking farther out in the bush, parallel to the main body to protect it from ambush, snipers or some other surprise attack. As the column turned a sharp left near a bend in the trail, a few of the flanking Marines were suddenly ambushed, cut down by machine gunfire. The wounded Marines were all critical and could not move. All the other Marines, including me, were gripping the ground, hiding from the snipers.

"Corpsmen up! Corpsman!" we all screeched.

Our brand new U.S. Navy medical Corpsman ran from the rear of the column, from where he had previously been banished. He crouched behind one of the idling tanks, surveying the tall grass where the wounded Marines were down, then, suddenly, he bolted into the grass

Amtracs taking us out in the "boonies" photo: L. Fernung

and zigzagged running in a combat crouch from one wounded Marine to the other, treating their wounds and bellowing orders for their fellow Marines to come and get their writhing buddies. Like the lead goose in a migrating flock, the Corpsman had transformed into an inspired leader. He would pierce the wind and lead the way. He entrained us emotionally, if just for that moment. Leadership in Vietnam was transitory. It would rotate – each person would eventually be tested as a leader, one way or the other.

In less than 10 minutes, the new combat corpsman had stunned the Marines with his skill, courage and resoluteness. He was in. He was one of us, ("a *combat motherfucker*"). In a few weeks he would treat me for a freak accident on a night patrol. In another few weeks he would earn a Purple Heart and later a Bronze Star for his bravery.

~ AIR SHOW ~

Three different times our unit found itself fighting in the mulberry field on Go Noi Island – May 28, 29, and June 5, 1968. It was odd and ironic – each time we were in the exact same spot, running essentially the exact same mission, blazing away, shooting with everything we had into the dark, densely forested tree line. The NVA were deeply dug in throughout this area and rooting them out was a chore. Each time we tried we ran into fierce opposition, as they fought back with intense automatic weapons fire, mortars, and deadly accurate snipers. Firefights are noisy, inaccurate, confusing affairs. We would shoot blindly into the forest to suppress the NVA gunfire, and they would shoot blindly back hoping to prevent us from advancing.

The first time we were there, our assault had ground to a standstill, even though tanks reinforced us. I was still eager for the fight, but the effects of heat, confusion, and fatigue were starting to accumulate. We seemed to be fighting for the sake of fighting, not winning or losing, just fighting. Everything we could hurl at the NVA horizontally was being poured into the tree line. It was always the same. This particular day, and it is difficult to untangle the intermingled memories of the three similar days, the tanks suddenly stopped-firing, and moved away from the tree line in reverse. Firing from our concentrated positions slowed at the same time, and gradually ended. Only the NVA were firing, but even their fire gradually slowed and then stopped. An eerie silence gathered over the battlefield. From our fighting positions we just stared straight ahead wondering why we had ceased firing.

The answer came soon enough in the form of Navy fighters, A-4 Skyhawks. They came in from the right of our position, the roar of their jet engines trailing some distance behind. As they approached the troublesome tree line, they released their canisters of Napalm. The long, tapered, oblong, green cylinders tumbled end over end as they fell to the ground, erupting on contact in an enormous, elongated orange and yellow fireball looking like the head of a giant match being struck in slow motion against the earth. A second jet followed the first, its lethal ordinance dropping from the underbelly of the Jet and out of our sight into the thick, black clouds of smoke quickly billowing up to obscure the devastation. Another jet followed, repeating the same sequence. The entire forest quickly became engulfed in flames and thick, curling clouds of smoke.

The heat was intense and sucked the oxygen from the air to feed the furious blaze creating a brisk windstorm as the air rushed in to stoke the lapping hungry flames. Even at 100-200 yards away, we felt the heat of this incinerator on our faces and chests. The wind rushing past us evaporated the sweat from our soaked clothing and cooled our backs.

Above the carnage, the jets banked right, lifting higher, distancing themselves from the battlefield as they quickly disappeared out to sea or to whatever safe haven they had come from. The attack had taken only seconds. In front of us the inferno of burning gelled gasoline consumed everything: the tall, vine entangled trees, the light green broad-leafed banana palms, and God only knew how many enemy soldier's bodies withered and crackled in the intense heat – although we never gave that a second thought at the time.

After only minutes of viewing the devastation, our trances were broken by incoming small arms fire coming from the NVA still entrenched in the smoldering forest. It was on again and we dutifully began returning fire, only to have the battle interrupted again by another group of jets. This time Marine F-4 Phantoms came screaming in. They were on the same flight path as the others but lower and they came in, it seemed even faster, delivering a series of highly explosive bombs from under their wings onto the target area in rapid succession. BOOM! BOOM! BOOM! The concussions shook the earth around us as the jets pulled up and banked away, rocking their wings in a wave, as if to say howdy from the Marine Airedales. ("Airedales" – a derogatory nick name for anyone associated with the Marine air wing/or air craft)

The last Phantom came in much lower than the others. A Marine lying on the ground next to me, in a very matter of fact, all-knowing way, said, "Bachelor."

"How do you know that?" I asked curtly, pissed off at his presumption.

"Just watch." He was implying that any dare devil Marine this audacious and willing to face court martial and the consequence of this slightly suicidal act had to be unmarried.

The monosyllabic Marine turned out to be right. The pilot dropped his bombs then jumped his aircraft skyward at an extremely steep angle, rocking his wings in a parting salute to the Marines on the ground. The throaty, grinding turbines straining against gravity created a deep roar. He was showing off and received a series of wows and whoas up and down the line of Marines on the ground. Faint cheers could still be heard over the din of gunfire as we went back to applying suppressing fire on the tree line again.

The side show of fire and fury provided by "the bachelor Marine pilot" had been very entertaining, but now it was back to business. Or so I thought, until I looked out toward the sea and saw, in the distance the bachelor carving a large circle in the blue sky as he arched back away from the sea and toward us; he descended lower and lower, picking up speed as he returned for his encore. Coming in just above the burning trees he rolled over and flew upside down the length of the battlefield. The entire shooting gallery of grunts on the ground stopped to watch. He cocked his head toward the Marines positions, clearly looking "eyes right," then refocused straight ahead, turned his aircraft with a sudden jerk and barrel rolled, waving his wings a final time. BAM! His afterburners kicked in, thrusting the plane forward at a steep angle. Then he was gone. Discarding caution, I spontaneously jumped to my feet, cheering, "Get some!"

As I did, I looked around to gauge my overwhelming response compared to the others. Every Marine was on their feet, wildly cheering the bachelor. I looked again at the Marine to my right. He had a wry grin on his thin dirty face, and he calmly said, "Out-fucking-standing."

That Marine: the pilot with balls of steel had made our day. We were all inspired by this overachiever.

~ Suicide is Painless ~

Riding into combat on a helicopter was always wild. As we landed into the unknown with the whirlpool of windblown sand roaring below us, I became more excited each time. It was simultaneously exhilarating and frightening. Helicopters increasingly delivered us to our missions and I grew to both fear and derive excitement from the whoop-whoop sound of the rotary blades, and the noisy blast from the engine.

Our war was intensifying daily. The stifling effects of the heat, ever present and the realization that you could be next, tempted some Marines to self-inflict wounds in the hope that they could escape the "boonies" and the chance of receiving a more serious, mutilating wound or being killed. You didn't have to be in country long before you had seen legs and arms blown off or mysterious chest wounds where Marines would disappear, screaming into Medevac helicopters and no one would hear how so-in-so was doing after his injury. If the Marine was a FNG – a new replacement – very often you didn't have time to know his name and didn't want to in most cases. Personal relationships were a liability—best to fight among nameless faces.

A wounded Marine we loaded on a helicopter had a mauling groin injury. He lay screaming in agony aboard a chopper as the Corpsman worked on him. The Marine was always showing pictures of his pretty high school girlfriend to anyone who had the time to look at them. After the explosion, I guess the prospect of a sexless life without a penis and testicles was too much for him to bear.

We were all hunched over, trying not to get sandblasted when the shot went off. Then we heard "Jesus Christ!" shouted by the Corpsman as he crouched over his charge then a very loud, dull thud from inside the chopper. The Corpsman screamed, "Oh my God! He shot himself!"

In his agony aboard the helicopter, the mutilated Marine pulled the .45 caliber pistol from the Corpsman's holster, chambered a round put the muzzle to his face and pulled the trigger. Then the chopper bolted into the sky, kicking up thick clouds of sand in its wake. The Navy Corpsman stumbled out of the helicopter, fell to his knees in the cloud of swirling, stinging sand and sobbed. That was that.

~ FRAGGING ~

Artillery support, from distant fire bases, strategically located around Vietnam, was very often the saving grace for Grunts, both Marine and Army. Also known as "Arty," 155-millimeter howitzers, could drop high explosives (HE) or white phosphorous ("Willie Peter") rounds almost anywhere, and do so with astounding precision. One hundred meters between you and the enemy was the accepted tolerance, but if a position was being overrun, some courageous officers would call the artillery in on their own men and themselves ("danger close.") Many Marines believed that it was a preferable alternative to being swarmed over, shot, and bayoneted to death; the logic being that at least that way we'd take some of them with us.

We were using our entrenching tools to dig in late one afternoon, preparing for night company-sized patrols. As we were completing the construction of our fighting holes, rounds from automatic weapons poured into our perimeter. Mortars soon followed. The attack seemed far more intense than the harassing and brief "nighty-night kiss" of one or two sniper rounds we received so often just at dusk. This was an assault, and we were taking casualties. A Lieutenant made the decision to call for artillery. After reading his map, he radioed in the grid coordinates for our position and asked for a marking round of flesh burning White Phosphorous ("Willie Peter"). The round landed some distance from us. The Lieutenant made corrections to adjust the trajectory of the artillery rounds and probably gave the standard order, "Fire H.E. (High Explosive) for effect." On the other end of the radio, the Marines at the artillery fire base made the corrections and fired their salvo, the fire control Marine responding, "Shot, out."

Most of the time H.E. does its duty, arriving on time and on target, but this afternoon as the sun was setting, the last light of day dancing through the trees, a round fell short, exploding in the middle of our ring of fighting holes. When we heard the round coming in, we raced for cover but one Marine, a grunt jumped into a hole filled with too many other Marines. He lay exposed to the bombardment sprawled across the top of the hole already filled to the brim with other Marines. The massive explosion sent shrapnel ripping through our encampment, and a piece of the razor sharp hot metal sliced the Marine's ass cheek off. As he lay in the open, bleeding, the enemy disengaged and silently withdrew farther back into the bamboo thickets and disappeared for that evening.

As night fell around us, a few disgruntled Marines were were incensed. They believed the young officer had tried to call the artillery in too close to our position or had given the wrong coordinates. They talked about revenge, determined to extract their own pound of flesh. Tension mounted as they gossiped how they would frag (a derivative of fragmentary grenade) the naïve, unseasoned, and unaware officer.

Weeks later, as the story that was passed around, the Lt. walked down a sloping riverbank to approve a spot to ford a wide but shallow river. There, as he approached the water's edge, he snagged a booby-trap trip wire. The concussion threw him several feet from where he had been innocently looking into the distance across the surface of the shimmering water. He was trying to find a safe place for us to cross the river. Rather than respect, he had earned disdain from the disgruntled and exhausted Marines by a mistake he most likely did not commit. To be clear, the story about the Lt. and the possible assination, most likely did not happen. The Lt. was seriously wounded by an enemy surprise firing device (a booby-trap).

He was carried by his wounded arms and legs to a clearing and was laid face up on the sand, to stare into the hot sun. A "dust off" medevac helicopter was called in. The Lt. lay there alone, waiting, twitching, and moaning, sucked forever into a horrific, life-altering spiral of unlikely circumstances, removed from his command, superseded by the cruelest of fates. Our ceaseless patrolling continued; the mutinous Marines satisfied with their having heard the Lt. was wounded. The Marine officer continued his military career successfully. Years later we met again, and he asked about the incident. I denied any knowledge of the rumored circumstances of his injuries – he'd earned peace of mind and my respect.

Often fragging was a death sentence for an infraction of some private unstated rule by an aggrieved individual or a conspiracy of a small estranged splinter group. Other times, it was self-inflicted. Either way, it was cowardice. With one Marine, we knew it was self-inflicted.

The Marine, we called Cat, simply did not have whatever it took to be in this war. He had had enough. He talked out loud about fragging himself; to get out of Vietnam, if not in one piece, at least alive. One late afternoon, after a long day of moving across the sand of Go Noi, Cat wandered off into the bush alone. Once there, he would have tilted his helmet back, to protect his neck, then pulled the pin on a hand grenade. Before tossing the grenade backwards over his shoulder, he would have lifted up his private parts to protect them. After it landed nearby, the grenade probably rolled across the ground, spinning first, then wobbling as the timed fuse burned exactly at its prescribed rate. The deadly oblong grenade would have skid

61

across the loose sand, slowed and rocked a little end to end before coming to a stop. There, it would lie as the fire in the fuse would burn furiously round and round the circular core. The fuse would heat first and then ignite the tightly packed chemically sophisticated explosive charge. Cat must have waited for what would seem like an eternity. Alone, as the setting sun back-lit the quaking bamboo leaves twisting and turning in the gentle breeze, he probably gathered his thoughts regarding what he was doing. He had cast his lot now, his fate would be sealed. He was joining a different Corps. He probably clenched his teeth, biting hard as every muscle in his body tensed, turning rigid in grim anticipation. He undoubtedly counted the seconds off and may have even asked God to understand, probably just a "Dear God." There wouldn't have been time for an eloquent plea or elaborate summoning of any celestial powers. Assured of his decision, convicted to his purpose, in these last moments Cat was undoubtedly convincing himself of the obscure heroism associated with fragging out. He would have already rehearsed the lie he would have to tell over and over to explain, for the rest of his life, the evil day he was removed from combat in Vietnam. Then, BOOM! The impulse from the expanding searing gas and red-hot metal fragments ripped him to the ground, face down in only one sudden millisecond.

We heard the explosion and the scream which sounded like *Ouch* and *Oh, God* smeared together. In unison we ran to the sound and found Cat lying on his side, pathetically smiling at us. The pain hadn't started yet. I had seen wounds like this before. Cat had no idea what was waiting for him. He said he had tripped a booby trap and although he stuck to his story, none of us believed him.

We were a long way from anywhere and the sun was setting, darkness rapidly approaching. Cat's luck had run out, for no medevac choppers would be flying out to fetch him this night, there were battles all over Vietnam and real Marines needed help. Cat would just have to wait.

Designing hand grenades and calculating the wounds they will inflict is no doubt an applied science. There is probably an entire governmental agency dedicated specifically to insuring that the wounds from a grenade explosion are traumatic. Cat's were. The back of his arms and legs had been deeply lacerated by the almost square, serrated fragments from the grenade. It was only a short time until the pain became excruciating. It might be inappropriate to judge someone else's moral conduct, right from wrong, good from bad, and the choices they make during war. There is a categorical imperative, however, you can question a person's timing. Here is the existential import: don't frag-out at dusk, you'll have to wait a long time to get medevac'd ("dusted off"), especially if everyone knows you did it to yourself.

Cat's luck returned, after hours of agony. A nearby patrol was ambushed and a Marine was shot and seriously wounded. A medevac was called out and Cat was able to ride to the field hospital with him, at around 0200 hours. A medevac extraction is extremely dangerous after dark. It draws enemy fire to the hapless helicopter and leads them to the location of Marines on the ground. Fragging was a loathsome, dangerous reality of the war in Vietnam. Twice I had been the only survivor in our squad after an engagement – the only man not killed or wounded.

22 may,

Dear Mom & Dad,

We just got out of the boonies —
after 12 days. Our Company
is slowly being wiped out.

My fire team leader was
dinged yesterday. We were
on a four man patrol I was
humping the radio. we got sniped
at & hit it. we were pinned down
I called in — but another fire team
had hit a booby trap about the
same time and needed medi-vac

Our team leader ran over
to my position. I was laying on
my back trying to get the C.O.
as he slide right be side me
his legs were sticking out ZAP
one round blew a hole in is leg
the size of a quarter. I patched
it up with a battle dressing.

He was hurt'n bad. laughing
and swearing at same time

Well I switched the freq. to
35:50 (medivac) but no response
So I tried to switch back to
preset. freq. but it wasn't preset —

So we were 2 miles away

with no radio - snipers - and
a wounded team leader - gee!
what to do? We were saved -
2 Hours later by an ARVN platoon
and our platoon. To say the
least we were P.O'd after 2 hours
in the sun. Sorry about
this mixed up letter, but am
hot, tired, P.O'd and just plain fed-up
groovey huh? Well I also satifisfied
that I can do this _____ job.

I ast night had a 10 hr. patrol
and almost got it by our own
artillery, groovey! God Save The
Grunts. I dig it. but bitch alot.

Tell people (gramma, others
that am fine but can't write in
the boonies but will try.

KEEP THE FAITH.
LOVE,
GEORGE

TELL
HI
MAC
LTC

One time my squad was riding security on top of an amphibious tracked vehicle (AMTRAC- nicknamed "coffins") on its way to a large river, where my squad would swim and otherwise relax. I had been held off the duty for disciplinary reasons, (questioning direct orders) and for punishment had been assigned to unloading resupply helicopters – hot, dirty, exhausting work. While the squad was driving to the river, the AMTRAC they were on hit a land mine and everyone was wounded.

Photo: Associated Press, 1968

PJ my fire team leader at the time arrived that afternoon by resupply helicopter. He had been in the rear area where he periodically received malaria treatment. That evening, because we were it, all that remained of the squad, we shared a fighting hole. At twilight, mortar rounds started pouring in on our position in a symphonic requiem. I was angry and despondent because of the events of the day, so I told PJ that I was going to frag myself by sticking my leg up out of the protection of the fighting hole, hoping that some shrapnel would hit me. Lying on my back I poked first one leg then the

Photo: L. Fernung

65

other out of the hole. PJ fought to keep my legs down, but each time I pulled away and poked it right back into the air. When we realized the ridiculousness of what we were doing, we laughed until we had no more strength.

Resting between the exploding rounds, we agreed to peer over the top of our fighting position (hiding place) and look at the carnage. Slowly, cautiously we raised our heads and looked out across our dug-in patrol base. There were arms and legs sticking up from fighting holes everywhere, some had even rolled up their shirt sleeves and pant legs. Astonished, using the sidewall of the hole for a brake, I slowly slid back down and started laughing. It was unbelievable. I looked at PJ for confirmation of what I had just seen and heard. Wow! The entire patrol base was loudly, defiantly laughing. I don't know what touched it off. Pick something: the heat, the war, officers, politicians, the Jodie motherfucking cowards back home, banging our girlfriends, the NVA or us, farcical characters in a ludicrous setting. There must have been twenty naked arms and legs in the air at the same time looking like porcupine quills. It was amazing.

~ THE GRAVEYARD ~

My fire team, coincidentally all came from Illinois, except one, a Navajo from Gallup, New Mexico. We were "the boys for Ill-in-noise," and everybody had a nickname. There was Smitty (Black), JR (Puerto Rican), Rat (Polish) and Chief (Navajo) who hated whites in particular, non-Indians in general, and this stupid white man's war almost as much as he hated himself. My moniker was "Bergy" or "Iceberg," depending on the day and the circumstances. When it was *Iceberg*, a more sober response was being requested. We patrolled

Photo: L. Fernung

66

mostly at night, with short patrols during the day, totaling 14-18 hours. The sand would shift like ball bearings beneath our boots during the endless plodding.

It was exhausting and sleep was at a premium. On some patrols we would take turns sneaking catnaps ("copping Z's"), at the checkpoints. Some of the team would sleep while the others monitored the radio and kept watch. Rat consistently went to sleep on his radio watch. He must have had narcolepsy, because when he was scared, he would doze off. He got disciplined ("the shit kicked out of him") more than once for falling asleep on radio watch.

Out in the countryside, the Vietnamese sometimes bury their dead on raised graves that are about 3-4 feet above ground. They are usually marked with wooden or sometimes stone plaques with the deceased's name and other information on it. Small Buddhist shrines also marked some of the graves complete with incense holders and bolts of silk adorned with calligraphy describing the deceased. Over time the graves get neglected, become covered with grass and blended in with the natural surroundings and the older graves.

One night, around midnight, we set up an ambush in a graveyard. The raised graves provided excellent cover and afforded great protection. The irony and symbolism of being protected from death by a grave escaped me at the time. We assigned radio watches and took turns listening in the darkness and looking for any sign of the enemy. Normally I resisted napping when we were on patrol, but this time, exhausted, I took my turn. Rat assured everyone that he could stay awake, and we took him at his word. I had no more than dozed off when the sound of automatic weapons woke me up. My eyes flew open! Muzzle flashes were everywhere, appearing from all angles. Rounds flew into our position, zinging in all directions. It was mayhem, Marines shouting, rolling around on the ground looking for cover and a place to return fire. A VC patrol had walked past the sleeping Rat undetected into our position. Here's my bet - the VC were as surprised as we were. However, we claimed a victory, after all we had set up the ambush the VC had walked into it, a Marine had fired the first shot and we think we killed one VC and wounded another. For his dereliction, we sentenced Rat to two full weeks of Ham and Lima Beans, the worst of the various C-Rations we ate twice each day.

~ BIG TRUCKS ~

Sometimes we would go by truck from the 27th Marine headquarters (HQ) area to the North. Prior to leaving, the truck drivers would bravely get ready by sandbagging their vehicles, cleaning their rifles, or otherwise preparing for the long, arduous drive. Anywhere *north* was serious. The grunts would ride in the back of the big trucks open to the elements and enemy fire to wherever, running the risks of snipers, mines and ambushes along the way. We would stay where we were dropped off, alone in the bush, cursing the truck drivers for taking us there and knowing that the drivers would be back at HQ that night in time for evening movies, showers, and hot chow—maybe even a beer. There was a gross disparity in the Vietnam experience. My early patrols were mostly local. They were dangerous, but local. They had not been in the North, or on Go Noi Island.

~ POT ~

Going "North" was fearful. North was a dreadful place, and it didn't really matter where it was, if it was North of Da Nang, it was bad. Whether it was the Ashau Valley, Quang Tri, Hue, Khe Sanh, Con Tien, or the "Demilitarized Zone" (DMZ), they were all deadly, scary places where most of the Marines killed in Vietnam would die. By March 1968, half of all Marine infantry was located in I Corps, the farthest northern reach of non-communist Vietnam. I Corps was one of the four military operational areas and was the most critical and dangerous. Marines would die in the mountains, the blue-green forests, the coastal plain, and the rice paddies, but it seemed they always died in the North - *up country*. The most dangerous place on earth at the time.

One group of grunts, who had been in the boonies up north, near Hue for weeks, had just returned to our base. They cleaned their weapons, took showers, ate a hot meal, and were authorized two beers each. Then they were left alone but together in the warmth of the Asian night to sort out and make sense of their experiences in the North. These Marines were keenly aware of each other. They were also keenly aware of the thousands of Marines in the countryside surrounding them, the thousands of Marines who had come before them and the thousands of Marines who were still to come after them. They were aware of the Marines encircled at Khe Sanh and they were surrounded by "the old corps" Marines, unseen and invisible, though nonetheless present. But now – on this night *They* were the Marines.

I walked into the 20-man tent where they had gathered to talk and just be together. The night was an angry eggplant black except for faint stars twinkling in the dark sky. My long hot summer in Vietnam was just beginning. In the distance, booming artillery rounds were being sent somewhere, spiraling out into the darkness. In the tent, the case-hardened Marines back from the North were gathered in an odd circle. They were a close-knit fraternity – teenaged men who had experienced extreme danger together. The cots had been pushed to the edge of the tent, out of the way and in the middle of the circle of Marines wooden artillery round boxes were neatly stacked. A single large candle provided a flickering, eerie light. Jimi Hendrix music blasted in the background from a battery powered phonograph. The same 45 rpm record was playing over and over again. The shirtless Marines were laughing as they upended and threw back their government issued beers. Then, unannounced, one Black Marine lit a joint, a marijuana cigarette dusted, I found out later with either opium or heroin. He inhaled deeply, and with a broad, confident smile held his breath and when he couldn't hold it any longer, he choked and coughed through his nose making a squeaking noise in the back of his throat. He then passed the joint, pressing it with his thumb into the index finger of the Marine next to him. Laughing in anticipation, the next Marine did the same, each Marine in the circle trying to hold in the potent purple smoke longer than the others. They

26 MAY

UNITED STATES MARINE CORPS

DEAR mom & FAMily,

Sorry about not writing but that's the way it goes. We are going on a Big operation in the morning so we came in to form up we are going by Chopper. Am seeing moderate to light action as the papers would say

I sent a picture of <u>Stork</u> and self to Joanne I hope she shows it to you. like most am reluctant to write details of what am doing but will have Stories and such to relate at a later date if I remember — you know how mind works. Tell Gramma I appreciate letters and think of grand dad in WW <u>I</u> and gordon in WW <u>II</u> He's (both are groovey) can't think of anything to write except war barf! Oh you can send 3 pair white cushion sole socks to absork persspuration. maybe pictures of family car junk house

Say Hi to people tell mark to cut hair and start working now to get in shape for F.B.

Love Gers

tell to dad to by new sports coat on me with 275.00 am sending soon.

also get hair over →

& see how much money I
have counting 275.00 on the way
next week. income tax, ETC.

love,
George

Think
about
family
often.

will
try to
write
more
soon

would laugh louder as the joint was passed, Marine to Marine, forcibly breaking the hold the experience in the North may have had on them.

"It ain't nothing. North ain't nothing motherfucker! Charlie ain't shit" They would bark, referring to the faceless enemy. The cauterizing of raw emotions occurred right before my eyes, blocking whatever had happened to them, keeping it from seeping deeper into their inner-worlds.

Some of them debated the right or wrong of Marines from our Battalion being investigated for the murder of five Vietnamese civilians who had been shot and hung at Xuan Hoa hamlet. The debate followed a logic of men who spent their days surviving and killing. *Killing civilians is wrong man, but were they really civilians? War is about killing – they die, or I die. Most civilians are VC – gotta kill them before they kill us. You can't win a war without winning over the people, and you don't win over the people by killing them. I ain't here to win a war; I'm here to survive for 13 months!*

The debate was soon eclipsed by the music and dope. The dilemma became clear. Some of the Vietnamese who had been killed had been lynched. The process for those killings took the longest to carry out, and the killers had to be up close and personal with their victims. Therefore, their logic went, hanging was the least moral. The argument being that when killing someone, the distance you are from the victim exponentially decreases your responsibility for the victim's death. The farther away you were from the person you were trying to kill, the more chance came into play. To hang someone required cutting and measuring the rope, deciding weight, balance, where to position the rope, pulling the rope tight, then listening to the victim gagging and watching him jerk until he finally just swayed, limp and lifeless. It was combat logic of young men, but everyone leaves combat one way or another. When the social context changes, can the justification for one's actions also change?

Does the distance from killing perhaps an unseen, unknown enemy allow you to evade responsibility? Without some mechanism at work to distribute guilt, how could these men be free of the responsibility of their actions? They were determining a biography that would be inconsistent with their actions.

Things having to do with morals are different during war, and social constraints are relaxed. Guilt and anxiety are distributed to the group. We become more emboldened by the presence of others. We do things we may not have done were we alone. Responsibilities and consequences are also diffused. Is a homicide that may aid your own survival justified? Many attempt to atone later, when the fog of war clears, but the tie that binds remains knotted tightly around warriors. Individual actions and consequences are inescapable over time, regardless of any previous distribution. The chickens do come home to roost. Murder is murder. War will come back to those warriors who fought in it in a long elliptical loop and stare back at them from the warrior's own eyes.

I had never smoked pot before, let alone Vietnamese pot with its well-known, well deserved, and internationally admired reputation for its virility. I turned to beat feet out of the tent, but the exit flap was guarded by two nasty looking tautly muscled Marines, who just smiled flatly at me. I was going nowhere. I rejoined the circle, enjoying the experience, even more now that I knew the inevitable. As I counted the Marines around the circle in; 5-4-

3-2-1 Marines I would be smoking dope for the first time. I could hardly wait, and the others couldn't wait either. Everyone knew who the new Marines were, and we needed to be tested. This was one of those tests - Pothead or straight/ trustworthy or not?

I watched and learned how to receive the joint. *Nothing to it*, I thought. Finally, it was my turn. The smoke from the crumpled hand-rolled joint was thick, and it tasted strange. I gulped down three large mouthfuls as the others smiled and cheered the ubiquitous, "Get some!"

I passed the joint and stared upwards, my eyes closed tightly. Bonk. It hit me immediately - Stoned. On the next round a new joint was passed and I found out how to use an M-16 rifle as a bong and to blow smoke deep into another Marine's lungs. After an undefined time, I wandered out of the tent and into the warm tropical night laughing. The stars were still there and the outgoing artillery was still outgoing, pounding sonorous bass rhythms into the night, providing the back beat for an invisible choir, the accompaniment for some fierce battle being fought somewhere in the bush where angels were being made. As the moon and the clouds played hide and go seek, I wondered what would happen next. May 1968 was going to be a personal growth month for me. I laughed to myself about the vise I was trapped in. What was I doing here, stoned, in my cut-offs and flip-flops? I had made a central discovery that evening: a profound revelation. All of this – the war, killing people I didn't know – was stupid. The dizzying euphoria of the pot was like a slow soothing piano solo.

I hooked up with one of the Marines from my fire team and together we wandered through the battalion area. We accidentally stumbled into the "Guns" tent, where the M-60 machine gun crews stayed when they were in the rear area. Somehow, they felt we were trespassing and made certain we knew it, as they loudly jeered and shouted insults, primarily, "Fuck you!"

The only thing I remember was taking three steps farther into their sacred sanctuary and offering them a blessing in return. "Fuck you all. Y'all gunners ain't shit."

I woke up the next morning with the blazing sun beating down on me and found that I was lying on the hot sand in a bloody, bruised pile of me. I never smoked pot in Vietnam again but tolerated others who did. My only requirement was that no one gets high a few hours before we were to go on patrol into the boonies.

~ OFFICERS ~

My feet were rotting. Layers of flesh – soft, white, spongy skin came off with every change of socks. "Immersion Foot" was the technical name and almost all of us had it. "Bad" feet were part of the bargain for service as an infantry Marine in Vietnam. Tropical fungus grew rapidly in the ideally suited warm, wet, dark spaces between our toes.

I was sitting on a green towel in the already withering morning sun, administering to my tender feet with a bottle of Absorbine Jr. that had come in a "care package" my grandfather had sent from home. The bottle came equipped with a circular sponge applicator tip. As I dabbed the stinging fluid on my toes, the pain became more intense each time the bottle top touched my flesh. I winced and whined and finally, in frustration, tore the top off the green bottle. I took a deep breath, for courage, decided where I needed to pour the antiseptic fluid, turned my head away and upended the bottle. The green fluid quickly seeped under my skin, into the cracks and sores. My eyes burned and teared instantly, and I let out a profane yelp, "Jesus H. Christ - Son of a bitch!"

I continued to whine and curse as more and more of the medicine found each and every exposed nerve of my shredded precious feet. In the middle of one outburst a pair of clean jungle boots, the number one sign of an FNG, appeared in the field of my downward focused vision, and a voice said, "Wow, that must really sting. Does that stuff really work?"

"Of course not, dumb ass!" I snapped, "I'm just doing this for the entertainment value. What the hell do you think, for Christ's sake?"

The calm, deliberate voice replied, "Do you need anything? Those look pretty bad."

I was about ready to tell the dumb ass to buzz off, but I looked up instead, to find a Marine officer with a concerned look on his face and an oak leaf cluster on his collar. "Oh! Sir, I'm sorry sir! I didn't know it was you!"

"That's OK, son," the Major replied, "Carry on. And take care of those feet."

I nodded, watching as he slowly walked away to give face time to other men in the area. That Major (Major Skipper) was good at that. Many Marine officers stayed with their men and lead from the front, but some, regrettably did not. In the Marine Corps we call commanders, Skipper. So we naturally called this Major "Skipper Skipper" redundantly. A few weeks earlier, when Skipper Skipper was wounded, we expected him to have himself medevaced to a rear area, and that we would never see his spit and polish, college educated ass again. Instead, the next day, as we were departing our base on Amtracs (Amphibious Tractors), I climbed onto the third or fourth track in the column and was stunned to see Skipper Skipper climbing into the lead track. His arm was wrapped in bandages, but he was there, back with his men, still leading from the front. He could have sat this one out, but he didn't. He was on the first track, the one most likely to hit a mine and be disabled.

I remember now how I felt to see him there. I never have forgotten the obnoxious, self-absorbed, arrogant officers, nor have I ever forgotten the really good ones, the ones that connected personally with their men, shared the misery, danger and fear, and still kept their cool. The good ones inspired us all to trust their training, abilities, integrity, and judgments and to follow them – unfortunately, not all officers were good ones – but most were.

~ WATER ~

The heat and humidity rapidly pulled moisture from our bodies, sapping our energy and stamina. By noon on most days we were soaked in our own sweat and our rifles were so hot the black metal of the M-16 rifle burned our hands. The two canteens of water we carried were quickly finished off and out of necessity we had to use local sources to refill them. The water purification tablets (Halizone) we had to use gave the water an iodine taste, so many of us requested Kool-Aide to be mailed from home to kill the taste as best it could. We got water from tepid streams, bomb craters and hamlet wells. The NVA and VC would poison the wells of unsympathetic villagers with their dead bodies, weighing them down so they would sink and be undetectable. The Halizone couldn't kill all of the virulent strains of exotic bacteria—exotic at least to our western immune systems.

We all got dysentery and diarrhea a few days after drinking from a local source or spiked well. The consistency of hot latex house paint was all we could hope for. We sometimes stayed in the bush for weeks at a time with few creature comforts, eating two meals of C-rations a day, but gradually we got used to it. Life was very simple – kill the enemy ("gooks") – try to stay alive.

~ CHIEN TRANH STRATEGY ~

One of the basic tenants of North Vietnamese strategy, Chien Trish is commonly known as the 50-year-war thesis. This tenant makes it clear that politically and militarily, the Viet Cong were prepared to take as long as necessary to produce victory. Ho Chi Minh used the same basic philosophy for his war against the American military forces as he did for the French. The basic principle was simple: Even if you kill ten of my men for every one I kill of yours, you will lose and I will win. For you will tire of sending your men here to die before I run out of people for you to kill. You may not want to lose, but you do not have the desire necessary to win.

Having such a commitment gave PAVN Command General, Vo Nguyen Giap, wide latitude to mold his tactics and stage his battles at the time and place of his own choosing. This was indeed fortunate, for Giap's strength was in logistics rather than tactics, as can be seen in every set battle waged under his command, from the Battle of Ia Drang Valley to the Tet Offensive of 1968, which all failed to produce a real victory for Giap.

Military experts say that Giap's conduct of hostilities evolved five different times, but through most of 1968 Giap was still using Regular Force Strategy, which consisted of two fighting techniques. The Doc Lap Cach Danh, or independent fighting method, which was basically a series of simultaneous small scale military actions, none of which were important on their own, but combined were important as an irritant to the enemy, producing casualties, increasing stress and anxiety, reducing self-confidence and creating doubt.

The second fighting method, Hop Dong Cach Danh – coordinated fighting – called for specific large attacks against relatively important targets, with the stipulation that the attacks must be "perfectly planned and flawlessly executed." When the time was right, the two fighting methods would be combined into a full campaign in which military activities would escalate and intensify over a period of several months. Finally, his "comprehensive offensive" consisted of a massive assault on an important target, the loss of which would bring the enemy to surrender. Diem Bien Phu and the 1968 Tet Offensive are two examples of the tactic, one successful, one a serious defeat that, ironically, lit the fuse that would eventually produce victory.

~ MAY AFTER-ACTION NARRATIVE (USMC)~

May 1968 tested the Regiment's prior training and experience. Within two days after the 1st Battalion returned to control of this Regiment, the 27th Marines were directed to take operational control from the 7th Marine Regiment of Operation ALLEN BROOK, which was being conducted on the GO NOI Island, south of the Regimental TAOR. Previous enemy activity on the Island had resulted in a considerable infiltration north, and the island had been a relatively safe haven for both VC and NVA elements of regimental size or larger. Contact with the enemy was made resulting in heavy fighting immediately upon assuming OPCON of the operation. Elements of NVA were located in heavily fortified trenches, bunkers and fortifications and were considered to be high caliber fighting units. The Regiment pressed the attack on the VC and NVA units, supported by substantial air and artillery support, and was able to inflict heavy casualties on the enemy. Problems were few, and operational efficiency was considered to have been commendable. The one problem which was not surmountable was the intense heat encountered within the area resulting in a large number of heat casualties. This problem was alleviated substantially by the removal of flak jackets by the troops, thereby lightening the load and reducing the number of heat casualties.

The Da Nang area of operation still required saturation patrolling with particular attention directed to the areas defined as the rocket and mortar belt. The mortar belt was established on the 20th of May in an attempt to prevent future mortar attacks on the Marble Mountain Air Facility. The 27th Marines were assigned the responsibility of coordinating with the 51st ARVN Regiment, the 3rd Amtrac Battalion and 1st MP Battalion for the establishment of an effective counter mortar program. The counter mortar program requires extensive patrolling activities within the region designated as the mortar belt. The mortar belt has been established south of Marble Mountain Air Facility extending in a 3000 meter arc from the southern tip of the airfield at coordinates BT067732. Since the establishment of the mortar belt, there have been no reports of mortar attacks originating from within the area.

JUNE 1968

Summertime Blues - Blue Cheer

~ SUCCESSFUL AMBUSH ~

ON ONE LONG AFTERNOON PATROL we were ordered to travel a route that would take us on a circuitous loop ending back at our PPB (Platoon Patrol Base) after dark, which meant a higher probability of trouble. I was tired and pissed off, so while walking point I decided to try out one of the new baseball shaped M-33 grenades we had been issued. The old M26 grenades were oblong and had replaced the classic "pineapple" style grenades of World War II. Now we had the newest design, the "baseball" grenade, easier for Americans to throw. Curve ball, sliders, change-up, we all knew to how to throw baseballs.

"Fire in the hole!" I yelled, a military courtesy borrowed from the mining industry and then I pulled the pin and threw the grenade into a deep fish pond between some rice paddy dikes. The blast threw water in the air breaking the monotony and silence. PJ got angry, complaining that the noise had compromised our position and could help the enemy hone in on us. He was right, as it turned out.

This random, impulsive tempting of fate and baiting of the enemy was stupid, but I had started to feel a disregard for dying - like running up hill to jump in a coffin. I ignored PJ's complaints and kept our patrol moving at a slow steady pace. I moved us around the dry rice paddy dikes and away from the worn paths, both of which were likely places for the VC to set trip wires for booby traps. At sundown we took a zig-zagged course, to throw off any enemy observers. Once it was dark, we set up an L-shaped ambush along a three-foot high rice paddy dike. As we settled in, I could hear the sounds of the day transition into the sounds of night, tree frogs and crickets singing their rhythmic songs against the backdrop of the perfect stillness of the evening. We could feel the air temperature slowly drop. I always closed within myself at night, growing more cautious and alert. It was like pulling the bed sheets and blanket over my head as a kid.

The moon was rising. It was serene, almost peaceful sitting there, until whispers came down the line, "Heads up. Something's coming."

The alarm traveled in hushed voices, passed from one Marine to the next. "Stand by!"

"*Bullshit*," I thought to myself, someone around the corner of the L is hearing things. Straining to hear for myself, I held my breath and sat motionless. All I could hear was my own heartbeat thumping in my chest. Then, I heard it too, loose ammunition jiggling in a backpack, or in someone's pocket. It is surprising how far sound travels in the night air. As the sound came closer, we could even hear clothing rubbing – they were running toward us. The strides seemed farther apart and faster than a person just walking. Slowly, ever so silently, we all moved the safety on our weapons forward. Pressing our backs against the dirt of the rice paddy dike, we patiently waited for the enemy to enter the kill zone. Although frozen in place, my whole body was keyed up. My heart was pounding, the adrenaline rush had brought all my senses to life – I could see, smell, hear, and taste everything. Suddenly, over our heads an illumination canister exploded, launching a brilliant flare suspended by a parachute that began a slow descent toward us with a pronounced rocking motion and a distinctive hissing sound. Night instantly became day.

Jesus H. Christ, I thought, staring for a moment at the intense light of the flare. *What are they doing? They gave our position away.*

We had just lost the element of surprise. When I refocused my eyes straight ahead, I could see five NVA soldiers jogging across the rice field headed right for us. Our ambush opened fire on full-automatic knocking all five of the NVA backwards. They disappeared into the shadows as the flare burned out. A Chinese Communist designed ("Chi-Com") grenade landed in front of us, sending shrapnel and debris in every direction as it exploded. We all hurriedly rolled over to the other side of the dike for cover and opened fire again. I decided this would be a good time to try out another M-33. I grabbed one of the baseball grenades from my webbing, pulled the pin; held down the spoon and readied myself to rise up and pitch it over the dike. I took a deep breath, steadied myself and thought, *here we go* – 1, 2, 3. I rose up on both knees, but as I did, inexplicably I lost my grip on the grenade, which rolled off my hand. In the dark I blindly followed the probable path of the grenade down and luckily caught it. Clumsily, I used a shot put motion to push the grenade with the palm of my hand up and over the dike. Then I ducked and yelled, "Grenade!"

As I went down, PJ rose up to unload another magazine of ammunition into the kill zone. As he did, my grenade exploded just on the other side of the thick rice paddy dike. The concussion and a single piece of shrapnel hit PJ and knocked him backwards. I thought he was dead at first. I thought I had killed him, but it turned out that the shrapnel had ricocheted off his forehead, gouging a furrow of skin from his scalp. Rather than penetrate the skull, it had just knocked him down leaving a square shaped wound on his forehead.

The firefight continued for a short while before the enemy withdrew from their untenable position. The shooting gradually faded away and then stopped all together. We took time to quickly collect our loose gear using red-lensed flashlights and then hastily made our way back to the PPB. The sun was just starting to rise when we arrived. It was probably now June 23, 1968. As soon as we got there, we were met with questions about the firefight. Everyone at the PPB had heard the gun fire in what was being called the "Arizona Territory" because of all the shoot outs. We got the Corpsman to treat PJ's flesh wounds and the cuts and abrasions I had sustained.

As he was treating our wounds the Corpsman said, "Well Marines, you may have just earned yourselves Purple Hearts."

It seems the blood from the cuts and the small shrapnel wounds plus the bruises and dirt were not enough to earn a Purple Heart medal – a low honor at the time, many of us dreaded and derided as a symbol of not being able to duck or run fast enough. PJ looked at me with a scowl and I silently returned the inquiry with shrugged shoulders and raised eyebrows. What could I have said?

A patrol was sent out to search the ambush site for enemy bodies, but returned with only a few backpacks and some ammunition. The episode had dented PJ's head and my pride but not our friendship; we even joked about it for the next few days, with PJ wanting to know why I had fragged him. The Corpsman did not record treating our wounds. I think the fact that I threw the grenade, and our surly attitudes, persuaded him we did not deserve medals.

~ BOOBY-TRAPPED ~

We continued the journey toward our rendezvous after medevac helicopters and trucks removed the wounded to the rear. Our journey had just begun and the attrition from the heat, booby traps and the NVA snipers was already escalating. The next few weeks were not going to be a pleasant experience. We were going into their backyard, an NVA stronghold in the foothills that overlooked Go Noi to root them out of their ancient tunnels and caves.

Hours later, our company broke away from the tanks and we formed up to take the point on the assault.

The plan was that we would be first to make contact with another unit of the 26th Marines, then together, we would move on line into the mountain strongholds. The relentless 110-degree heat, humidity and razor sharp grass took its toll. We had to stop frequently, rest and regroup. One Marine refused to move out after one rest period was over and threw his M-60 machine gun belts to the ground. He wouldn't budge. I was the point man, so I picked up the machine gun belt of ammunition he had thrown down, slung it over my shoulder, and started walking into the bush—a small price to avoid charges of a mutiny (combat refusal) and the wrath that it would bring from the noncommissioned officers and new junior officers. Later, relieved of his burden, the Marine reluctantly moved forward with the rest of our unit.

Farther on, another Marine, exhausted, gave out under the blistering sun and drenching humidity. He could not continue and needed help with his gear. I took his "starlight," a night vision monocular rifle scope that gathered any light from the darkness and magnified it thousands of times. The view in the scope was a mint green circle that illuminated almost anything light-reflecting or light-producing in its field of view. It gathered any available light and magnified it. One could see into total darkness with that scope. I put the strap over my neck and slung it opposite the extra belted ammunition I was packing and then dutifully moved out.

We slogged through the grass and brush and came to a barren field, the main channel of the Song Thu Bon on the left and a dense tree line 200 yards to the right. Ahead of us, about a quarter of a mile was an elevated berm crowned by railroad tracks, the old National Railroad. The shoulder of the earthen berm was covered in grass, overgrown brush, and small trees. As I stepped out onto the field, I got the sinking feeling that this was not a good idea. As I continued forward, I pivoted my head left, right, center, left, right, center, searching for any hint of ambush. I had to be careful and step over the dried dirt clods that were about the size of footballs. It looked like the grey ground had been plowed wet, rolled up, and then allowed to dry out. A gentle wind kicked up dust from the field and small whirling clouds spiraled upward, creating a light greyish-brown haze that blurred distant images.

Footing was awkward and the forward pace slowed accordingly. Then sniper rounds, from the railroad tracks, began to hit around us. The bullets whizzed only a few feet from my head, and at first I didn't realize what was happening. The bullets sounded like very large, fast, buzzing bumblebees. It was only a moment after the deep tenor whir passed within feet of my head that I heard the faint report of the rifle – POP-POP-POP! I looked over my shoulder and saw the bullets landing behind me, kicking up towering plumes of sand.

The shots came from hundreds of yards away – the railroad tracks. I dropped to the ground as the rounds started hitting beside me. Again, I could hear some of the bullets passing over my head, snapping loudly as they broke the sound barrier. You could feel the power in the tiny bullets as they sped by. I dreaded being hit by one—the damage would be horrific. I turned my head toward the river to get lower to the ground and saw a Black Marine beside me, piling dirt clods in front of him to build a makeshift wall to hide behind. I started laughing because he was laughing. He smiled at me and just kept piling up his protection. He seemed to always have a smile on his face. It was a strong smile, full of comfort, joy and strength that opened even the darkest heart. He was one of those guys you just had to like. Weeks later, while crossing a river in full gear, Vietnam took him without a sound. He was on an inflatable air mattress that rolled over and because he couldn't swim, he simply slid beneath the water, weighted down with the burdens of war.

From a prone position I aimed where I thought the shots came from and squeezed off two quick rounds. After only the second round, my M-16 jammed. Frustrated, I started reaching for clods of dirt and stacking them up in front of me. We lay there for about five minutes. I used some of the time behind my little fortress to clear my rifle. The Marines whose rifles worked laid in suppressing fire. I continued stacking clods, building my protective fort. It seemed more immediately relevant than returning fire with a rifle subject to jamming. The sniper fire stopped eventually, and, with no actual signal, we all seemed to just quietly stand up in unison, dusting ourselves off and looking around to see what damage was done. No one had been a hit.

We calmly gathered our gear and again pushed forward, toward the railroad tracks. We had spread out on line, trying to put as much space ("interval") between each of us as possible. I finally approached the toe of the slope of the berm and started up toward the tracks, twisting one way and then the other, forcing my way through thick, waist-high brush. I clambered to the top and inspected the aging rail bed, an old French colonial public works project. To the west, down the tracks, I saw what remained of an old rail trestle across the river, long since destroyed. The whole situation reminded me of exploring an old, abandoned house – its creaking roof about to collapse.

Because I had gotten to the tracks early, I waited on one knee for a time and then decided to find a comfortable spot to rest in the shade on the reverse slope. I knew we'd eventually regroup and form up on line for a new go at our combat sweep. The straight line created by the tracks was the logical place to do that. I saw a comfortable- looking spot and gently lowered myself and my new increased burden to the ground. It felt great to get that load off my back.

It would take some time to get everyone there, so I laid back and closed my eyes. As I settled in, I felt a hard lump under my buttocks. I reached around to find out whatever it was and as I lowered my right arm it caught on a piece of thin nylon fishing line.

Odd, I thought to myself. As I shifted my weight and grabbed for what I thought was a rock, the tension on the line increased. The line was attached to what I was sitting on! It was a grenade.

"Booby-trap!" I yelled as loud as I could.

The Marines near me scurried for cover behind; trees, downed logs or just fell flat, faces to the ground, arms covering their heads. The wire was connected to an American M-26 grenade in a C-ration can with the pin pulled. If the grenade, whose time delay fuse had been cut to zero, was pulled from the can, the firing mechanism would release, and it would detonate in a fraction of a second. There I sat, motionless with both hands under my butt holding the can, the nylon fishing line, and the grenade together. Because I wasn't instantly blown to pieces, after a few minutes, folks began to stir and more Marines were coming up behind me.

"Trip wire," I yelled again, and the stunned new arrivals looked around for clarification. I yelled, "Hold up!

 God damn it, I'm sitting on a grenade."

Marines were milling around exchanging expressionless glances, waiting for the explosion. I could almost hear them thinking, *The poor dumb shit's going to get cut in half at the waist. He'll only feel it a couple of seconds before he buys the farm.*

More time passed and I just sat in a frozen stalemate, both hands locked behind my back around the can and grenade. I was getting scared. I'd had time to contemplate my own destruction, the pain and how my death would crush my family. My grip tightened on the can. I leaned my head back and looked skyward, pleading, "Hey God, get me out of this. Let's talk. Can we make a deal?"

Then I heard a deep voice, in an affected, exaggerated fake Mexican accent, "Hey bro, ju got in some sheeet maann. Hold still, Bro, I'll get ju outta here!"

The man behind the voice, who turned out to be Corporal Marty Garcia, knelt down, clasped his hands over mine and pushed down on the can, making sure his hands controlled the can as much as mine. He was taking no chances. When he was sure of his control over the canned grenade, he slowly released one hand and grabbed a safety pin that he had brought with him. (Safety pins were used to adjust the length of the cloth magazine bandoliers of ammunition that we carried across our chests.) He inserted the safety pin in the hole in the spoon of the grenade and pulled the grenade out from beneath me. Smiling, he handed me the now-harmless grenade.

"There you go man. Be cool," he quipped, and walked away.

I stood there stunned, like a plastic mannequin, holding the grenade. War sometimes magnifies compassion and accentuates contrasts. I had just had a full measure. My knees were quivering, and my whole body was starting to shake convulsively. Then an officer I'd never seen before rushed up to me and started yelling, "I give the orders around here. I'm the only one who can give an order to hold up."

"Fuck you, sir!" I yelled (not really loud enough for him to hear clearly) and started walking toward him when two arms grabbed me around the chest from behind, picked me off my feet and carried me backwards into the brush as I punched and kicked the air in every direction.

"Settle down, man, it's over. Let it go or you'll go to jail. Let it go," my rescuer repeated as he set me down on the ground. Had he not interfered, I might have beaten the officer bloody and would have, no doubt, been brought up on charges before a general court martial. I was full of adrenaline from my closest call with dying so far. I never knew who the arms belonged to, just some Marine, I guess.

~ LITTLE DRAGONS ~

After weeks in the field, we had to shave where we could. Clean water to shave with non-existent. I used the steel pot of my helmet to scoop water out of a bomb crater to shave with. As I wet the razor and started to drag it across my face, I happened to look into the upside-down pot and found that the water in it was alive with small insect larva and pollywogs. Repulsed at first, I just continued to shave and watched as they twisted and turned in the warm, dirty water. They appeared like miniature sea dragons, arching their backs then submerging down into the brown soapy water. I watched their small, complex world and wondered how they had found their way first into the bomb crater and secondly into my helmet. When I finished shaving, I poured them all back where I had found them. Somehow, I felt they were survivors and therefore close to my wild, and now, misfit heart.

We all acquired some sort of gastric abnormalities from the local bacteria in the water we drank. The resulting diarrhea and dysentery created a variety of problems, not the least of which were merely walking and just staying hydrated. Vietnam seemed to be home for every type of dung beetle, small and large and everything in between. They were genetically encoded with the ability to instantly locate excrement of all kinds, fly to it and process it, either laying eggs and rolling it into a ball or consuming its nutrients on the spot. They would blindly smack your butt and fall into the recent deposit even before you could hike up

JUNE 7,
9:30

UNITED STATES MARINE CORPS

DEAR MOTHER AND DAD,
WE ARE STILL IN THE BUSH, CHARLIE CO.
IS STILL IN TACT... BUT WE ARE TAKING
HEAVY CAUSALITIES. STORK GOT IT....
I'VE SEEN IT ALL AND DONE MOST OF IT

IN THE SHORT TIME I'VE BEEN HERE.

MY SQUAD LEADER SAVED MY LIFE
AND I'M GOING TO TRY TO GET HIM UP
FOR A BRONZE STAR OR NAVY ACCOM, WITH
A COMBAT V FOR VALOR.

I SAT ON A BOOBY TRAP AND NEED
Someone to put The PIN IN while I held
The spoon down. He PUT A SAFETY PIN IN
IT. OH WELL!!

A LOT OF MY FRIENDS HAVE BEEN Hit,
AS A matter OF FACT MY WHOLE SQUAD,
WAS WOUNDED, EXCEPT THE SQUAD LEADER
AND I..? (12 men) I will come Home with
with a purple heart.. NO BIG DEAL

I'VE GOTTEN ALOT OF N/H Gear... but
Trade IT TO THE CLEAN UP MEN..... For
COOL Aid, Gum, money, THE GRUNTS DO IT ALL
AND THE TANKS, AND choppers FINISH IT
I HAVE BATHED OR SHAVED IN 20 days
UGH..

JUNE 14,

CRAZY
IDIOTS

UNITED STATES MARINE CORPS

Dear Mom,

A-OK, but we are getting our ass kicked "Charlie Co. is almost being wiped out, this junk is crazy the way the do things but I'm just a snuff!

can't write much but see what you can do about CPL. Marty H. Garcia he saved your sons life

Maybe write our Congressman or rep. or Have dad write my CO. Charlie Co. 1 Bn. 27th marines.

and suggest a navy accomadation with a combat V for valor.

OH. I'm the only one left of a 12 man squad besides Garcia who is my squad leader all have been causalties.

this pen is being shared we stole it. HA so must close.

KEEP THE FAITH.

INCOMING MAIL IS SEMI-REG. A-OK DROPPED by Chopper.

tell dad to write that letter as only a military man con. He should know how

tell Hi liz mal stive gramma papa Kick Este gordon all

Love George

83

your trousers. Plainly, Dung beetles would hurl themselves into your bare ass, and they hurt. Your semi-private moment interrupted by a spiny hard-shelled creature eager to eat your bowel movement even before it hit the ground. We couldn't even defecate without being attacked by something Vietnamese.

Sparrow Hawk missions were challenging. The chore is to lie perfectly still, stay alert, and monitor enemy movements. Some of the time, while you are lying on the ground, in the rain, you could also experience violent stomach and lower gastrointestinal convulsions. Then, as I have said, there were the rats, poking around for leftovers, and add in the ever-present vampire mosquitoes, with their sucking, buzzing and signature high-pitched "Z" whines, whose life work is to suck your blood. Remember, the job is to stay awake all night, stay alert, stay vigilant, stay silent, and stay undetected. More often than not, at dawn we would slowly rise and quietly disappear back to our base camp to be nourished, while letting the rising sun revive us as we recharged our blood supplies.

~ OPERATION ALLENBROOK ~

On the helicopter landing zone (LZ) in the midday sweltering head, we waited for the word to saddle up. The 1st Battalion, 27th Marines was in the process of assuming operational control of Operation Allenbrook on Go Noi island from the 1/26th Marines.

Tension and anticipation were building. We were all anxious. The ramps of the idle, twin-bladed C-46 Sea Knight helicopters were down waiting to take us out to Go Noi Island. We lay against our backpacks around the landing zone parallel to the helicopters waiting for the order to go. We had been briefed earlier that morning and had been instructed to carry a certain amount of ammunition, food and two canteens of water. The officers were moving at a quickened pace now. They walked in the intense heat of the tropical sun like men with a purpose. They seemed very serious, which was not uncommon for Marine officers, but you could tell this was different. This time the situation seemed more serious. The officers' bearing signaled this excursion into the boonies was going to be more intense.

An officer walked up to the side window of the lead helicopter and joked with the pilot for a few minutes. Laughing, he backed up and gave him a thumbs-up signal. When he cleared the landing zone the helicopter's engines started. The machine produced a shrill whine and blue-black puffs of engine smoke, then the rotor blades began slowly turning, bouncing and flexing as the spin increased. The limp lumbering blades stiffened and awakened as they turned faster and faster. The dust kicked up and swirled higher and higher shrouding the entire LZ. We averted our eyes, either down into our shirts or over a shoulder. The roaring engine noise became deafening.

Because no one could hear or see clearly, elbows and backhand slaps, conveyed man to man, the signal to stand up and board the impatient roaring machines. Orderly lines were formed at either side of the ramp and two by two Marines disappeared inside the bellies of the helicopters. There was a collective sense of urgency as all the aircraft quickly filled. We sat down in the rumbling hollow metal tubes on webbed canvas seats and packed ourselves together as tightly as possible shoulder to shoulder. An air crewman hurriedly paced down and back inside the beast making sure the boarding process was to his liking. Satisfied, he yelled something into his headset microphone. Then, as the rear ramp door closed, the engines wound up to full speed, the whole helicopter shifted, vibrated faster and faster, then whop, whop, whop, the noise roared into an earsplitting bawl.

The chopper pitched to one side, then jumped into the air, nose down, and lunged into the blue sky. We climbed quickly and the low coastal mountains soon disappeared from the view out the circular portholes that dotted the chopper's green fuselage. The miniature landscape below was beautiful, an odd contrast to the war raging throughout the picturesque countryside. The textured carpet of green, the mountains, coastline, and the surf, breaking on the shoreline with wind-driven white capped waves of first robin's egg, and then deep cobalt blue combined to paint a tranquil scene.

The aircraft climbed higher and higher, and the ride smoothed out. Some of us relaxed enough to look around. Others smiled and bounced to the rhythm of imaginary tunes; others just stared straight ahead in a fixed trance – deep in private thought, dead calm. Disjointed Jimi Hendrix and The Doors lyrics raced in and out of my mind. The music of the mid '60s, mostly Jimi's music, became a narcotic. Hendrix's music transported me away from the rigors and fears of combat and into the arms of a nubile fantasy princess.

The sensual dream world allowed me to step out of my body, to float above Vietnam and what had become my grim new reality. My dreams produced a powerful unconsciousness that surfaced as a mountain wind carrying me away from where I was. The dreams I enjoyed of women neutralized the effects of an extreme male environment, of brutal isolation and the fear of a death among strangers. The beauty once again moored my psyche back to the civilization I had known. I yearned for home and its human qualities. There was a larger force at work in my dreams of imaginary women. Real women were spirits, specters now, figments of a disintegrating consciousness, the progressive conversion to pure bestial male Warrior. It was their sex, their body parts, their gooey lips and what women represented – eternal life; that the violence of war and images of women fit so neatly together in this madness was both pleasant and troubling.

The haunting memory of the real world and real women vaguely reappeared as shadows in the word "Fuck!" The 'F' word and the act it represented were our breakfast, lunch and dinner, and our kiss goodnight. The word and the act were primordial expressions of dominance, power, control, and of all things conceived to be male. The 'F' word was a verb, a noun, an adverb, adjective, and a hand gesture. The 'F' word and all its incarnations were durable, omnipotent and ever present. The 'F' word was our job description. The 'F' word was a subconscious remnant of our sexuality, which was subverted by the war experience. How could life and death— the sacred and the profane—ever be so closely aligned? The 'F' word was the adhesive force, the boundary layer, between these diametrically opposed concepts – Thantos and Eros - life and death.

The helicopter jerked, pitched left and started a gradually tightening downward spiral.

My ephemeral escape over, I quickly returned to lucidity. Marines started checking their gear, adjusting their helmet chin straps, and squirming in the canvas seats. The anticipation of landing was palpable and hung in the hazy air of the interior of the hot, dusty, cramped aircraft. We dropped rapidly out of the sky and the hard rubber tires rammed into the ground and the ride suddenly was over.

The rear door ramp cracked open and the bright blinding sunlight flashed into the dimly lit cabin. The ramp was just a quarter of the way down when, astonishingly, bare hands, fingers spread wide, began to appear at the edges of the lowering ramp door. The hands yanked and jerked on the side of the door, coaxing it lower, trying to get it down faster. Then faces appeared—silhouettes backlit by the glare of the direct sunlight. Ghoulish blood-splattered faces of wounded Marines, their anguished faces twisted and turned in the dusty light. The powerful downdraft of the helicopter was mixing the sand in the air with the helicopter's exhaust, turning the hard quartz sand into stinging biting missiles. The door was only half down but the wounded Marines fought their way aboard, even as we, their reinforcements, deplaned onto the white sand.

Marines who were wounded themselves struggled with the critically wounded they carried in ponchos. Some of the wounded men were hoisted, one arm around the waist and the other arm securing the wounded Marine's arm around another Marine's shoulder. Other Marines limped and hobbled up the ramp, protecting injured arms, legs and shoulders. Pain and fear were imprinted, undisguised on all their faces. Their hands, covered in dirt and stained by dried blood, reached for the canvas webbing, some literally throwing themselves on to the seats just as they were vacated by the inbound Marines.

I hustled out the door, amazed at what I had seen. The hasty exchange of bodies – intact ones for damaged ones – lasted only minutes. I stared at the helicopter containing the wounded Marines. As the hydraulic door slowly closed, the faces of the wounded sadly said, *Good luck, brother. My war's over for now.*

Again, the entire bizarre process took only minutes. In a whirling storm of sand and noise the helicopter strained against gravity and then rose straight up to gentle the effects of the ascent on its new more delicate cargo. As the chopper climbed skyward, I peeked through my fingers that were guarding my face from the ballistic sand. On the side of the chopper in black capital letters, I read MARINES and said to myself, "You bet!"

The helicopter quickly disappeared over the distant treetops. It was time to punch the clock and go to work, I thought as I ambled to catch up to my squad, who were headed toward a line of trees. I wanted some pay back for the bloody mess I had just seen.

~ RUSH TO THE TREES ~

The average Marine grunt was usually more remarkable for his disinterest in the war and the alien culture than for his viciousness that was about to change. Sporadic small arms fire could be heard crackling up ahead. We assembled in a small line on the edge of the trees and started into the high elephant grass to our left. Once through the grass, we stopped and lined up ten feet apart and started out into the neat rows of miniature mulberry trees. The mulberry trees, used to grow silkworms, were between one and two inches in diameter and usually six to ten feet tall. The worms eat the leaves for food and spin their silk cocoons among the tree branches. The rich sandy soil was perfect for growing these trees, and they probably have been part of the landscape here for hundreds, if not thousands of years.

We were about a third of the way through the mulberries when gunfire erupted from the tree line of a nearby forest. THWACK! The bullets hit the small mulberry trees and blew them into fragments. Some only splintered, stood, and then gradually eased over. We ran toward the safety of a dry irrigation ditch that separated the cultivated mulberry orchard from the dark hardwood and bamboo forest where the intense but sporadic gunfire had originated. We had done this exact maneuver before, in this same place, but this time we had walked into a trap. More and more bullets flew through the air, cutting whole trees in half and dropping leaves and branches on us as we ran for the safety of the ditch. It was butchery. We had been caught in the open. In only minutes, wounded Marines lay everywhere out in the mulberry trees and along the ditches.

I had started to run for cover when someone motioned with his arm for me to follow him up a hill into the forest toward the source of the incoming rounds. I didn't know who it was, so I didn't follow the order if that's what it was. I sat down and pretended I didn't see him signal. The battle raged on but for some reason, I decided this wasn't my fight - not today anyway. The idea of acquitting myself like a 'true Marine" and having no fear of death unraveled. I had regained full possession of a self I was determined to preserve. I reinterpreted my military purpose for this day – stay alive.

Unvoiced thoughts raged through my mind. *Fuck you*, I thought. *I'm not doing it. This is bullshit. I'm tired of this shit. What's the fucking point? We'll just end up like those dudes on the LZ, all fucked up for nothing.* I was stupefied. I intellectualized and rationalized the fear, but it was raw paralyzing fear nonetheless. My new chore that day, I decided in one momentous conclusion would be tending to the wounded not war fighting.

After listening to the horrific noise of the battle building up around me, I heard the voices of the group of Marines returning from their rush into the forest. They had destroyed a machine gun position, caught a few NVA in the open fleeing uphill toward their bunkers, and killed them all—except one prisoner—a young boy. They had the packs, knives and rifles of the dead NVA to prove it. One of the Marines received the Silver Star for his participation, but he died in the process.

As they approached, someone asked, "Where were you man?"

"Right here," I replied.

"Hey, where's your rifle?" he said, not pressing for an answer to his question and bypassing the first question - my absence from the ad hoc team.

"I don't know," I yelled back, defiantly. In the confusion, I had somehow actually lost my rifle, the most serious and cardinal sin a Marine can commit, especially in a battalion-sized firefight. *What have I done?* I pondered, *What just happened?* With one mistake had I made

June 16

UNITED STATES MARINE CORPS

Dear Mom, & Dad & herd

I'm writeing this letter on my knee sitting on a grave in the sun (100°F) watching (on guard) the operation we are now engaged in is called "Allen Brook" We lost 3 more (charlie company) men this morning. We will be out of this valley (Rocket valley (Happy valley) in about 5 or 6 days.

The 27th is so chewed up that we may be sent to okinawa to "lick our wounds" and regroup. a welcome rest.

Every officer in "C" has been wounded Almost every platoon Sgt. also.

P. I'm glad to hear about your job. and the Grad. issue telegraph was also welcome (am using a piece of cardboard to absorb perspiration from brows and hand to no avail.) "rat-tp"

them I've gotten alot war soveniors, but trade it off to the, Engineers, motorman, etc. and others who come in after it's over to "clean up" HA! you can imagine a grunts openion of a person who comes in after it's over, but we couldn't carry all the garbage anyway and they can so we trade for most anything, sometimes even water & cigs I don't smoke still

I can imagine the stories their girl friends get — HA!! — Bastards !!!

I find myself.. PETRIFIED before
a firefight but WHEN IT GETS THICK
you forget it and do it

We CAN'T GET PACKAGES IN the field
but we do get letters almost everyday

Am in Good shape,, but fear for
my smarts. So in every letter send
a new vocabularly word and definITION
your AND JOANNes (sometimes) LETTER) MAKE THIS
Place bareable, Thank gramma for writeing
explain NO ANSWers pliz! WOULD LIKE TO HEAR
FROM EASTER AUNT KICK if possible,

Believe me I THINK about All
of my Groovey family And How Locky
I am.

I TRY TO STAY objective.... BUT IT'S HARD
I'VE PUT ALOT OF PEOPLE I KNOW ON TO THE
CHOppers Bleeding. IN FACT LAST NIGHT I PUT
THE LAST MAN OF my orngIONAL FIRE TEAM ON A
medi-VAC. IT'S OK BUT HOW WILL IT END?

P.S
DON'T SEND
LEATHER NECK HA
NEWSWEEK WAS
MOST
WELCOME
RobT.
KENNEDY
God!

LOVE,
George

SAY
HI ALL
PS HAVE JUNGLE ROT
WHAT A BITCH
BUT IT'S CLEARING.
UP

myself a pygmy Marine, a shit bird? Had I just fallen short of my goal to be like all of my grandfathers for generations?

Just then, mortar rounds exploded around us, hurling shrapnel in every direction while rocking the ground and throwing dirt and smoke into the air. Damn, this forest is no longer safe, either. I took off for the mulberry groves on a dead run. At least it was farther away from the tree line. I ran past several dead NVA and Marines. I grabbed an M-16 from the ground and slid into the side of a raised irrigation dike. Mortar rounds continued to drop in and detonate all around us. A mortar round landed directly in front of me and buried itself in the sand. Mesmerized, I just stared at it unable to move. For some inexplicable reason it didn't explode. It was a dud. My life was saved by an unexploded mortar round! Small arms fire from AK-47s ripped the open field, kicking up fountains of sand. It seemed the onslaught lasted forever. I aimed my rifle (the new one) from behind the dike at the offending tree line and shot at the sound of rifle fire. I felt only rage.

Suddenly, Marine tanks appeared behind us and just stopped. KA-BOOM! The tanks blasted the enemy positions in the densely forested area on the hillside. The tank cannons were pounding the forest where we later found an NVA sanctuary with a highly-developed network of interconnected tunnels and vast caverns. The complex housed hospitals with surgical suites, supply depots, and a sophisticated Soviet-supplied electronic communication and command center, all underground.

~ REDEMPTION ~

More Marines began congregating near the dike. I recognized some of them from my Company and we regrouped. I heard familiar voices. A Lieutenant and a red-haired career Marine Staff Sergeant were acting as our leaders. They organized a semblance of a squad, about 10 of us, around one of the idling tanks. We formed up at the rear of the tank for protection. Crouched over, we could hear the bullets ping off the tank's front armor.

Without warning, the tank suddenly revved its engine and lurched forward. I heard one of our new leaders yell over the distinctive chirp and squeak of the tracks of the tank and din of combat, "Let's go!"

We were assaulting the tree line. The tank rumbled forward, gaining speed and we jogged, bent over behind it. KA-BOOM! Without warning, the tanks triggered another round that rattled our bones. My ears rang, then everything fell silent, my hearing was shot out. I was deaf. I crowded closer to the tank for cover but the heat blowing out from the grilled exhaust at the rear of the tank was intense. The diesel fumes were choking; it coated our throats and stung our eyes.

We continued moving forward at a hurried pace, protected by the tank, safely behind our hulking shield. Then the tank rocked to a sudden stop. Instinctively, I knelt down to get away from the heat and diesel fumes and to be able to attempt to hear or see what was next. The Staff Sergeant was carrying a 45-caliber pistol that day, highly unusual for an enlisted man. I saw him chamber a round and look side to side gathering his men for

Photo: USMC

what I believed would be an immediate rush to the tree line 30 yards ahead. Bullets were still plinking off the front of the tank when I got the nod from the Sergeant. His eyes said, "Go-go!"

I stood up and sprinted toward the trees with my borrowed rifle, blindly zig-zagging along the way. I held my rifle across my torso waiting for a bullet to rip through my chest. My eyes were drawn tight but up ahead I saw the irrigation ditch that separated the sloping forest from the flat, sandy mulberry field. Out of breath, I stumbled forward and dove headlong into the trench – my imaginary end zone. Touchdown!

I was in a deep ditch protected from enemy rifle fire. Whoa, I was safe. I rolled on my back and looked at where I'd run from, thirty yards of prayer, and broken field running through a hail of enemy fire and not a scratch. But where were the others? Didn't we assault this tree line together? I quickly realized that I had made the trip alone. No one else but me had run for the ditch in the tree line. When I focused on the tank, I could see the helmeted heads furtively bobbing back and forth, hoping to get a glimpse of what was up ahead, where I was.

~ DITCHED ~

Damn! Then another complete surprise, the irrigation ditch was full of Marines just lying there. Some were intently looking toward the tree line, clutching their rifles; others were fidgeting with their gear; still others were tending to wounded Marines.

I crawled over to one of them and asked, "Hey man, what's up?"

The Marine said he was with the 26th Marines and they had been pinned down there for nearly an hour. They were supposed to hook up with the 27th Marines and take the

NVA stronghold, "But those stupid mother fuckers got hacked up crossing the mulberry field. We've been stuck here for hours, waiting for them to get their shit together."

I just nodded in silence, not acknowledging I was with the 27th Marines. I'd had enough craziness for one day, and the day wasn't half over yet. I crawled away, farther down the ditch, trying to find a more hospitable place to sort out this confused mess.

The ditch took a sharp curve, revealing another entirely different aspect of what was now developing into a major battle. I crawled to where NVA bodies and live Marines shared the same part of the ditch. The dead North Viets were grotesquely sprawled and scattered on both sides of the ditch bank; heads pointing up and down, most with their eyes and mouths open. The 26th Marines had assaulted them on line. The dead ones probably couldn't retreat fast enough or else they got caught by artillery. It didn't matter. They were dead and in significant numbers.

~ NUTS ~

I continued to crawl until I encountered an odd-looking, wide-eyed ruddy Marine who was lying near a dying NVA, who was making quiet gurgling noises as little translucent red bubbles of blood and saliva formed on the side of his half-open mouth. The red ooze trickled down his face in thin diluted ribbons. The dying enemy soldier sucked in air in a sudden heaving motion and exhaled slowly, his lungs wheezing.

"Hey, where ya from?" I asked the red-headed Marine.

"Tennessee," he replied with a wide upturned grin.

"Cool."

"Where y'all from?" he asked.

"Illinois," I said.

We were silent for a few seconds, then he asked, "Hey, do you want to nut this fuckn' asshole?"

"What?"

"Yea, you know. Cut his balls off. I got a knife," he volunteered. In fact, he already had his K-bar knife drawn and was slowly, maniacally slicing the air with it.

I reasoned to myself; let me process this offer to castrate the dying enemy soldier. First, one of us (you) will have to unbutton his trousers or pull them down entirely. Then grope around between his legs and go fishing for his now shriveled pint-sized penis and testicles. Then stretch his package until it's tight and saw through the sinew and tissue until it's severed. Then you'll have a fistful of soft, spongy, bloody organs, all the time listening to the screams of pain and horror coming from the NVA soldier. Mortally wounded, he'd no doubt still perk up a tad for this. Now what do you do with these disconnected parts? Well, let's say you throw them away. If that's the case, you'll have to tighten your grip on them. Then they might ooze through your fingers and drop onto your lap. If you stand up to throw them, you'll get shot and die with some guy's nuts in your hand—a fitting end for a halfwit, inbred piece of shit. Disgusted, I crawled away, keeping my bizarre images to myself. To this day, I have never visited Tennessee other than for work and a battalion reunion hosted by a fellow Marine.

~ FAST EDDIE ~

Sneaking down the trench, I came across a Marine from the 1/27th. He too was pinned down by the intense gunfire, so we took shelter together in the ditch and tried to figure out what to do next. As we sat there, he said he saw our good buddy, Eddy P, get shot.

"As we rushed the tree line, there was a wounded NVA hidden in the ditch. He had leg injuries and could not walk so he played dead until Eddy P jumped over the ditch. As Eddy was in the air, the NVA shot him. His AK-47 had been on full automatic. The rounds hit Eddy in the left shoulder turning it into bone meal. Eddy was so surprised that he threw his rifle at the wounded enemy soldier hitting him in the head. Eddy then took off running, at a full gallop, back to the landing zone where we had arrived this morning."

"No shit?" I replied sincerely. "That's the second goofiest thing I've heard all day."

"What's the first?" he asked.

"You don't want to know, but it's about 20 yards that way with a knife. You'll stay here if you know what's good for you."

I peeked over the edge of the ditch and let my eyes sweep the panoramic view across the growing battlefield. It was a massive spectacle. I was struck with the sheer magnitude and reach of the destruction, the number of lives that would be radically altered forever and the amount of raw energy being transferred into light, noise, and heat.

Nothing can prepare you for an encounter with the awesome power of technologically supported combat; I was numb and stunned.

The sanguinary fury of Operation Allenbrook subsided for the time being, so we started to venture out to see what had happened. There were bodies of dead and wounded Marines and NVA everywhere. Now the task of reclaiming them had to begin. We teamed up and began carrying the wounded on ponchos to the landing zone. The primacy of Marine selflessness emerged. We were all damaged in some basic way; battered, cut-up, tired, hungry, but other Marines were down and they had to be taken care of. The morose chore of body recovery continued hour after hour in the parboiling 110°F tropical sun.

~ ICE CREAM ~

With another Marine I grabbed a dead Black Marine by his wrists. As we pulled him up by the forearms, his sun-roasted dark skin peeled away like kid gloves, revealing the new pure white skin beneath. I just stood there horrified with handfuls of rolled dark brown skin, staring at the new white layer of fresh skin below. Vietnam was so hot in the summer of 1968 that in the hours from start to finish of that battle, the bodies had already begun to decompose in the heat and humidity. Nearly one-third of the casualties suffered in Vietnam were from heat-stroke alone.

"Hey! Pick him up and carry him!" It was the voice from the top of a nearby tank. The black tank commander resented us dragging the dead Marine, so I enlisted the help of other dazed Marines, and we packed the dead man, carrying him by the feet and shoulders, to the LZ. The tanker never bothered to dismount and help, he just barked orders from his exalted perch. *It's a little tougher when you actually have your feet on the ground*, I thought to myself.

When our grizzly duty was over, we gathered around a small, shaded clearing and rested. Some of us smoked and ate our C-rations; others just sat quietly. Off in the distance, a C-46 helicopter with a webbed cargo net slung under its belly approached and hovered, releasing the load from its hitch 50 yards away. The load in the netting was vanilla ice cream, in stacked 5-gallon cylinders. We were invited by the officers to eat the rapidly warming ice cream.

Although on the verge of exhaustion, some of us shuffled, with little enthusiasm, toward the huge pallet of snow colored ice cream and ate as much as we could tolerate. I happened to sit in front of a pile of naked, twitching, dead NVA, and ate cold vanilla ice cream in the hot tropical sun of Vietnam. My boyhood was now completely gone. I had gone directly from boy to Marine. Somehow, I felt I'd skipped an essential step. Where was the growing into manhood part? Sadly, there were not enough Marines left standing to eat all the ice cream and most of it melted slowly into the sand, to probably be consumed by the surprised but grateful insects.

~ COUNTING THE DEAD ~

In time, we were given the order to finish gathering the rapidly rotting dead NVA, finish stripping them of their clothes, personal effects, unit insignias and stack their skinny, little dead bodies like chord wood. Few of us cooperated. The stench of death was starting to spread and would soon overwhelm us. The unlucky compliant Marines (the ones who followed orders) got stuck stacking the dead until the gruesome job was done. Hours later, combat engineers arrived on their bulldozers, laughing and joking victoriously. They casually dug deep trenches and rolled the piled bodies into makeshift graves. The dead would become part of the vast sea of sand, part of the geology of Go Noi. We just watched the Combat Engineers as they energetically went about their task of burying the logs that only hours ago had been young men. I despised the engineers for not being in the battle, yet relishing its aftermath and claiming its spoils. They had not fought the NVA or contributed to their deaths. They just buried them.

~ THE LAST OF FAST EDDIE ~

On one of my laps carrying wounded Marines to the LZ, I spotted Eddy, lying in pain on the sand. I knelt down to talk to him. As I fumbled and stammered for comforting words, a Medevac chopper approached. The down wash of the rotor blades stirred up the sand so I gently lay over Eddie's face with my chest, thinking I'd protect him until we could carry him on board. Instead of helping Eddie, the accumulated sand on my lap spilled onto

Marines Dislodge NVA From Bunker Sites

By Sgt. Robert M. Bayer

DA NANG—"There were North Vietnamese soldiers (NVA) all over the place, but they didn't open up on us until we were 10 feet from them," said Lance Cpl Thomas R. Thuesen, (Walnut Creek, Calif.) as he described a bloody four-hour battle during Operation Allen Brook. *US God DAMN IT*

An element of the 27th Marine Regiment, 1st Marine Division was moving into a treeline on Go Noi Island, south of Da Nang, to reinforce another unit already in heavy contact on the right flank.

"We took four casualties crossing an open area, but we managed to get into the treeline where the point element was," Thuesen said. "As soon as we got up front the NVA pinned us down with machinegun and sniper fire."

The NVA occupied three well-hidden, reinforced concrete bunkers. The communist gunners had a clear field of fire at the assaulting Leathernecks.

"I worked over the bunkers as best I could with my machinegun," said Thuesen, "but it didn't have much effect. I started concentrating my fire on the snipers in the trees."

The Marines were so well pinned down by the NVA that they couldn't move their rocket teams up to knock out the bunkers, and they could not bring back their casualties.

Marine helicopter gunships and jets were called to pound the NVA positions.

"Some of the bombs and rockets hit within 30 meters of us," recalled Thuesen. "I think the only thing that could have knocked out the bunkers was a direct hit."

"I knew we had to get help, so I ran, crawled and slid back to the rear. I got a corpsman to treat the wounded and picked up another squad," Thuesen continued, "and managed to guide them forward to the trapped men."

The Leatherneck directed the fire of three machineguns at the enemy bunkers while the casualties were pulled back.

At dusk the Marines were assisted by a smoke screen and a heavy artillery barrage.

The next day, the Marines found that their persistence had paid off with 45 NVA dead and several machineguns and rifles captured, along with a jeep load of assorted equipment.

Skirmishes: Things were bad enough already. Gen. William Westmoreland, the U.S. commander in Vietnam, was stating simple fact when he declared last week that "the intensity of the war has greatly increased." Although American commanders were under pressure from Washington to "pour on the heat" to offset the enemy's "talk-and-fight" strategy, there were as yet no spectacular victories or defeats, but rather an endless series of bloody minor clashes. Notable was Operation Allen Brook, where 105 marines were killed in a drive to disrupt an enemy buildup around Go Noi Island, a traditional staging area for attacks on Da Nang, 15 miles away. More typical, however, was a skirmish which developed when a Marine road-clearing force ran into an ambush 2 miles from the U.S. base at Khe Sanh. Eight marines and 60 enemy soldiers were killed in the fighting that followed.

The cost of these countless, obscure skirmishes was made painfully plain in the casualty lists. According to one U.S. intelligence officer, American troops in I Corps alone have killed an average of more than 1,500 Communist soldiers a week ever since the Tet offensive four months ago. But U.S. casualties have risen proportionally. For the two weeks that ended May 18, the U.S. death toll reached 1,111—higher than in any other two-week period of the Vietnam war. And given the enemy buildup, it seemed clear that there was worse to come. Increasingly, the struggle in Vietnam showed signs of falling into the pattern

Mute testimony: Helmets of marines killed in Operation Allen Brook

June 3, 1968

TIME MAGAZINE

L. Cpl. George Berg, 21, 819 E. Third St., Dixon, wounded Aug. 20 while on combat duty in Vietnam, has returned to the Great Lakes Naval Training Center Hospital after spending a convalescent 10-day leave with his parents, to undergo surgery later this week.

Berg, a 1967 graduate of Dixon High School, attended Sauk Valley College prior to enlisting in the U.S. Marine Corps Nov. 8, 1967. He had served in Vietnam since April.

George P. Berg, 1967 senior class president of Dixon High School, has been recently pro-

L-CPL. GEORGE P. BERG

moted to Lance Corporal in the U.S. Marine Corps. He enlisted Nov. 8, 1967. After completing basic training at Camp Pendleton, Calif., he was sent to Vietnam.

Lance Cpl. Berg's life was saved this month during Operation Allen Brook when his squad leader came to his rescue in an incident involving an enemy booby trap.

Lance Cpl. Berg is the son of Mr. and Mrs. Charles H. Berg, 819 E. Third St., and grandson of the Herbert N. Parkers. He has a brother, Stephen, student at NIU; a brother, Malcolm, at DHS, and a sister, Elizabeth, in the seventh grade at Madison Elementary School.

Lance Cpl. George P. Berg, 2380364, USMC, "C" Co. 1st Bn., 27th Marines, 1st Marine Div., FPO San Francisco, Calif. 96602.

Exchange Fire . . .

Two Marines exchange fire with the Viet Cong in bunkers while a 106mm recoilless rifle, background, blasts enemy positions built to withstand the explosive force of an air strike. Action took place on Go Noi Island in area south of Da Nang. (AP wirephoto)

A Muddy Track

Ask our Hero *did he do this?*

U.S. Marines find the going a little sticky in a field south of Danang. They were part of a two-week operation which swept through numerous villages seeking out enemy soldiers in the Dien Ban area. (AP Wirephoto)

makes me "mad" - poor kids.

Can't swim in this?

VC Weapon Hard as Rock

DA NANG, Vietnam (Special) —A Leatherneck stationed at Liberty Bridge, southwest of Da Nang, can't decide whether to be happy or mad after a Viet Cong hit him in the head with a rock.

Pfc. Fred S. Wilson, 18, of Wayzata, Minn., a rifleman with the 7th Marine Regt., 1st Marine Div., was standing perimeter watch in a one-man fighting hole next to the bridge.

Early in the evening a number of Viet Cong began to probe the company's lines with rocks and grenades attempting to discover the location of the Marine fighting holes.

"I had my flak jacket on, but I was wearing my soft cap," said Wilson. "Suddenly, something I thought was a grenade hit me directly on the head. It bounced into my foxhole and I figured 'this is the end!'" After some long moments Wilson discovered it was only a rock.

"I was so mad that I returned the VC's rock, along with about five or six real grenades," he snapped.

me, I, e
mark it

The Situation Is Well in Hand

A Marine reaches out to give a buddy, neck-deep in water, a hand as Leathernecks cross a monsoon-swollen stream in a valley west of Da Nang. Units of the 27th Marines were searching for enemy troop concentrations in the area. (AP

Corpsman 'Thankful To Be Alive'

By LCpl. Art Kibat

Da NANG, — "When I woke up on the helicopter I though I was in heaven. Right now I'm thankful to be alive."

That was the feeling of Hospitalman Third Class, USN, Paul A. Benech, (Canoga Park, Calif.) after his brush with death during Operation Allen Brook, southwest of Da Nang.

Intense fire hit his company, of the 27th Marines.

"I remember carrying our executive officer to safety and tending to his wounds. Then I dragged two Marines suffering from heat exhaustion to a small pond," Benech recalled. "But after that I didn't know who I was patching up. I was just running everywhere I heard Marines yell for a corpsman."

Halfway across an open field, the enemy opened up on him. One round hit his pistol. Other bullets ripped through his pack and parts of his flak jacket. One round tore a huge hole in his helmet and creased his head, knocking him unconscious.

[AP Wirephoto]

Patrol Climbs Hill

United States marine corps patrol moves up hill, pocked and shredded by artillery, near Hiep Duc, South Viet Nam. Site is 30 miles southwest of Da Nang.

June 26,

Dear Mom,

Sorry about Bitching but was feeling sorry for dudes in squad as well as self. but for now the worst is over.

I'll try to get a picture for you of my fire team, all from Illenois except a Navaho Ind. from New Mexico.

Thank everyone, granna, aunt Mary (esp) for letters, packages of which I have recieved all - absorbine Jr. helps feet 100%. Aunt Mary sent an inspiring little book. Thank her in person or by phone but do. however it's words come no where close to yours. I guess thank that's what moms are for, people always say "you take things for granite." That's never really understood until one is taken out of the enviroment - SMACK AS YOU SAID "RIGHT IN THE FACE." GET IT!

Enclosed is promo. warrant Telegraph is nice —

A·OK ——→

OH YEA PLIZ! Add up MY INCOME
TAX RETURNS AND THAT'S THE MONEY
IN BANK - IF SPENT OK ! & $275.00 (MAd ON The
way IN ROUTE AND $150.00 I WILL send
home SOON FOR (JUNE) 425.00 & INCOME
TAX. & BANK ACCOUNT
      "promotion ceremony"; I shot bourbon
2 beers, ice cold, I took ANOTher shot !
CO ASK about who wanted more map
reading class. - we All said yes -
Then we gave money for beer and ice
$10.00 $8.00 $12.00 Etc for The PLATOON.
what blast (IN The wind)
      I'VE GOT 3 operations IN MY
record book "Allen Brook AND operation
"NO NAME" 1 & 2 I'm GETTING There
      I was promoted with men IN The
corps 3-4 years - I got it IN 8 months

                          Love
                          George

During Operation Allen Brook, August 1968, members of the 27
Marines patrol near Go Noi Island.

HELICOPTER TO GOI NOI ISLAND,
OPERATION ALLENBROOK

Eddie's face and directly into his open eyes and mouth. When I sat up, I realized what I had done. I stuck my index finger into Eddie's mouth and dragged as much of the dry grit out as I could. I tearfully begged his forgiveness.

"Man, Eddie, I'm sorry," I repeated over and over and over, tears pouring down my face.

When he could breathe without hacking and choking, he sort of smiled and mouthed the words, "That's OK, man - it's OK."

I helped carry him to the chopper and said adios to the gentle Lance Corporal reservist from Louisiana, and I never saw or heard from him again.

~ STOLEN MOMENTS ~

Carrying wounded Marines to the helicopter landing zone was exhausting grim work. Having to watch the helpless suffering of other young men, Marines in fact, and watch as they endured the pain of their mutilating wounds was itself a trial, leaving a nasty indelible mark on most of us.

On one trip to the LZ, carrying a wounded Marine, cradled in a poncho, I tripped and dropped my corner of the makeshift litter. The Marine was mortally wounded in the back, most of which was gone, his shirtless torso mainly a bloody gaping hole. When the poncho corner slipped from my hand, the Marine screamed and died when he hit the ground. All of his dark red blood, which had pooled in the poncho, flooded out onto the sand.

While carrying ("humping") him to the LZ I had cruelly yelled at him ("to shut the fuck up"). He had been screaming loudly about dying here without seeing his family one last time and was delirious with pain. We were all dying a little that day, but he was dying a lot. I should have prayed for him, but I hollered instead and kicked his boot, which was hanging off the edge of the poncho. He was evolving from Marine to cadaver in slowly leaking seconds. I wanted him to go gently and quietly. In the end - he did.

We picked up the now dead body and carried him to the morgue area of the LZ and laid him beside the others. My shouting had not killed him, but for many years I thought I had stolen precious moments from his life.

~ LISTENING POST AT NIGHT~

Even with the high number of casualties, we stayed in the field that evening and formed a protective circle— hastily dug fighting holes. They were occupied by 2-3 Marines and they ringed the company command post. Listening posts (LP), established farther out were manned with two Marines each but sometimes a solitary Marine would be sent out by himself. The purpose of the LPs was to listen for the approach of NVA sneaking up on our positions. The Marine on the LP was to either report movement on the radio or fire on the enemy. It was a very tense, nerve-racking experience that lasted up to four hours in the stillness of the night before being relieved by another Marine. Every few hours Marines

June 26,

Dear Mal,

Recieved your letter of 7th
The best news I've had in a long time —
your A's The 2nd best is that you ary' an MAKEING
effort to be the best soph. qtback. A. To
play quarterback is sometimes hard.
B. It is more of a challenge C. more responsiblity
F But good for 1 thing to give a young man
a taste of what it's really like to work, sweat
for something you want. — In a way I'm
glad your haveng trable passing — ?? wonder
why — now you have a definite obstacle to ·
over come. you know what you have to
beat - your arm - learning to throw straight
over your ear and useing your wrist to spiral
the ball — then work on distance, then short, fast
hard - "bullets. there is method to learning
it. — with your $ — you can buy groovey
garbage - work hard
        You'll never guess what I found
in a river - that's right a football —
some other jar head must have lost it
I throw it for relaxation at night (evening)

I'm not going to discuss viet-nam, to boreing. Do you run alot? who is competition? how much do you weigh? hught? do glasses bother you. Do you think you will hit hard (I do) if you get pissed off bad enough write and tell me what subjects you took write about work-outs, weights etc. I dig that stuff.

The one thing that is **MOST** important is you <u>ARE</u> <u>what you think you are</u> if you think you are. if you think you are a quarter back damned if you just might <u>be</u>. If you want and think you are a scholar a try to improve vocab. (a scholar's vocab. can be a measureing stick for his intellect (some ass hole said that)

Do you know where I get my most (besides Ahh! ? cunt) pleasure? I'm doing something better or faster or more completely than another person could do it. I try to be precise, slow- to provoke, (calm) to keep my head in all situations (4 down & 1 yd, or under sniper fire both) IN SITUATIONS The right decision could mean Succes or Tragedy

1 bad thing about me - I hardly ever am willing to take a gamble - but do (unwilling) because it's Necessary - but never like <u>to</u>.

I like to take control of people, act fast, an then calm down <s>to</s> right after the "shit hit the fan." - a few days ago after our platoon was in "shit" all day I wrote our mother a letter she detected that I was disturbed about what I am doing as a grunt. it was the most trying day I've ever spent. but for some who went spastic - heat stroke, shell shock battle fatigue etc. it was, HEY. About 115° on white sand. reflection almost blinded you. We where carrying alot of ammo, gear etc. a then got hit. from tree line. talk about mad! I cussed for 2 solid hours - to myself. but helped other dudes calm down.

One guy who had passed out (heat exhaustion and stroke are 2 different things) I almost broke my god damn hand slapping his face to keep him alive (awake, conscious) woops! talking about VN sucks. Thank mom for letters and have gotten all mail & packages sent also Tell mom TO THANK AUNT MARY FOR LITTLE BOOK I read it - IT'S TRUELY INSPIRING - BUT NOTHING helps like words from mom & dad & you AND LIZARD Breathe - Steve's Traveling to much to write - rationalize rationalize, rationalize.

P.S. PRACTICE
PLAYING
THE BEATLES
SONGS I SING SONGS
SGT. PEPPERS
All day and night
TRIP-OUT
AS AN ESCAPE
BUT STAY ALERT

DEVELOPEING YOURSELF INTO WHAT YOU WANT TO BE SHOULD KEEP YOU BUSY—

Some people it takes 3 or 2 or 1½ year to make lance corporal it took me 8 months

Just Thought I'd brag a little -
it's in the family also am a
team leader, groovey write as
you can,

Love

George,

PPS.
AT YOUR JOB -
GRAMMA AND MOM ALWAYS
SAID "WHEN I'd GET A NEW JOB
WORK hard BUT don't KNOCK yourself
OUT" ASK Them MOM ABOUT THAT quot
I SAY - KNOCK YOURSELF OUT - IT'S
FUN - THEN YOU CAN DRAG YOUR
TIRED ASS HOME AND HAVE A REASON
TO ACT MEAN - BECAUSE YOU KNOW
YOU CAN WORK AND EARN YOUR OWN
MONEY. EVEN IF IT'S PART TIME
THE BERG'S HAVE HAD IT SO GOOD
WE HAVE TROUBLE - MOTIVATING OURSELVES
SO GET BITTER - "LEAN & HUNGARY LOOK
ABOUT HIM
                    SHAKESPEAR'S
            SAID CEASAIR ABOUT MARK ANTHONY
    I KNOW LIZ'S POSTURE IS IMPROVEING
I JUST KNOW IT
I JUST KNOW IT
        KNOW IT
            RIGHT LIZ GOD
                          DAMN
                            IT

106

would noiselessly crawl, clinging to the ground, out into the darkness to trade places. The rotations started in the early evening and lasted all night until dawn.

During the night, at preset intervals, the handset on the PRC-25 ("prick 25") radio was depressed and a hissing squelch-coded noise was sent back to the center of the circle to indicate, almost silently, that everything was OK. Silence was essential or the location of the LP would be compromised. In reality, the LP occupants were sometimes live bait. Like goats tethered for prowling tigers, the LPs were a way of intercepting the enemy, who were very skilled at sneaking up on Marine perimeters and killing Marines not paying attention.

The potential sacrifice of a Marine on an LP was necessary but a chore relished by no one. We all understood why, but nobody wanted the duty. LPs were also the domains of shit birds—those who screwed up or pissed off someone during the day were doomed to LPs at night. It was the law of the jungle. Don't be an idiot or risk being staked out and spending part of the night in your own small terror filled hole in the ground far away from the protection of other Marines. LP duty was always a harrowing experience. On Allenbrook, due to the high number of casualties, sometimes solitary Marines manned our listening posts. The area was saturated with NVA, and at night they would crawl for hours in the dark, taking all night to inch toward the Marine perimeter. The NVA infiltrators were able to get up on Marines who weren't constantly vigilant and silently kill them.

Because of the danger and fear, occasionally a Marine on an LP would indicate that an attack was about to occur and would come hauling ass back to the perimeter and safety. Said plainly, they'd fake an attack to get out of having to stay out there all night by themselves surrounded by pissed off, highly motivated NVA. They had AK-47s that worked. We had M-16s that routinely did not. But more often than not, the NVA used knives to kill unsuspecting Marines out on LPs.

On the second night after the major tussle with the 308th NVA Division, I was listening to hushed, whispered radio transmissions to and from an LP. The Marine in the LP was indicating he was hearing sounds and movement directly in front of his post. We thought he was making up a cover story in order to escape the LP so he could bolt for the patrol base. Then, listening to the radio, we could hear his voice crack, and he whispered that someone was creeping up on his position. The palpable fear in his voice grew more intense, but I was sure he was a fraud. Without warning, three shots from an M-16 were suddenly fired.

Then we heard shouts, "Don't shoot! Don't shoot! It's me! I'm coming in!"

And the Marine from the LP ran right at us. He was out of breath, stuttering, slurring his words and on the edge of madness as he explained again how he thought he had heard the enemy slowly crawling through the wet, mist covered elephant grass. His LP was positioned on the margin between the sandy mulberry field and the tall, restless sea of grass. The hysterical Marine's LP duty was almost ended anyway, so another, more fortified Marine crawled out to the LP and finished the cold dark night, doing his duty, just listening – listening to the little sounds in the dark; chirping, buzzing, thumping, snapping.

In the morning, just as the sun cracked open the light, the Marine on the LP suddenly let out a howl, "Holy shit!"

As he walked back to the perimeter, he yelled, "Hey man, you gotta see this!"

Several interested Marines followed him back to the LP where they found two dead NVA sappers, not six feet from the LP, both shot by the Marine just before he had run back to the perimeter the night before. He was vindicated and the two NVA were buried in a shallow, sandy grave.

We ate a C-ration breakfast and then began that day's patrolling, humping the sand and bush.

~ IT'S THE LAW ~

The rattle of automatic weapons fire made our hearts race and our eyes dart, searching for the location of whoever had fired the rounds. It would take minutes before we could breathe easily again. It was always the same. The only thing I could hear was my own heart, the tension in my skin and the bundling of my intestines. This time the bullets had come from a large cluster of bamboo in front of us. Our patrol, part of a platoon-sized sweep, was stopped; we had gone to ground and were now pinned down.

Next to me, Smitty stared straight ahead, searching for a muzzle flash to give away the enemy position.

"There! There in the trees!" he yelled, pointing to the right side of the bamboo cluster.

When we moved, the snipers would open up with what sounded like AK-47 rifles. We were held in check for an interminable amount of time. Then I suggested to Smitty, a Black Marine from Chicago, "Let's take them out."

"What?" he exclaimed.

"Let's take them out! We can grab a couple LAWs, sneak up there and dust 'em." I was half kidding and half daring him to take me up on the suggestion. LAWs are Light Antitank Weapons, hand-held portable rockets that neither of us had used.

He thought about it for a few seconds, and then said, "Sure. Let's do it!"

I slid away, down to where some other Marines were and then crawled back with two LAWs. To Smitty I said, "Here's the deal, we'll run, zig-zag, behind the rice paddy dike..."

"Then what?" he asked.

I pointed to a spot some 30 yards ahead of us. "Well, we can stop over there and catch our breath and figure out the rest then."

"Oh, good plan," he smiled, then with a sudden confidence he added, "It's cool man. Let's do it!"

We both now understood that we didn't know what we were doing with our cobbled together plan, but we were going to do it just the same. It was kind of like the "go deep and I'll throw it to you" play in sandlot football, with about as much chance of working. Nonetheless, before we knew it, we were both off toward the bamboo, running as fast as we could, first in one direction, then the next, all the time trying to keep the tallest dike between us and the enemy. In one hand I had my rifle and in the other the long, thin, green tube of the LAW, like carrying luggage and running through a crowded airport.

We stopped, quickly caught our breath, looked at each other and then got up and sprinted some more. The crack of the snipers' rifles was now really loud. We were close, within 40 yards maybe. We stopped again; breathing hard as we lay on our backs, looking up to the sky and preparing to draw very direct fire. We read the instructions stenciled in high contrast yellow on the side of the olive drab rocket. Then, looking skyward again, thinking and reading some more, we tried to understand the firing sequence.

"Do you understand these instructions?" Smitty asked me, doubtfully.

"Yeah," I replied, "Pull this, push that and then squeeze this and that's it."

"You'll only have from 2 to 3 seconds to get this done," Smitty reminded me. "Any more than that and the gooks will have us dialed in."

"I know," I replied, stoking myself. "Alright! Let's get some!"

We rose to our knees, the fully extended telescoped tube of the LAW ready to fire. We identified the clump where we knew the snipers were. My helmet fell down over my eyes, but I cranked my head enough to get one eye in a position to aim the LAW where the snipers were. I pushed down on the electronic trigger and waited for the jolt of the rocket and the hot exhaust to cover my face. I imagined the small rocket spiraling through the air, leaving a dense cloud of smoke and cork screwing sparks in its wake, then landing just where I'd aimed. I could even imagine the sound of the explosion tearing apart the pair of snipers. Then there would be the satisfaction, the after-action glow, of whacking not one but two gooks with one shot. It would be a shot; I reminded myself, that we were able to take only after considerable initiative and risk. What I heard and felt, however, was nothing. The LAW malfunctioned - it failed to ignite!

We both dropped back down and stared at each other in disbelief. We waited for a few seconds to see if we were drawing fire. Nothing. The snipers must not have noticed us. Feeling safe, Smitty said, "Let's go back and get the other one."

We had left the second LAW at our original site. With no more thought than we had put into any other phase of this venture, we both jumped up and ran, retracing our previous steps back to our beginning. Once there we caught our breath while reading the instructions again. Yep, they were simple, pull this, push that then squeeze here. We waited a few more minutes before darting back across the rice paddy. Once there I removed my helmet, grabbed the LAW, pulled the safety off, and pulled on the tube to telescope it out. I took a deep breath and jumped up, sighted the LAW in on the enemy position and squeezed the electronic trigger located on the top of the launcher. Nothing! Really angry now, we ran back to rejoin our platoon, where we complained loudly and profanely about receiving faulty munitions. I found out later that in order to fire the LAW, you had to suppress the safety and squeeze the trigger at the same time. The debacle was a lapse in good judgment and training combined.

Lloyd Fernung Squad Leader

Goi Noi 1968

~ Night Mortars ~

On the second night, our squad was up. It was our turn to patrol the area around our company command post. With PJ leading the patrol, I stepped out to walk point. It was dark, with only a sliver of moonlight to help guide us slowly out across the sand and into the groves of small mulberry trees. About a half hour later and 200 yards away, we heard the distinct sound of rounds being tubed in a mortar. We mouthed the word incoming, without making a sound. A flash and then the sound of a deep metallic thunk was followed rapidly by two more. Thunk! Thunk! Thunk! Three fast rounds were quickly heading almost straight up into the night sky. While we were on patrol, the company perimeter was being shelled by NVA mortars.

Clicking my M-16 on to full automatic, I pointed my rifle in the direction of the noise. I wanted to rake the area with a full magazine of rounds to stop them cold, but PJ grabbed my shoulder and stopped me by quietly stating, "We're all going to be killed if you open fire."

I argued silently with a disapproving stare and pulled away. As soon as I did, another, the fourth mortar round exploded around us, and we all hit the ground. The round was right on target. They had us perfectly sighted in. But only that single mortar round exploded near our patrol, as the Marines in the perimeter returned fire and suppressed the NVA mortar men. The surprise attack was over.

As we stood and collected ourselves, we heard the muffled moaning of a wounded Marine. PJ and I rushed to his side. He was standing up, holding his shoulder.

"God damn, it hurts!" he said. "Where?" I pleaded.

"My shoulder. I'm hit here," he replied, pointing upwards toward his wounded shoulder blade. PJ had a flashlight with a red plastic filter over the lens used to read maps at night. He shined the dim light closely to the Marine's shoulder. A two-inch piece of smoking steel fragment was sticking out of the Marine's shoulder blade and arm. The deeply embedded metal shard had blindly found its mark, exactly where his flack jacket stopped and shoulder and arm were joined. "Wow," PJ and I said almost in unison. "Cool. Look at that thing ("fucker") smoke."

The red-hot metal was vaporizing his blood creating a thick gas that curled rapidly toward the ground. It was fascinating to watch the bloody steam in the narrow column of red light produced by the small flashlight.

PJ and I laughed aloud at the oddity, and we couldn't take our eyes off the freakish horn sticking out of the now wincing Marine.

"Hey," I asked wryly, "Can I pull it out?"

"Fuck you," he replied as we wandered slowly, silently back to the perimeter to get a corpsman to treat the wound. Our patrol that night was over.

~ Kiem Thao ~

One common theme in the Vietnam War was that we didn't understand our enemy. Many times we didn't even want to understand, but more often than not, we simply couldn't. The social-cultural heritage their common soldier experienced was just too dramatically different from the way an average 19-year-old American Marine was raised. Regular North Vietnamese military units were expected to do more than fight, they were, for example, expected to be productive and engage in activities other than military actions. The government would provide these units with food for nine months, but expected them to feed themselves, through their own cultivated gardens and such, for the remaining three months. NVA troops were expected to have political ties that would ensure loyalty to the party first, and they were expected to win the hearts of the people, although fear tactics and executions were not only acceptable, but time tested means of obtaining that goal. It should be noted that while all the reported qualities of the NVA look good on paper, their desertion rate throughout much of the war was equally as high as the soldiers from the south, the ARVN.

One practice that separated them from their American counterparts was the concept of Kiem Thao (self-criticism), where every soldier, even those in combat units, is required to spend an average of one hour each day criticizing themselves. The concept is designed not so much to reinforce ideas or doctrine, but rather to combat indifference.

~ UNHINGED — RICE JARS ~

I yelled at a little Vietnamese boy, maybe twelve years old – a beggar who I also threatened with my rifle: "...I'll shoot your dumb ass if you don't buzz off and leave me alone." He pulled up his shirt exposing his thin infantile chest and yelled in Pidgin English, "Shoot me! Shoot me GI! – numb'a ten!" (number '10' was one of the worst insults one could hurl to or from a Vietnamese) His small brown eyes expanding in enraged saucers, staring at me defiantly. I had not meant what I had said. I was trying to shoo him away, to scare him. He did mean what he had said. His home and family had been destroyed by the war. He didn't care about dying.

Nearby in his bombed-out village, there were the rice jars sunk into the ground exposed by the now flattened homes. They were thick vitreous clay terracotta pots for storing rice. They were long maybe three feet tall and slender with thick lip openings at the top and tapering down from 10" to 8" at the bottom. They were meant to be impervious to water, rodents and were buried below the dirt floors of the villagers' "hooch's" for convenience. I led a patrol through an abandoned "ville," and strayed into a roof-less bamboo hooch that a few weeks ago was a family's home.

Suddenly the compressed dirt floor gave way. One foot went into a rice jar all the way to the bottom, my other leg buckled slamming my testicles into the rim of the jar. As I pulled myself up a mongoose raced up my leg out of the jar and into the banana grove outside the abandoned village. Rats live near broken disserted rice jars, cobras eat the rats and mongooses eat the cobras. I gathered my composure and moved on only to fall through another jar, just a few feet from the first. This time, my shins battered and skinned, I moved away swearing to myself. Later, on the return lap, I routed the patrol past the *ville* to stop and see where I'd fallen into the rice jar traps. I was outraged that I'd fallen in the hole not once but twice and my shins still hurt. Moving closer to get a better look - I fell through a third jar. Without hesitation I pulled the pin on a grenade and tossed it into the basketball sized rim of the jar blowing it into fragments. Huffing back to our patrol base no one mentioned what had happened. We just walked in silence.

~ WEST SIDE STORY ~

June 1968 in Vietnam was miserable in every conceivable way; hot and humid, the operational tempo was exhausting. Although we were inflicting very heavy casualties on the enemy we were being depleted daily. We were taking more than our fair share of the enemy but that gave us consolation only briefly.

Most of us were too tired to be afraid any longer and the primary feeling for me, anyway, was loneliness. It was abject, absolute "Damn, I'm in this shit storm alone" – loneliness. We ran patrols all day and trudged around the sandy island looking for the NVA that remained in their very well concealed caves and bunkers. At night we'd form a protective, more or less circle, and then dig a "fighting hole" (fox holes are for the Army) and wait for sleep or an attack during the night – whichever came first.

The enemy was still very much engaged even after taking massive casualties, firing rocket propelled grenades, B-40 rockets, mortars and shooting rifles into our positions. They targeted resupply helicopters and were occasionally successful shooting them down. That left us with low supplies of ammunition, food, and fresh water but the most valuable of all: mail. My normally positive attitude was eroding quickly but mail would always improve it, if just for the moment. On one particularly hot afternoon, as I was finishing digging my "house," a Marine crawled over to my fighting hole in the ground (it was too dangerous to stand up because of the snipers), yelled "mail call" threw a single twisted and crumpled envelope into my hole, and slithered away making crunching noises as he twisted his knees and elbows over the hot irregular sand.

My high school days were now in the very distant past – thousands of miles away in time and space. The big deal at Dixon High School at the end anyone's senior year was the spring musical. Football players and the actually talented were invited (some drafted) to participate. I was drafted by my speech teacher and the drama coach to try out for the part of Bernardo (the Puerto Rican gang leader) in West Side Story. My grades were so poor I had no choice – I needed all the allies I could get to be able to graduate. But there was an interloper; Marty – a better looking, more talented, olive skinned, great singer who had been hand selected by the music director. Dixon High School was striated, just like most organizations into cliques. This guy was in a group that I thought were – well, let's say not the football players. Immature, silly, childish all come to mind as I think back to those days long gone. To put it plainly, I didn't like Marty or any of his friends. I didn't have a good reason for it – I just didn't.

I was temporarily given the part of Bernardo because Marty's family was on vacation during the try out and rehearsals. However, the music director was determined Marty would be a better Bernardo and confronted my supporters (the drama teacher) with a bargain. I agreed to take the understudy role, if and only if I got a dance solo, could pick my partner for it, and be the lead Bernardo on one of the weekend performances. The bargain was struck! The musical went well, it was fun and with few challengers, I was voted "The Best Dancer" in my senior class. But Marty will always be remembered as Bernardo.

In my lonely hole in the ground, tired, hungry, filthy and generally pissed off, I slowly tore through one end of the mysterious envelop to see who in the hell remembered or even cared enough to write a letter to a "butt plate infantry Marine" in a very unpopular war. I slowly read the words. As I remember, the letter read something like this:

"Dear George,
I am writing to thank you for your service to our country. I admire you and all the other Marines that have volunteered for this difficult task. (There was more in the letter I can't remember) Once again, thank you for serving our country.
Very sincerely, Marty"

I was gob smacked; almost everyone in the world hated the war and the warriors that were fighting in Vietnam. Yet, here was a high school acquaintance and competitor taking the time to write. It reminded me there were people who actually cared about the warriors fighting the war. I folded the letter slowly, put it in my breast pocket and carried it until the heat, rain, sweat, and finally blood, dissolved it into an unrecognizable pulp.

~ JUNE AFTER-ACTION REPORTS (USMC) ~

During the reporting period the Battalion operated in two separate areas, Go Noi Island and Da Nang (Operations on Go Noi Island and Da Nang constituted Operation Allenbrook). On June 5th, the Battalion had orders to proceed to Liberty Bridge and link up with the elements of the 1st Engineer Battalion. The route of march to Liberty Bridge was on the northeastern sector of the operating area. Company B, 1st Battalion, 26th Marines moved into the vicinity of CU BAN (4) (AT9453) and encountered heavy resistance. Company C moved south until it encountered the northernmost element of Company B, then swung to the west and deployed on line with the 1st platoon on the left, 3rd platoon on the right, and second platoon in reserve.

It is of interest that this was the third time Company C had assaulted this area, to assist other elements that had been pinned down by the enemy, from virtually the same location. The first time was on 28 May when Company C moved to the relief of Company I, 3rd Battalion, 27th Marines and recover 11 casualties from that unit that had been pinned down on the battlefield. The second was 29 May when company C assaulted the area in support of Company B, 1st Battalion, 26th Marines. During the action of 29 May, Company C with a section of tanks in support had secured the objective with no casualties and inflicted significant losses on the enemy.

Now, on 5 June, the same two units were in the same situation as on 29 May. Unfortunately,

Just after promotion "Ceremony" to Lance Corporal
at Liberty Bridge, July 2, 1968

July 2.

Dear Folk,

How's it? The picture was taken this morning - I was summoned to the CP to correct the pay roster - and a dude had a polaroid. I was mad because I had to walk over - after a night patrol. but I am happy, the picture is bad but - note the 30 lbs gone!

hair is unkept usually combed ha sun was right in my eyes !

I sent "150⁰⁰" home oh! ... unindorsed or unsigned - nothing.. but put in account. forge signature of something?

a got a letter from Julin and one from Dunlop. so have ack. may write Lt. col. Julin.

Gramma's cinnamon rolls were - molded! ugh!

275.⁰⁰
150⁰⁰
+ bIKE
+ INCOME TAX RETURN
+ BANK ACCOUNT
_____
?

the results were nowhere near as favorable as they had been on the earlier occasion. The Company Commander and the Lieutenant next in the chain of command were wounded by mortar fire as they approached the battlefield; tanks were not present; a proper base of fire was not established; enemy positions were not accurately reconnoitered. The 3rd Platoon advanced over the open area and came under intense fire from well-entrenched enemy at extremely short range. The attack lost momentum, faltered, and stopped. The fierce fighting and the close proximity of the enemy to the friendly troops restricted area fire support weapons and air strikes. Company A, which had proceeded to Liberty Bridge to provide escort for the engineers, was ordered back to assist Company C, and a section of tanks that had been at Liberty Bridge was also committed. Upon the arrival of Company A and the armor, an all-out drive was made by Company A and Company C, which secured the objective.

JULY, 1968

Love Me Two Times - The Doors

WITH OUR PARTICIPATION IN OPERATION ALLENBROOK finished, 1/27th spent July moving from one Tactical Area of Responsibility (TAOR) to another. In early July we conducted saturation patrols with elements of the 51st ARVN Regiment throughout the Rocket and Mortar Belts. Around the middle of the month the Battalion took over the TAOR of the 3/27th, with our Company assigned the desert AO and patrolling with Marines from the Republic of Korea (ROK) TAOR to provide security for a detachment of the 7th Engineer Battalion.

~ THE ROCKET'S RED GLARE ~

The patriarch of our family, Herbert N. Parker, was born July 4, 1895. During World War I, in a gasp of patriotism and the yearning for adventure, my grandfather joined the Canadian Army infantry, and then trained as a fighter pilot. He later became an American flight instructor and flew in France in 1918 and returned a hero, larger than life to all of us. He was a gentleman, a member of the landed gentry, and already living a privileged life made possible by a modest family fortune, being educated at the University of Wisconsin, and a Phi Delta Theta fraternity brother. The collective bar for measuring accomplishments had been raised for everyone in the family forever, some fifty years ago by a war in Europe, far from the long fields of corn and soybeans in Illinois. Now it was my turn to measure up, only in Asia.

We were assigned an evening patrol on July 3, 1968. The *Green Gun Show* was now our squad nickname. We all wanted to be rock stars. Music and mail were our last connection to the world and those connections were becoming tenuous at best, thinner by the day. So we made our own music. Our rifles became air guitars and the M-79 grenade launcher a microphone. Nightly, as the sun set, we sallied out into the bush singing songs from the late '60s. It was, in part, to add merriment to the dull routine of endless patrols and ceaseless combat. Our laughter was like hanging a jeweled necklace on a skull. The *Green Gun Show* name also set us apart. No other squad had their own rock stars or sung rock n' roll in the face of the ever-present threat of being blown apart by booby traps or shot by a sniper's bullet. The singing quieted our fears, and we were braver because of it, but we were just another cheesy cocktail lounge act.

Walking out into the jungle; "Good evening, ladies and gentlemen! Welcome to the green gun show. On lead guitar, you have *A -Man*. On rhythm, *Chief*. On drums, *Bergy*, And your lead singer, the incomparable *PJ*!"

"Dumb ... dee ... dum-dum ... dum ... dum... dee . , . dum. Dumb!"

With the downbeat we loaded magazines in our rifles, steeling each other, staring into each other's eyes to confirm the Marine Corps bond. There were no braver, finer Marines in this war. Of the 27th Marine Regiment's Jr. enlisted Marines, (71%) would eventually be killed or wounded in just seven months.

In our minds, the houselights dimmed, the crowd roared – it was our time. "Lock and load ladies and gentlemen, it's show time."

We were young, we were Marines—we were ready. We walked out of our protective perimeter, bouncing rhythmically into the darkening landscape, softly singing in a whisper and playing our M-16 Fender air guitars. We sang, to the best of our abilities, the lyrics to the songs du jour – *Dance To The Music, Mony-Mony, I Heard It Through The Grapevine, Born To Be Wild, Jumpin Jack Flash*, and all the rest we could remember. It may have been happenstance, paranoia, or just plain coincidence, but we got ambushed every time we sang the lyrics from *"I Wish It would Rain."* It happened four or five times! Our superstition finally got the best of us, and we never sang *"I Wish It Would Rain"* by the Temptations ever again. Never! I still get the willies whenever I hear that song.

Because it was the eve of our country's independence, a Noncommissioned officer (NCO) gave us a stern warning, telling us not to celebrate by wastefully discharging ammunition, especially tracer rounds, or hand-held flares. "Aye, aye roger that..," we agreed, noting that we wouldn't want to give "Charlie" (the VC) the advantage of knowing our position by uselessly discharging U.S. Marine Corps ordinance, particularly tracer rounds.

Tracer rounds were used to help adjust rifle fire at low light levels. A small pellet of a chemical compound, which burned with a brilliant light, was embedded in the back of the tracer bullet. It only needed to burn a second or two, and the shooter could see where the bullets were hitting. I never used them; they fouled barrels and were corrosive if used in excess. I never used them, that is until July 3, 1968, when I appropriated a box of twenty and loaded them into my magazines.

I was going to be celebrating the 4th of July in style and they could throw me in jail if they wanted to. Military justice and the brig (jail) had been the coercive threat the officers used to convince us not to go nuts for the 4th of July. The brig was not enough of a threat however, not on July 4, 1968. Not in Vietnam, where 10% of all the on-the-ground fighters were Marines and 25% of the eventual deaths, and more of the wounded, would be Marines. More Marines would become casualties in Vietnam than during World War II. Marines in World War II spent an average of 40 days in combat over four months. Vietnam Marines spent an average of 240 days in combat in thirteen months – primarily thanks to helicopters.

As the weeks and months that we were in country grew, we grew fond of saying, "Fuck the brig. What are they going to do, cut my hair and send me to Vietnam?"

That night we walked a patrol route that took us to the side of a small hill overlooking a broad flat valley of small hamlets and rice paddies. We settled in, sitting down to wait for darkness. After some time resting against the brush and cool damp ground, I took a short nap, dreaming of home. When I awoke, it was twilight the morning of July 4, 1968. Off in the distance across the expansive valley, we heard an artillery bombardment start. The thunderous rumbling was constant for the next hour at the opposite end of the long valley. Later the carpet-bombing air strikes of the B-52 made the earth roll, even though their targets were miles away. It was going to be one hell of a night for the NVA.

Some poor enemy soldiers ("gook bastards") were getting their asses shot off, I thought as I loaded the magazines with tracer rounds into my rifle. Just as I raised my rifle muzzle to the sky, ready to celebrate, the festivities began throughout our entire Area of Operation (AO). From patrol bases and from individual patrols below us and on the hillsides surrounding the valley, it seemed like every American in the whole country was firing off anything that produced light or sound. The darkness gave way to an eerie strobe-lit gigantic party. The brilliant flashing lights and booming noise were everywhere. It was mesmerizing. The dull hum of the Air Force planes circling above the valley turned into a long deep winded whirr as they unleashed their mini-guns, releasing an unbroken line of reddish orange tracers speeding to the ground at 2,500 feet per second, aimed toward unknown, unseen targets. One out of five rounds coming from "Spooky" or "Puff the Magic Dragon," as the gun ships were variously nicknamed, was a tracer and the speed and volume of their bullets created the illusion of a solid orange line of bullets, one bullet per square foot, the size of a football field in only a few seconds. First the curving stream of light, then a long deep guttural "whooo" sound that lasted for minutes.

From the valley floor, occasionally a green-colored tracer would rise from a village or bamboo thicket. It was the NVA shooting back into the sky at the planes that were raining hell down on them. The hard-core enemy soldiers ("gook pricks") were actually shooting back up into the sky with their green tracers. Spontaneously, we cheered THEM on. "Get ya some!"

We all admired their courage, especially on the 4th of July, the day we celebrate to remind ourselves that we had been freed of the tyranny and oppression of our own British overlords. The VC and NVA had done the same to the French and had fought them, more or less, since 1857 when Napoleon III ordered the invasion of Da Nang. One hundred and eleven years ago, twenty miles north of where we were, the same war drama had been played out, using muskets and swords. The invaders then were turned back by a determined people, the Vietnamese, fighting for their homeland. What was it about those history lessons that we had not learned or understood? I thought – "*God, they are tough little fighters ("fuckers")*.

"Get some!" We yelled and whooped. As more bases and patrols added themselves to the celebrations, Vietnam was illuminated into daylight. It lasted for hours before, finally, the sanity and discipline of the Marine Corps was able to stop the celebration, via terse radio messages. We had no officer with us; ours had all been casualties. We stopped only because we ran out of tracer rounds. Tired but happy, we walked the remaining part of our patrol in silence. After all it was, by now, the 4th of July 1968. The holiday will never be the same for me. Fireworks in city parks have turned anemic, void of emotional content and pale by comparison – they are too tame. The guilt and sadness of surviving when others died and the sheer joy of being alive all collide for me on the 4th of July, in a thin soup of watery melancholy. July 4th, 1968 in Vietnam will be a part of me the rest of my born days, forever etched in my memory.

~ An Oasis in the Forest ~

Patrolling was a constant in our lives, just like the rising and setting of the sun. It was a never-ending task that we may have grown accustomed to, but few enjoyed. There was the drudgery of the patrol, venturing out on a prescribed path, usually in the dark, in search of VC or NVA. We walked with great care, usually in the habitual combat crouch, sometime with heavy packs on our backs, enduring the forced quiet and stress of having to be hyper-aware of every sound and nuance of our surroundings. This was a world manifest in the subtle. And, of course, there was the danger. Instantaneous danger could erupt without warning, at any time, at any place. Mostly we patrolled at night, but daytime patrols were almost as dangerous with small ambushes and booby traps being the norm whether it was sunny or dark. We hugged the ground and converted our world into tiny islands of cover (protection) where we were safe for the time being from enemy fire. Our world became simple to understand – safe or not safe.

Although we normally patrolled within our own area of responsibility, we were occasionally assigned longer patrols that put a lot of distance between us and our patrol base, sometimes many miles. If we ran into trouble on these patrols, we were on our own. On one long range patrol, in the "rocket and mortar belt" around the Marble Mountain area near of Da Nang, we hiked over various types of terrain, thickly canopied jungles, mostly bamboo, open rice paddies, and a leg of the patrol that took us to the South China Sea and along China Beach. During that one day we experienced four different landscapes and microclimates.

When we came to the beach checkpoint, we just relaxed and watched the warm, gentle breeze push the waves to shore, each of the light blue waves curling and breaking on the white sand in slightly different patterns. Vietnam is a truly beautiful place. I remember thinking that I would one day return to Vietnam after all this was over, to enjoy the beauty without the distraction of war. Naturally, my vision was to return as a triumphant victor of this American war.

"Saddle up!" PJ yelled, just when I was working up some Aloha, and we started our last leg of the patrol, back into the thick bush and the dark bamboo groves, where only fingers of light could penetrate between the narrow, slim leaves. When the light did filter through the canopy, it played almost magically on the leaves, the sun reflecting off one leaf then another, varying the colors in the grove from greens to yellows to blacks. Sometimes the leaves, washed by rain and direct sunlight, would turn gray, but always the dominant color was green – thick, rich, and varied. The tall, skyward reaching bamboo canes creaked and whined in the wind, sounding like loose floorboards in an old, abandoned house. The cane tops spend their days and nights, their entire existence, swaying in the sea breeze. The sharply pointed leaves at the top gently rustle together, making faint hissing sounds as they sway first in one direction, then in the other, playing the same tune over and over again. The foot of the thick bamboo canes formed a clump where years of decaying leaves pile up, producing a stillness that is inviting and foreboding at the same time. Bamboo clumps are a place designed by nature for a hunter to hide in and wait. Bamboo groves were places of delicate variations of colors and tone, subtle shades of difference from beautiful to dangerous.

We were moving in a line slowly through the thick jungle and bamboo cane groves, like a slender green snake when we heard sounds, maybe voices, up ahead. Whatever it was, it was loud. Instinctively we knelt behind cover and tried to identify the source of the ruckus. Gradually, we crept forward, painstakingly, an inch at a time to get into position for a better look. To our surprise, in the middle of the vermilion forest, we found a Navy Construction Battalion (Seabee) base camp and these Seabees had it good. They had generators to produce electricity and container cars full of provisions, air-conditioned hooches, equipment repair shops and, on the other side of the compound, a saloon, complete with red lights, a lacquered bar with stools, music from a juke box, dim lights, a rotating mirrored disco-ball, and a bartender.

We stood up, abandoning our cover and, without hesitating, walked nonchalantly into the miniature city. We smiled when we looked at each other and, without exchanging a word, headed to the bar. We walked in, discerning patrons that we were, and ordered beers. The bartender hustled drinks to our congested table of six and collected his money. We drank a few beers, harassed the occasional sailors that peeked in to see what six combat Marines were doing in their bar, and thoroughly enjoyed our unexpected reprieve. The bar was actually an insulated boxcar (a Conex) that the Seabees had converted with air conditioning powered by diesel generators they called Gen-Sets. After finishing our beers, we gathered up our gear, opened the door to the blast furnace of outside heat, and returned to our real world.

As we walked out of the compound and back into the jungle, the experience seemed even more surreal. We had actually gotten a midday beer buzz in the middle of the jungle, and had been served the drinks without question by a bartender, even though many of us were still minors – most of the Marines in Vietnam were 18-20 years of age, but the term "minors" was in no one's vocabulary.

We took a different route back to the coast, moving slowly and carefully, truly back into reality now that the bush was closing in and surrounding us. On our way back we crossed a wide, shallow river which seemed to be leisurely making its way to the South China Sea. We zigged and zagged across the terrain until we came upon the ocean. A large earthen dam at the mouth of the river backed the fresh water into a large pool, maybe 8-10 feet in depth at the point nearest the dam. As we crossed the dam, PJ noticed a whirlpool on the side of

July

Dear Mom,
Got packages - grape aide - cool aide
was good. We got out of bush last
night - a shave, a shower a hot meal
a beer or 2 or 3 ...!
Next month will be transferred
to a new out fit (the 27 is going
home) the 5 or 7 or 1st marines
probably. I hope.
Enclosed is an article from
newsweek you sent me about
"gonad" island (Go Noi) - that's where
"C" co was and got their ass kicked
yok!! now going to liberty bridge
for security there
it was 126°F here about a week
ago but didn't know it. I've lost
30 lbs but feel stronger?

love
lance corporal/USMC
George P. Berg
was promoted June 1
but didn't even know
myself.

morale high, confidence up
am learning more,

the dam, spinning round and round, making loud slurping, sucking noises. Curious, we all stood transfixed on the dam, maybe five feet above the swirling vortex and idly wondered where it went.

Perhaps some of us had cheated on our beer ration at the bar for, unexpectedly and suddenly, PJ dropped all his gear into a pile, pulled off his boots, socks and shirt, and dove, headfirst, into the water. He slowly surfaced and grabbed a handful of tree roots protruding from the dam and slid over to the two-foot wide whirlpool. He looked up to us, smiled, took a deep breath and disappeared under the water, down into the swirling dark hole. Just that quickly he was gone, but moments later, actually before any of us could do anything, PJ popped back up, bobbing like a cork on the other side of the dam in the ocean, his hair matted down on his face, a huge Cheshire Cat-like smile on his face and his hands raised in the air signaling touchdown. We laughed until we cried.

~ AWARD CEREMONY ~

After a few weeks in the bush, we got word that we were going back to Battalion Headquarters for a little celebratory get-together. The rumor was that we were to participate in the "pinning on" of recently earned medals. We were dirty, hadn't bathed in weeks and we were going to the rear area. Our clothes were tattered, and our jungle boots were rubbed suede. Simply put, we all looked, acted, and smelled like hell—like combat Marines. Nevertheless, we were herded to the Battalion area in trucks. When we arrived, we dismounted and started walking toward the center of the compound. No one knew what was going to happen or where we were going. We were unsure about what we were supposed to do, so we weren't much interested in marching in military formation. We sashayed down the street with a *roll in our stroll* and a *slide in our glide* attitude. We didn't care much for precision drill and laughed and joked our way toward where we thought the ceremony would be held.

As we drew closer to the center of the compound, a Marine officer hurriedly approached, his face a bright red as he yelled furiously, "Who is in charge of this cluster fuck? Fall in God damn it, you are Marines. Who is in charge of this herd?"

I couldn't help wondering who the real Marines were, this starched and cleanly shaven "in the rear with the gear," officer, or the smelly "butt plate,

Photo: L Fernung

July 13,'68

Dear Folk,
    Well, we go back to the bush
in about 3 or 4 days - ugh!
    No News just routine patrols
an ambush that I set up, was
sprung, we had 2, possibly 3, VC
in it but no confirmed kills.
It was the first ambush that
was even a partial success
in otherwords, we had the only
ambush to have VC walk into
it. Alpha Co. yesterday had 21 cas.
in one (1.) booby trap (a 155 mm. shell)
    Also a patrol I led (8 marines
4 ARVN's) was sniped at by 2 AK-47s'
in a semi-cross fire both fired
automatic they had us pinned
down for about 1hr. in an open
rice paddy (105°F)

needless to say I was terrific at fire control, radio comm. posit, and support and other military garbage, - I'm great.

Thanks for the finance report - Aunt Mary's molten choc. was "S OK". Don't press the Garica thing. If you haven't done it yet let's just let it "phase out" OK!

Write Col. Julin, I'm mucho busy!

Well thats it for awhile Say Hello and etc. to Family Grama etc.

Tom shaw bought telegraph it comes pretty reg.

Love,

George

leather neck" horde roaming up the street. In some unbalanced way, I guess we both were. I was beginning to question the rigid structure of the garrison Marine Corps – I liked combat. The Marine Corps seemed bi-polar – a focus on both; combat skills and spit and polish seemed diametrically opposed.

We dutifully complied with the officer's request, formed into a column two abreast, and were led to a tent where we could clean up, which meant we had time to wash our faces. We were then marched into a large open area complete with a Marine Corps band where we stood in the hot sun in our ragtag uniforms for the duration of the ceremony. I wondered if this was how it had been done on Iwo Jima. I found out later that it was a General that pinned the medals on the few brave Marines who received the recognition they rightfully deserved. The rest of us got beers. When the ceremony was over, we were hustled back on the trucks and returned to the bush – where, I for one, felt more comfortable.

~ FOOL AND SNIPERS ~

Sometimes the less you knew about your fellow Marines, the more there was to like. When one person has disdain for another it shows, no matter how hard the person tries to conceal it, or how clever he might be. Hate, distrust, scorn and disrespect are more obvious than a fake smile. "The Fool," as I called him, was a chattering idiot. He was, in fact, insipid. He made friends like a used car salesman, as if collecting Marine "buddies" would provide an invisible shield and protect him from harm. The constant currying of favor was solicitous, transparent and, more than anything, irritating. Maybe it was me; I couldn't get beyond his veneer. It was an intense self-focus, a need to preserve beyond the interest of the group – our platoon. He wanted something more and was willing to suck it from whoever was near him. Self-preservation is important, but the loss of self allows the joining of group to be complete. A "band of brothers" has a lost sense of self and a higher adherence to the group. In Vietnam there was intense sharing, bonding and camaraderie, but another reality was also as true. We sometimes live alone in our thoughts; we die alone and only receive comfort from others on rare occasions or inspired moments, such as: tragedy, fear, and love of family.

The Fool Marine was a portrait of neither excellence nor ineptitude but rather of numbing mediocrity. He was just pretending to be a Marine most of the time. One hot evening, while we were digging in a patrol base, the wind slowed and the few birds stopped their chirping. Stillness suddenly took charge. Night comes quickly near jungles, light to dark, first one star, and then another until they clutter the sky. As we all slid apprehensively into the darkness, the Fool stepped up on the rice paddy dike and stood there. His fatigue pants caught my eye as they suddenly billowed out, like a dark green wet balloon, then collapsed back onto his leg. His jungle fatigues grew darker and darker with his blood. Then we heard the sound of the shot that ripped the bullet through his upper thigh, and just as suddenly he fell to the ground, like a stone. Up, then down in a fraction of a second, followed by his mewling yelp, "I'm hit! I'm hit!"

An NVA or Viet Cong sniper had put a single round through the meaty part of his leg from a tree line a hundred yards away. We carried The Fool on a poncho to a safe place and waited for the dust-off helicopter.

As we waited he made a list of things we needed to do for him. He put on a thinly plastered, contrived brave face as he boarded the rescue helicopter. Then he was gone, like a little kid smiling and walking swiftly and whistling loudly passed a graveyard, he was lifted from the wind-weighted grass and gone. The next morning the sun rose with a jerk. Suddenly it was light. The birds awakened, first one then all the others. Another night had passed, another clear hot day began.

All of this is now a dream sensation that I talk myself through on paper. My own words soothe what bothers me, and what bothers me is that Marines like The Fool got so much from other Marines. What bothers me is the grizzly reality we Marines now carry with us, linked forever with a set of experiences that were jumbled, at best decades ago, and are even more jumbled and disjointed as time passes. The smells of warfare last decades afterwards and trigger recollections of burning villages, freshly turned earth and diesel fuel. The sound of the whopping blades of helicopters will always excite Vietnam veterans and quicken their pulse. But there remains the need to finish what can't be finished, to finish a tour of duty, to finish an emotion; to cleanly kill someone or to be killed by someone. That won't happen, but the bindings are there, tied tightly to those who went to Vietnam, and maybe every war. Vietnam won't go away for either the veterans who served there or for the national collective consciousness. It is part of our history.

~ Monsoon Rain ~

The torrential rain in Vietnam, driven by the wind, sometimes horizontally, pounded the bamboo leaves and sounded like a thousand people snapping their fingers. The intense rain drowned out all other sounds but its own. The hissing, muting rains sometimes came and went in only minutes. Other days, the rain lasted for hours, the accompanying rolling thunder only vaguely distinguishable from a distant artillery barrage. A loud deafening boom would sound, and then a rumbling that tapered off into nothing – silence, then, defiantly, it would start over. The patter-patter of the cold rain beat out a rhythm on anything it struck. The air was almost instantly cleansed by the rain, cleared of the acrid dust and the stale smell of the tropics. Freshness took over and suggested, momentarily, that if we really leaned into this deal, we could work it out and all of us could go home. Not a chance. This argument, this war would be finished toe-to-toe in the dirt.

In these downpours the salt from our own sweat, government-issued mosquito repellent, and the dust of Vietnam would all wash down our faces, sting our eyes, and foul our lips. The monsoon deluges were enough to blur vision, one way or the other. In the monochromatic mist, the hard, flat light, mixed with the greens of the elephant grass and bamboo bleach all colors to shades of gray.

When it rained, visibility was negligible. Now was the time for the NVA to crawl out of their caves and burrows and begin their haunting probes of Marine positions. Rain, was the great equalizer. Rain could neutralize any American made technological advantage. The monsoons were called "gook weather." When it rained, it was obvious that an attack of some sort was imminent. The enemy ("gooks") would be coming to kill us in the rain, and they'd be here soon. When it rained we, the veterans anyway, would automatically start bracing for the attack, and the FNGs would quickly follow our leads and key in on the excitement. Our entire shivering bodies sensed the new proposition. It was show-time at the "OK Corral." The war was coming alive in the rain. The shoot-out was on.

"Bring it on!" Someone would yell. "Somebody is going to die tonight!" In the cold rain, in the mud, either he or I would die. The duel started whenever it rained. The monsoon rain made it personal, intimate, one-on-one. We were all teenage predators and looked forward to the inevitable fight.

Our hearts were paced by the weather. The weather, especially the rain, was a metronome. The rhythm that was happening outside our bodies happened inside. Everything was alert, all our senses elevated. It was dreary and exhilarating at the same time, a twisting helix of mixed emotions.

During our patrols, we learned to stalk silently. Our hearing was acute; the snap of a twig even at a distance sent a jolt of adrenaline coursing through our bodies in alternating cycles of being rigid, holding our breath, and then relaxing as we walked. Our eyes saw everything and searched in a scanning motion back and forth, up and down. Our heads were mounted on swivels. When we smelled the smoke in the villages from the small wood cooking fires, we could tell whether the fires had just been started, or were burning themselves out. All of our senses worked together when we were in the "boonies," and provided the information needed to make decisions about what step to take next and where to place our feet. We were blending into the bush and had become part of the landscape of Vietnam at a deeper level than just our green clothes. Like the war, this synchronizing of our bodies to the climate and soil was part of the Vietnam War experience. We became organic, like the earth, a mixture – grounded.

~ MUSIC AND THE MADNESS ~

The rain started lightly at first, just a few droplets falling through the grey mist, first recognizable in the still, brown puddles of water that were remnants of last night's storm. The unannounced raindrops, falling one by one, made small, telltale ripples in the quiet pools. A change in the weather was about to occur. Another monsoon storm was gathering, but we were prepared. Four of us had constructed a makeshift shelter by tying our ponchos together. As more and more raindrops continued to hit our tent, we checked the stakes and guylines – everything was secure. The raindrops got larger but everything was ready for the monsoon or typhoon or so we thought.

As the raindrops continued to beat against the shelter, I realized that I was becoming what I wanted – a combat Marine. I was learning what it would require for surviving and succeeding in this ordeal. I was getting what I wanted, but learning the price, which was to go numb, forget about home and especially about its comforts. Don't think of the future, either. These were part of the price – the toll I was paying for the transition to "going bush."

The four of us had planned to pass the time between patrols that night by memorizing lyrics to Beatles songs. Music would become our anchor, which we could haul out to slow our drift into the insanity of war and remind us of the "world," our homes, our family and our friends.

During my days in Vietnam our music ranged from dull to frightening. There were the subtle sounds which permeated our existence, the clack of metal C-ration cans, the chattering screech of men and machines, and the low buzz of insects with the accompanying harsh slaps that smashed the blood suckers. We could hear the sounds of sucking, squishing and squashing boots as we plowed through water filled rice paddies. Our percussion section usually consisted of the throbbing, pulsing, whop-whop-whop of helicopters and the ever-present kettledrum booming of artillery and air strikes, always near and always far away. The main melody, of course, was the staccato rattle of automatic weapons, and the occasional solo appearance of the sniper's round.

My younger brother had sent me a booklet of Beatles music we intended to memorize, but as the rain continued to intensify only our shouts were audible in the close confines of the shelter. The wind was driving the rain horizontally through our tent, and anything that had been dry was now hopelessly soaked. The deluge mixed everything into thick green, indiscernible gravy— the cigarette smoke, cooking C-rations, the decaying jungle vegetation, our sweat, rifle cleaning solvent and the scent of the ground all blended together.

The chilling torrent of what felt like a typhoon continued for hours throughout the night. We fought the demoralizing, negative psychological effects with our smiles and laughter, until even the small patch of dry ground, all that we had, eventually betrayed us. We had dug a trench around our rubberized canvas home as a catchment to divert the rainwater. We had pitched the tent on the highest piece of ground in the area. Our efforts were useless. The relentless rain continued to pound, attacking the already water sodden, saturated earth. With nowhere to go, the water just continued to rise, deeper and deeper.

We defiantly sang louder, forcing broader grins on our faces as we slowly became immersed in the water. We had used our individual ponchos to make our shelter, so all we could do was lay there, smile, curse, and shake our heads in disbelief. The evening twilight gradually surrendered us to the full bleakness of the cold night. In time, we were reduced to staring at the sheet music as it floated in small circles, the ink smearing, and then disappearing across the pages. The edges of the paper slowly curled up. Gradually it was stained a brownish-grey and became just a paper glob that eventually floated away and disappeared into the black night.

The roiling wind and rain hissed and slashed that entire night. The bamboo made indecipherable little stutters as it yielded to the typhoon's rage with a flawless, feminine curved grace. As the sun replaced the wind and rain, shafts of light unrolled into vivid white and yellow, horizontal beams. A fine steamy mist rose across the soaked ground. We blended perfectly, at least that morning, with the ground. Mud and muck caked us from head to toe.

This ordeal, on that particular night in July of 1968, in the Republic of South Vietnam, made me stronger. I entered a less curious state of turbulence. I was resisting fatigue and mastering fear. As that night ended, I believed I could withstand almost any physical challenge and endure any discomfort or pain. I was utterly at peace with myself. I had washed up onto a strange new beach. *I'm a Marine*, I thought. After surviving the typhoon outside in the elements, I had little doubt.

My heart beat with a single, calm rhythm, but with the vagrant, clinging pang of too many dead Marines and not enough dead NVA.

~ BIG SNAKES, LITTLE SNAKES ~

We moved on and off Go Noi Island and sometimes ran patrols along the "Canal," which was a more relaxed duty, but hazardous nonetheless. The canal was a system of dykes and levees sponsored by the South Vietnamese government to shunt water to the rice paddies in the hope of harvesting a second crop. These structures were hotly contested, and our job was to protect them from being destroyed by Victor Charlie (VC).

We ran patrols day and night to intercept and interdict enemy activity. Our patrols were run to and from checkpoints where we reported our arrival at specific locations on a patrol map based on very specific coordinates, at an absolute certain time. It was extremely important to stick to the patrol route and be on time and on target, because at night, artillery harassment and interdiction barrages occurred without warning. You had to be at a checkpoint when you were supposed to be there or face getting blown apart by your own artillery stationed at a firebase miles away from where you were. The Marine gunners had no way of knowing who was down range from them, they just crammed the shells in the breach of the 155mm howitzers and pulled the trigger lanyards and the flying bombs were gone, hurling through the night sky, invisible, spinning mindlessly toward their designated end. The sky at night in Vietnam was full of indiscriminate, undifferentiated danger.

The ground, the jungle floor, and canal water were also dangerous. Tropical snakes of all kinds posed real and imagined threats. On one hot blazing afternoon, like many of the other Marines, bored and sunburned, I decided to venture into the swift current of the canal and take my chances. I stripped off my shirt and swam into a shallow shore area which was full of water hyacinths. The hyacinths were tall, green, waxy-leafed plants, with light blue flowers that floated a foot or so above the surface of the water. They were constructed with bulb-like flotation structures. Their roots hung down below the surface in entangled thick masses, which created an almost impenetrable barrier. I quickly found out you could swim into these root clumps and almost stand up. The root masses would support your body weight. I sat down between the hyacinths and took a nap with only my head showing above water. Without my being aware of it, the hyacinths slowly closed in around me. I awoke entwined in the plants. Panicked, I kicked and punched my way out. Treading water, I surveyed the area in 360 degrees. No one had witnessed my foolishness. My plight had been anonymous, unnoticed by anyone beside me. I recognized the terrifying effect the plants from hell had on me. I wanted to test it on someone else, maybe several other people.

I stayed concealed in the thicket as more Marines started slipping into the reddish-brown waters of the canal to cool off. Whenever a Marine would swim past me, going upstream toward the metal pontoon bridge combat engineers had built to get heavy equipment back and forth from one side to the other, I would grab him around the neck, cover his mouth with my other hand and drag him, silently screaming bubbles, under the murky water. I had leverage because I could stand and my hapless victim could only flail around as I dragged them under the water and into the hyacinths. I quickly freed my victims. Most took a swing or two and all of them called me a variety of colorful names, making reference to a body part or my heritage. I laughed at all of them and sneered at their helplessness in the water.

After pulling several Marines into my lair, I tired of the game and started to swim against the current toward the bridge, where most of my victims were hanging out, some still fuming. As I approached, I could see them milling beside the bridge rails, pointing at me.

"Snake!" One of them shouted, pointing in my direction.

"Too bad," I thought. *"You lost! The joke was on you!"*

Several of the others also shouted the warning and several turned, grabbing for their M-16's. As I swam upstream, I saw one Marine chamber a round and point his rifle toward me.

"Damn, this was getting serious," I thought. It must be a plot to extract revenge for my antics downstream. As I got closer, I could see the whites in their wide eyes, and I knew something really was wrong.

Were they that pissed off that their eyes still bugged out? As I got closer, still unsure about what was happening; they continued to yell, "Snake!"

I looked over my right shoulder several times. I could see beside me and behind me and there was no snake, just my wake. Nevertheless, their activity heightened. More Marines were grabbing their rifles and loading rounds. I looked over my shoulder again. Nothing. I was getting closer to the bridge and the Marines on it were still bouncing around excitedly. Then I finally thought to look over my left shoulder. I took a deep breath, then still face down, eyes open in the water, I rotated to the left. As my face cleared the surface, my eyes blinked with disbelief. There it was, the head of a huge water snake. It was swimming parallel with me, seemingly oblivious to my presence. It continued steaming ahead, only inches from my face. Its eyes never altered their transfixed gaze. Stunned by the size and nearness to my face, I slapped the water between the snake and me, rolled onto my back and crabbed to the bank, splashing water and tearing a hole through a colony of hyacinths. I bolted up the muddy, sloped sides of the slippery canal and stood there, out of breath, staring at the snake as it slowly disappeared down into the dark, murky water. The snake was gone in a split second. The chuckles from the bridge soon faded and the alerted Marines returned to their routine of whatever had occupied them before the entertainment began.

As my heart and the noise from the bridge quieted down, I realized I was on the wrong side of the canal – the VC side, unarmed, half-naked and exhausted. I dove back into the water and swam across in seconds. Safe on the other side, I returned to my fighting hole. The stars would be out soon, and we would start another night's patrolling in Vietnam. I was a long way from home, yet I could be there in my dreams. I dozed off, still wet, but smiling – another hallucination was over. And so was another day in Vietnam.

~ SAND BAGGERS ~

Night patrols were dangerous around the canal. We had "Victor Charlie," (VC) ARVNs, artillery, other Marine patrols, the elements, insects, snakes, and each other to contend with. Sometimes the risk and the effort needed to run the patrol correctly were out of balance with the benefits. Occasionally, we would lay up at a checkpoint out of fatigue and self-preservation. It was called sandbagging. We'd walk to the first checkpoint as planned and then, instead of relocating to the second checkpoint, usually half a mile or more away, we'd stay where we were. When the approximate time to be at checkpoint two had passed, we'd call in our position as if we were there, when in reality, we were still camping at checkpoint one.

"One, this is one-dash-one. Be advised we're at checkpoint two, over," We'd whisper into the two-way radio. "One-dash-one, this is one, roger that."

Safe now, two Marines would stay awake and the rest of us would "cop some Z's" (sleep). Most of the time it worked and the deception, albeit a dangerous practice, was a well-kept secret, widely known by all the grunts.

On one particularly long patrol, which was scheduled to last the entire night, we walked for miles into the dark bamboo thickets, the full moon darting in and out from behind gray clouds. The clouds created an eerie effect as they momentarily blocked the moonlight, then rolled past, pushed by slight gusts of wind. The moonlight seemed to race toward you, illuminating the area like a dimly blinking searchlight. You could see the illusion of moonlight traveling toward you. When the light was on you, you froze. We were silhouettes in the patchwork landscape of light and dark, the shadows dancing all around, continuously changing. We stopped and started all night until the moon finally set, and the inky darkness returned. We decided to sandbag at checkpoint three and at dawn walk back to our patrol base past checkpoint four. It was just too dangerous to continue playing hide and seek that night – we were too vulnerable in the ever-changing moonlit shadows.

At dawn, our charade complete, we radioed that we were coming in and we entered the perimeter, quietly walking past claymore mines and sentries stationed at the outlying LPs. No sooner had we set down our equipment to heat some C-rations than a Lance Corporal who had stayed in the PPB started yelling and screaming that we were "shit birds," jeopardizing the safety of the whole company by sandbagging. Confronted about the sandbagging, we all lied – naturally.

"Fucking assholes," he shouted! The Marine was enraged and continued to accuse us of the crime we most certainly had committed. Following each of us around for a few steps at a time, in a hysterical rage, he would berate us, moving from one person to the next. "You're all fucking cowards - Assholes!"

July 15, '68

Dear Mom,

We are staying at a dam for about 2 days for security, then on to the bush, around Marble Mountain the Engineers around here have it pretty good. - Gives us one night and we'll have a goodly portion of their goodies! - that's war

It's really quite warm - hum? 105-110°F. I got a field hair cut no longer retain the "Hippie in uniform look - it's cooler - my mustache is bleached out!

Thanks for the TIME & NEWSWEEK I dig them - We had a tropical rain storm - Remember Florida rains? - that's right! X10. The rainy season should be "wet and wild". - Cold.

Our squad was the vanguard ~~as~~, as usual, so we're the only one's here - We put the men in place for security HA. and the squad leader and the other team leader (AND PJ) are "SKATEING."

I "role my own" cigars a vet-marine showed me how. it's strong garbage - but it affects my image - for this week - I nuts" MA!

Well different schools dodge in and out of my brain daily - nightly all the time, maybe a voc. - in CONSTRUCTION Engineering or electricity - oh well but I will be trained or/and skilled - if not educated (LIBERAL ARTS TYPE). So many fields I may say be damned and become a conservation officer in Wiscon. or Ill. but no "$ing involved.

Love, your son,

George

PJ says Hi BUZAIRD SPANGLER TYPE ONLY - INSANE

HOW'S All - HOUSE CARS, JOB ANY $ TROB. FAMily.

Finally, frustrated and out of breath, he sat down, leaned against a tree and finished his C-ration breakfast. C-rations come in small tin cans and are precooked, prepared meals. You can eat them cold or heat them with the heat tabs provided. Heat tabs are small flammable miniature briquettes that you light, but many of us acquired a high explosive from mortar rounds, called C-4, to heat our meals, it burned very fast and hot, and got the job done quickly and efficiently.

C-ration cans are opened with a small can opener about an inch long and a half-inch wide, nicknamed a John Wayne. Officially the can openers were P-38's and everyone carried one on their dog tag chain around their neck. The preferred technique when opening a can was to leave part of the lid still connected so you could hold it above the flame of the burning C-4 with your fingers. After you ate your meal, you were supposed to bury the various cans and the boxes they came from.

The irate, battle-weary Lance Corporal had a habit of not burying his cans. On this morning, as he sat dozing under the tree, his empty cans lying all around him, a small but very poisonous snake, according to our Navy corpsman, crawled into one of his discarded cans, attracted, I guess, by the scent of food. Curious, I studied the snake for a while, watching its tongue flick around inside the can. Then the snake, with its head still in the can, tried to reverse itself, only to get trapped by the sharp, jagged metal edge of the can's lid, which had been pushed into the can. The harder the snake tried to back out of the can, the firmer it got stuck and soon it couldn't go forward either. The snake was trapped.

I walked over and picked up the assembly. The can and snake was now one wiggling unit. The thin black snake whipped its tail to escape the greasy trap, but my thumb kept the head of the snake securely in the can. It wasn't getting out unless I let it out. I began to menace my fellow Marines, showing the snake to anyone near me. Some sneered, and some just rolled their eyes. Then it was the Lance Corporal's turn. After all, it was his discarded can the snake had blundered into. I tapped him awake with my boot.

"Hey," I said, "Look what crawled over you while you were asleep. Don't worry. I caught this sandbagging asshole for you. Next time you may not be so lucky though." Then I crushed the snake's head in the can and threw it down beside the stunned Lance Corporal. He and I never did get along.

~ SPARROW HAWKS AND BALD EAGLES ~

With our platoons depleted by high casualties, our tactics were switched. Along with saturation patrolling we would also go out in small groups to the edge of a village suspected of harboring the enemy, where we would lay hidden and motionless through the night just watching. We would lie in the grass or brush for hours on end undetected and observe the comings and goings in that area. Once in a while, someone would see a Vietnamese carrying a rifle or acting suspicious in some other manner, and would call in a report but most of the time we just observed. The advantage of this tactic was that once we settled in, it was less likely that we would be discovered – no noise. Another advantage was that the physical exertion was much less, and we were able to get some rest, at least our feet did.

Of course, there were disadvantages as well. Lying perfectly still in the dark for hours was never easy, especially when you were physically exhausted and dangling at the edge of your physical limitations. Other disadvantages were the insects and vermin. The long nights were filled with insects crawling, biting, stinging and sucking your blood. Chief among these antagonists were the ever- present mosquitoes. Their high-pitched whine sounded like someone forcing the letter Z through their front teeth. The shrill noise was as irritating as the bites, and we couldn't move to swat or scratch as we were being bled, one bite at a time. The second, but more repulsive, nemesis was the vermin – rats. The rats were large, aggressive, and veracious. They would boldly crawl over us, sniffing and darting furtively to find scraps of food. Occasionally, someone would get bitten, receiving a nasty wound, when they were mistaken for food or were defending themselves.

On one of these long, overnight observation posts, which were called *Sparrow Hawks*, (Bald Eagles were reserve units) we held up in a bombed-out pagoda. Only the stone walls and part of the tile roof remained. In the front of the pagoda was a shrine with a raised stone altar, for placing offerings and burning incense. The rats gave me the heebie-jeebies, so I claimed the altar for my bed. The altar was cold and yes, hard as a rock but it was off the floor. While part of the unit was silently watching the village, the others rested, and some tried to sleep. In the darkness, once we were settled in, you could hear the rats racing from one Marine to the next. Muffled, murmured profanities broke the silence, "Jesus Christ! God damn it!"

Being in the Buddhist pagoda and being attacked by rats brought out a convoluted spiritual aspect in me, but the altar provided no sanctuary. In the dark I back-handed a rat off my chest. As I made contact, banging my closed fist into its ribs, the rat dug its claws into my chest, tearing away some of my shirt as it flew through the air. It hit the stone floor, squeaked a long single defiant note and scurried away, hidden by the darkness.

~ THE LUXURY OF SEX ~

Walking to the command post near the center of our patrol base along the canal, I stopped to figure out where they had moved the CP. A Black Marine, shirt unbuttoned, walked up and asked me for a cigarette. I didn't smoke but we struck up a conversation, mainly about the nasty scar he had on his stomach. He had large, matching round scars on his wrist and stomach where the two had been fused together in a graft to heal an earlier gunshot wound that had ripped through his arm. He had been in the rear recuperating and was just now reluctantly returning to the field. He said he had heard rumor that there was a whorehouse across the canal. After a brief pause, he asked, "Do you want to check it out?"

Without thinking, I said, "Sure, why not?"

I had not been near a woman in months and the sexual anesthesia produced by constant engagements was wearing off. Being stationed at the relatively uneventful canal was light duty by comparison to Goi Noi Island.

July 20,

Dear Mom, Folk,
    Enjoyed your last letter mostly about Sib- and my future. Golf.-- never.- ilve seen who plays it and why Lost Nation. Tennis (will learn) SCUBA, skiing, Karate (Korean) are more my bag.
    Sib's letters have been sparse lately - no time to wonder about what she's doing - but do sometimes.
    You wouldn't believe the jobs that ilve thought about getting and the schools ilve also given thought to.
    It's hot here - but am only 2 or 3 miles from S. China Sea. will be moving again. soon- We alternate 4 days in real bush - 4 days in an ARVN compound. Rice and squid! fish heads other garbage - we run patrols night and day- - There are a lot of mines and traps one jeep! 20 minutes ago and 2 casualties in 2 days.

time for me goes fast but
dread the monsoons
       of Tom Shaw sends the
Dixon Evening Rag. regularly
As take ~~this~~ note and save on
postage.
    <u>FLASH</u> ☆☆

    I was put up for Meritorious
Corporal (NCO) by my old squad
leader - I may get it in August
"BERG KNOWS HIS SHIT" is about
the highest compliment one can
recieve and <u>I do</u> I am good
and stay outwardly cool - but its
not (for probably the first time in
along while) a fascade.

        L/CPL   *Love your son,*
137.70 BASE
   9.00 OVERSEAS
 65.00 COMBAT
201.70 MONTHLY
         PAY - ALLOTMENT   George

    I DIG GREEN "S"

Thoughts of sex were a luxury in Vietnam. My experience in the field was numbing, out of many necessities. Errant thoughts of sex with a stranger, a Vietnamese woman, were suppressed. The Marine Corps had cautioned us repeatedly about black syphilis, a particularly virulent sexually transmitted disease. You did not want to get the "crotch" because, as jungle legend had it, if you contracted this particular venereal disease, your penis would turn black, shrivel up, and eventually fall off. In addition, the Viet Cong frequently recruited teenage girls to seduce naïve and unsuspecting Marines. These very young girls would torture and kill Marines in a variety of grotesque and hideous ways. Those were the reasons I didn't show much sexual interest in the few women we saw. The female villagers we did see, called *mama sans*, were culturally and politically conditioned not to respond to Marines. Besides, many of them were simply just not attractive. Most of them chewed beetle nuts, which stained their teeth an ugly dark brown. I was too busy staying alive, too mobile to be sexual; that is until this particular day. I was being overwhelmed by raw lust and an indiscriminate, undifferentiated desire for any woman.

He said he had heard that the price was a non-negotiable $10, (probably script money), so we hid our rifles, took off our green canvas jungle boots, stripped to our waists, and swam slowly, silently across the canal, with only our heads above the water. The anticipation of seeing a bawdy, perfumed, hopefully acrobatic, professional Asian girl dressed in nothing but delicately woven and embroidered red silk panties was all-consuming. The male hormone was already working, firmly and vigorously supporting my fantasies. Even the icy rush of the flowing water could not suppress physiology. It would be embarrassing and awkward scrambling up the opposite bank of the canal.

The other Marine loudly claimed "firsts," as we made our way, dripping, shoeless and shirtless through the bamboo thickets. We came to a clearing and there was a small bamboo hut (*hooch*), with a grey thatched roof made of dried palms. The walls were also constructed of split bamboo. What passed for a door was a faded piece of torn and threadbare brown cloth, weighted at the bottom, the Vietnamese version of a screen door. As I approached cautiously behind the other (first) Marine, over his shoulder I could see a woman's calf and shoeless foot. There was, in fact, a woman inside. My heart raced with excitement and anticipation.

Outside this small building, grass had grown up around the edges. There were no other buildings or structures around. Something was wrong here. It was suspicious and puzzling. This hooch was curious because village hooches were built with grass-thatched roofs and walls, not woven split bamboo. This structure was meant to keep something contained inside. Standing some 20 or 30 feet away was a grim-faced older woman, maybe in her 40s. Her black hair was pulled back in an ornate bun, which was unusual for a villager. Beside her stood a younger man, in black pants and collarless tunic top. He looked slightly nervous, guarded. He said nothing. He just stared past us dispassionately, but his presence was felt. He looked and acted like a sentry.

As the "first" Marine eagerly approached the hut, the old Madame motioned via an outstretched hand, for him to pay up. Mr. First walked over to the Madame and tried to haggle a better deal. The price was set. It would be ten dollars today. He begrudgingly complied and gave her the soaking wet bills he had carried in his pocket through the water. She examined them carefully, holding them up to the sunlight, as if she knew what she was doing. The man in the all-black outfit also looked the money over and nodded his approval. The woman then walked over to the hut and pulled back the curtain door for him to enter.

The older woman, her escort and I just stared in silence at the hut. Our eyes never met; they were fixed on the hut. Mr. First emerged minutes later, buttoning his wet fatigues. He walked past me, without a word, and headed straight for the canal. He didn't wait for even a moment. His transaction was complete. Rounding a clump of bamboo, he disappeared. I stood there listening to the cooing of Asian mourning doves in the nearby trees- reconciling what was about to occur. Then, in a snap, I realized I too had manly business to transact. I gingerly walked over to the older woman on the outside edges of my battered, raw feet and handed her the dry single bill I had carried across the canal clenched in my teeth. It was the only dry thing on me. I got the nod of approval. It was my turn. I pivoted around slowly, and made my way to the hut on my sore bare feet.

I pulled back the curtain and there, huddled up on what resembled a wicker mat on the floor was a naked girl. Her knees were tucked almost up to her bare breasts, her hand folded across, protecting them from my view. I just stood there and stared down at her. When she realized I was standing there in the door, she slowly rolled over onto her back and gradually spread her legs, her feet flat on the floor, her knees bent upward. Her face was turned away, looking to the sidewall of the hooch, her eyes tightly closed. The invitation was clear. She was signaling, with benign resignation, that the transaction could begin.

I quickly unbuttoned my soaked fatigue trousers. The weight of the canal water dropped them to the ground with a thump. Underwear was abandoned, usually after two weeks in the boonies. I kicked my battered and torn pants off my ankles and walked toward her completely naked. She looked at me sidelong with one eye, her face still turned away and lying flat on the mat. Her modest silk clothes had become her pillow, light, faded yellow silk pants and blouse rolled up to protect her face from the coarse, woven fibrous bamboo mat she lay on. I knelt down between her legs and just waited. I was very unsure about what to do and didn't touch her; the sublime taboos that maintain social control in America were operating. The conflict of male lust and Midwestern values of respect for women raged within.

Kneeling above her, between her widely spread legs, both of us naked, I found myself in the middle of a wide, psychic canyon. She was lying flat on her back, and she was still wet from her first transaction. Small pools of water transported from the "first" Marine formed on her flat stomach. The water droplets had beaded up and glistened on her smooth oily skin; *Mr. First must not have gotten naked*, I thought. *Am I doing something wrong?* She was very thin, almost delicate. Her skin color was that of a new copper penny. Her hair was long, lustrous, jet black and straight. Small dark tufts of thin black hair covered her below her waist, and a few, very thin hairs curled up in her armpits. Her breasts were characteristically small, but her dark disproportionally large nipples were grotesquely disfigured. Her nipples were rust colored and gnarled, looking like diseased galls on a tree branch.

As I waited, I began to genuinely enjoy viewing the body of the naked and fragile Vietnamese girl I had rented. I was in childlike awe. She must have sensed my being stunned and without turning her face toward me, she raised and outstretched her arms. When I continued to hesitate, she turned her face toward me. I immediately saw the plainness and simplicity in her eyes. I guessed she was the Vietnamese equivalent of an Illinois, high school-aged farm girl, pressed into prostitution by whomever those people were outside. Her fingers were rough, calloused, cut from working with her hands in the rice fields.

I raised her up and, while she was sitting on the bamboo mat, embraced her ever so gently. I just held her while she quietly wept. After only a few brief moments of indulgence, she stoically laid back and guided me inside her, without letting go of our embrace. This was my first rodeo, not hers. Cheek to cheek, the vibrations carried my thoughts to her. In my surreal mind's eye, I tucked her into imaginary sheets on an imaginary bed far away from the split bamboo hut. In one wholly perverse moment, I had transmigrated into her protector, her lover, customer, and liberator. This jungle ballet just was not right, but it became a luxury, nonetheless.

My own cruel and savage heart was healed, tamed for the time being by my kindness to her. I was hearing an echo of some humanity lost and now returning. It flew back to me like a wild bird, darting in and out of the trees of a dimly lit forest, not sure of where to land. The end was a merging of the profound emotions of pure joy and the simultaneous renewed validation of me as a human male. For that one instant, I was freed of the brutal, numbing circumstances of war. I raised myself, and still on my knees, and let out a long yell. In that sudden, single moment, the sun, stars, moon, and planets filled my head with a rush. God, I was still alive. I did not fathom what being forced to be an object for others meant at that time. I have a grasp of the concept now, and understand the dehumanizing, degrading effect war has on anyone who comes near it.

As I stood up and hastily pulled on my crumpled trousers, I looked over at her. She had returned to the fetal position. Curled up only slightly less than when I walked in. I said goodbye in English, and she smiled a weak smile, her mouth closed. She never looked up. I walked out of the hut and hobbled my way back to the canal on my spongy, sore feet. I cast a glance over my shoulder as I walked past the two pimps, probably VC or VC sympathizers, and gave them a "kiss my ass" disapproving stare. Expressionless, they turned and slowly walked in the opposite direction. All of their business was over, for this day at least. The girl stayed confined in her isolated cell.

Walking back to the canal, I still pumped mastic strings of reproductive, primordial goo. The genetic potential of thousands of beautiful, little round-eyed Americans would be left behind in the sand and be wasted, a misfortune of war. I made my way back through the bamboo groves and to the water's edge and dove in.

During the swim back across the canal, the cool water washed away the sweat, and the confused emotions of pleasure and guilt. When I finally straggled up the bank on the

July 24.

Dear Folk,
Now inside a bunker in
a white sand desert, burning INCENSE insense
during a sand storm. GROOVEY

We had a patrol this morning
PJ got his foot in a booby trap
it was a Chi-comm. grenade. It didn't
go off - he was the 5 man back I
was the 6. I had a grappling hook
PJ lifted his foot and ran like hell
nothing so We went up looked it over,
put the hook (REGIMENTAL order To carry one)
on the trip wire and pulled and ran
at the same time. By this time we
were taking it lightly. it still didn't
go off. Now this thing is laying on
the ground looking stupid - so I picked
it up and threw it. Nothing so I
said take it in - the chorus Arouse -
_ _ _ _ you! Finally Lloyd F. (squad leader)
picked it up put it in a mortar hole
threw in a frag (M-26 hand grenade)

OH! COOL AID — Good
WASN N' DRY
ABSORBINE JR.
PINEAPPLE
PEACHES
~~AN 18yrold~~

and blew it we picked up the
pieces and took them in

GRASS
DRIED LEAVES

TRIP WIRE

STEEL
STAKES TO HOLD IN PLACE

Wood

DIAGRAM duh!

another dude on another patrol
~~feel~~ fell in a punji pit and missed
the 106mm shell placed at the ~~p~~ bottom
↓ so today was a lucky day
                I never write or
            till JoAnne anything
        about this kind jazz — But
        it's good scoop! interesting

Your Son,

George

Hi Liz I enjoy
your letters
alot — love and
thanks

105°-110°
IN THE SAND
+
40 lbs
gear =

other side, I was greeted by the distant shouting of a sergeant. While I was gone, some Vietnamese, VC no doubt, had infiltrated the patrol base's perimeter and had stolen some rifles. Mine had been well-hidden, covered with brush and was now safely back in my arms. I felt oddly unfaithful to my rifle because of my tryst in the bamboo hooch across the canal, but the image of her sweet almond shaped eyes and her large, oddly deformed nipples lingered on. Smiling to myself, still sexually alert, I broke down my rifle and cleaned it for the next hour or so, trying to remember the lyrics to The Doors song, *Love Me Two Times Baby*, but the only words I could come up with were, "This is my rifle, this is my gun; this is for fighting, this is for fun."

~ ERODING CONVICTION ~

Back in States, irresoluteness and doubt about the purpose of the war were growing. That doubt was also spreading to the troops in Vietnam but in a different way. Our doubt was not about whether our involvement in Vietnam was just, on the front lines you don't worry about what is just, you only worry about how to survive. Our doubts were about whether or not America – its politicians, even had the guts to fight at all. The weakness of our National will was political and was starting to affect the Military. As the collective will of America turned from rock to sand, the NVA became encouraged and renewed, they became bolder and more assertive, even massive defeats, such as the Tet Offensive, were viewed as victories because of the unrest they fueled in the United States, and any success on the ground only fed their appetite for battle even more. The momentum of the war was shifting – you felt it, sensed it. The Marines were entering a new operational mode as the war strategy and tempo was being dictated by the U.S. Army, war protestors on college campuses and politicians in Washington D.C. We moved from an attacking offense to a defending force. We were fighting now out of respect for the brothers we fought beside, a determination not to let one another down, and a duty to ourselves and our families to survive. Although I didn't recognize it at the time, these have probably been the same – not patriotism, heroism, or honor – that have governed warriors since war began.

~ UNHINGED – THE LITTLE GIRL ~

A small girl maybe six or seven was rustling through our garbage—mostly cans from our C-rations. As we buried the trash in our fighting holes no sooner was it covered with dirt the little kids would dig it out with their tiny hands—mining the garbage for any morsel of food or anything of value. We buried our debris to deprive the enemy of anything that would possibly benefit them. I was never sure what that might be, but we did it nevertheless. We moved constantly from patrol base to patrol base into a series of airless dank and musty bunkers. But always we buried our detritus – the flotsam and jetsam of the war, we left behind.

On a rise in the terrain on the outer edge of the patrol base a Marine was scanning the tree line across the sand bars and swaying elephant grass. As he was comfortable with his surroundings, he began to unzip his fatigue trousers to relieve himself. The young girl unwittingly had moved into his urinary line of fire as he stared straight ahead out into the horizon. When he noticed the girl at his knees groveling for anything she could eat he doused the girl's head with his piss in a swaying motion as if he were putting out a small fire – his aim was deliberate, precise, and accurate. I had assessed what was going to happen minutes before knowing the character of the pissing Marine - like all of us, he was angry.

Outraged, I moved closer, picked up the little girl and set her down out of the way. While the grinning Marine was busy tucking away his extinguisher, I balled my fist tightly. Suddenly, before either of us knew what was happening, I hit him on the side of his head. He stumbled backwards and gave me a surprised look of disbelief. He zipped his pants and grumbled as he walked away. I would now have to watch my back because this would not be over anytime soon. My self-righteousness and moral outrage might be returned by a mishap of "friendly fire."

~ Dich Van ~

A strategic ploy of the political arm, Dich Van means action among the enemy and concentrates on the non-military population. Broken down to base terms, Dich Van was a public relations campaign aimed at the enemy's population base. In any conflict there will be people within the population of the enemy who are opposed to the conflict. Dich Van targets that element with the intention of sowing discontent for the conflict, while at the same time redefining the image of North Vietnamese leaders, people and communist ideology in a more sympathetic or even heroic light.

Through the successful implementation of Dich Van, a war can be won without ever winning a major battle, and turn a military disaster like the 1968 Tet Offensive into the catalyst of victory.

~ July After-Action Narrative (USMC) ~

Conducted combined patrols with elements of the 51st ARVN Regiment. Particular emphasis placed on saturation patrolling of the "Rocket Belt" and "Mortar Belt." Company C provided one platoon for security duty with 7th Engineer Battalion detachment operation in the RKO TAOR.

On 16 July 1968, the Battalion occupied the 3rd Battalion, 27th Marines Command Post (BT070656) and assumed responsibility of the TAOR. The Battalion TAOR was divided into three (3) company AO's to ensure positive control of all activities in the Battalion TAOR (See TU BAC). Company C established headquarters at BT069680 and assumed responsibility of the Desert AO. Company B and Company C provided one platoon each for blocking force in conjunction with ARVN clearing operation (BT0367 and BT0368). This operation was displaced on 27 July 1968 into the Mortar Belt, at which time Company C assumed entire responsibility for the Battalion's part in the effort.

~ SUMMARY OF ENEMY ACTIVITY ~

Since having taken over this TAOR there has been a definite increase of enemy activity on US and VN units throughout the area. Increased mining and booby-trapping incidents have resulted in 42 such incidents with 43% having been detected and destroyed. Remaining 57% have taken casualties of USMC and civilian personnel listed as (8) KIA, (38) WIA. The enemy at this time is using command detonated non-metallic box mines on the TU-CAU and MSR roads. Reports of enemy units in this area are of local force of which no designation has yet been claimed.

AUGUST 1968

We Gotta Get Out Of This Place - Eric Burdon

Patrolling activities revved up in August, as I Corps Intelligence anticipated that the NVA were preparing for a major offensive in our area of operations – Intelligence was calling it the "Third Phase Offensive."

~ Patrols Night and Day ~

Patrols became nonstop. Our platoon patrol bases were laid out in a long line to protect DaNang from invasion and were being attacked nightly by snipers and sappers. On this evening although it was still dark, someone heard the sapper as he slowly crawled up the side of the berm wall surrounding one of the encampments near us. An alert, albeit excited Marine, threw a grenade at the NVA and hit him in the head, knocking him out. In the excitement, the Marine had forgotten to pull the pin out of the grenade, so he grabbed his M-16, climbed to the top of the berm wall and shot the unconscious NVA. The dead soldier appeared to be about 14 years old.

The next day, August 26, 1968, a patrol set out in the late afternoon, heading west. Temperatures were well over 100°F. The patrol had been gone for about half an hour when we suddenly heard intense gunfire. Over the radio came a crackling voice, shouting that they had walked up on what appeared to be a large group of NVA, perhaps a company. The Patrol was pinned down in a banana grove where the NVA had constructed a well-fortified camp and they were taking casualties.

We got the order to saddle up. We were going out to help the beleaguered patrol. Hurriedly we gathered only our essential gear – flak jackets, helmets, ammo, and rifles, and out we went. Essentially on a run, we followed the sounds of the gunfire. Judging from its intensity, the Marine patrol was in a real shoot out. The Marine patrol had apparently walked into the middle of an NVA company-size base, catching the enemy by surprise as the Marines had quietly walked up on them. As more of the NVA realized what had happened, they entered into the fray and brought increasing fire on the Marines.

As we got close to the firefight we too came under automatic weapons fire and rounds from an American M-79 grenade launcher that, as it turned out, had been captured from a Marine called WB, who was well liked, professional, and could have been a model for a Marine recruiting poster. He had the look of a quintessential Marine, big, square jawed and tough looking. He had been killed when his patrol engaged the NVA at close range. The NVA recovered his weapon and were now shooting it at us. Pieces of shrapnel hit me in the left forearm and embedded themselves about a quarter of an inch deep into the meat of my arm. I blotted the blood with my shirt sleeve and kept moving.

Not knowing the exact location of the Marine patrol we were there to reinforce, we held our fire, even though we were taking heavy incoming rounds from the tree line and banana plant clusters directly in front of us. Up ahead, in the trees, we could hear Marines yelling back and forth to coordinate their fire. Bullets were tearing through the foliage and flying through the air in all directions. The beleaguered Marines from the patrol were putting up one hell of a fight but were being out gunned. Finally, they decided to bolt from inside the NVA encampment, where the enemy was well concealed and protected by bunkers built to withstand heavy artillery and air strikes. In a coordinated withdrawal the Marines stood up and raced across the dry rice paddy that was behind them as fast as they could. The NVA tracked them with their rifles and shot at the Marines as they were sprinting at full stride in the open.

As soon as we were certain that no more Marines remained in the banana grove, we opened fire with everything we brought with us to draw the NVAs' attention from the retreating patrol. As the Marines raced across the open field, bullets kicking up dust around them, we cheered them on. "Go! Go! Let's go!"

From our vantage point the escaping Marines appeared to be moving in slow motion. They seemed to hang in the air with each step. Up, down, up, down, step by tortuous step. As they made it, one by one, to the safety and protection of a paddy dike, we cheered even more. As the remainder of the patrol raced toward safety, a bullet caught the last man in the leg.

"God damn it - son of a bitch!" My heart broke as I watched the downed Marine curl up as the NVA peppered him with bullets. The lump that formed in my throat tightened my breathing. I was furious and despondent simultaneously. The Marine died there in the sand that late, hot afternoon, all alone, even though we were so near. His final words were not heard. When he was down to his last word, the only word left in his world, what word would that be? We would never know. I prayed that he didn't think he died alone.

With the patrol disengaged and out of the grove of trees, artillery and mortar rounds were finally able to rain down and pound the NVA encampment, pummeling them. They fled in small groups, running from their compound for their very lives, just as the Marine patrol had done. We hastily tried to follow after them, but they had panicked in many directions. We chased them with a vengeance, shooting at anything that moved, a flash, a shadow – anything. We could see glimpses of them in the trees and we just lit up the forest. After some time, we finally broke off and secured the area, retrieving the bodies of two dead Marines,

Aug 1.

Dear Mom,
Send another bank statement
I love it.
Will try to send some flicks
this week
By the end of Aug will be in
a new Regiment - 1, 5, A. - North
27 marines are going to Hawaii
We came back to the rear for one
day rest - Ha! haircuts, shave harassment
Can't write much - in small
different Patrol Base each night, so we
move fast and travel (hump) lite.
We are a reactionary force and go
where the action is. We lost 7 dudes (Lt + Cpt)
in a mine the other day.
JoAnnes scholarship was great
Tell folk Hi got granna's package the
Aberbine Jr. is great and helps - my feet are
100% better. A mayor ask about it and Sent
home for some
Tell Mal to work hard. its 105-115°
sometimes here + 50-60 lbs ~~~~~~, gear rifle
helment 3 canteens water one claymore mine
flak jacket entrencing tool poncho, flares gasp hook
4 grenade 400 rounds - and so on get the
picture -
thank Liz for TEA I use it
at dusk it's good

Well ~~eet~~ all my love
in high spirits

tell grampa to tie a fly for me
in 9 months, ill fish for blue
gills and bass again

I finished the Arrangement a groove
you'll never know how I read it
yuck!

Send ~~if~~ info about MGB or triumph & GT-6
pop!

Your Son

TRIMed
STACHE

17 agosto

Dear Gramma and Grand Father,
First, I apologize for not writeing promptly.
I am now squad leader in charge of nine men, a lance doing a Sgt's job is not uncommon. We had a patrol last night, it went off ~~~~ uneventful. I have 3 new men from the States, first time in the bush, so I left them behind, doing both a favor (the squad and the new men.)
We have sercurity for a dam being built to control the rains and insure a 2nd rice crop. The VC would be stupid to rocket or mortar us. They need the rice as much as the farmers. However they do mine the roads, a booby trap the areas in which our patrols venture out into.
ITs rained for 2 days now and I fear an early moonsoon It's cold and am wet all the time

2.

Fernung the old squad leader
got an infection on both shoulder
blades - that's why I was made
squad leader. I must know how
to read a map (areo picto type) use
a lensetic compass - shot azimuths.
Use a PRC-25 radio to call in
mortar support or Artillery. and
most important medi-vac choppers
   I act hard most of the time -
a necessity I guess.
   feet are in really good shape
now - absorbine JR.!!!
   I would love to travel, camp, etc
as you do but, now, have a job to do
I'm not going to BS and say I
enjoy it, I'd be nutz! Only 9 months
left - then out of USMC and school
   Well that's it - for now my tent
is holding it's own - Grammpa
we say "when an m-16 meets an
AK-47 you better hope yours
doesn't jam - because his won't
47's are the best weapon going

18 Agosto

Dear Mom,

In the morning my squad will be sent to AN ARVN camp to run night patrols with the viets. We will be there for 3 days, then to Regiment again.

the rains have been sporatic and indicate an early monsoon season. Kurtz, thanks for the car magazine and GT-6 and spitfire (the latter I like more) ads. Thank malcolm for the Sgt. Peppers Post card. Am busy most of the time now and can't write much - Patrols Patrols.

No Comments on family status - ok no comments. - I wouldn't offend anyone, I'm really tactxful - BS

Being Squad leader (Fawung has sores on shoulder blades) I skate alot. No work other than brain. no Police calls, etc. but I do the work each man does - if not more

I contend that to lead by example is the hardest and best way to do it. If they see you silently go to work if (they) (are) he's any type dude he'll start also, once started just sort of ~~bein~~ begin to supervise from within the and gradually supervise out of the picture Neat! It works.

Also with superiors I give them the idea I'm cold, hard never smile almost alien. That's so they don't think I'm wishy-washy or brownie, Just listen, nod then out of command post with map and orders and back to squad. Simple! am 2 dudes one cool the other hard — 1 for in the rear 1 for in the bush.

Love,

George

George =

Sib is cool isn't she!

August 2, 1968 Quang-Nam, Vietnam

Platoon Patrol Base
"Fort Apache"
photo: Crane Davis

their eyes still open, staring stonily into the clear sky. We carried their limp, lifeless bodies to "Fort Apache," the patrol base. After that we returned to the NVA camp and searched the area for weapons and ammunition, then slowly patrolled our way home. August was producing blistering heat, both in temperature and in enemy activity, which was definitely accelerating. As we came in after the patrol, a Corpsman, I didn't recognize disinfected and bandaged the wound on my arm. Dazed, I found a place to lie down and just stared out into the bamboo. Carried back silently, the bodies of the two dead Marines lay nearby.

I found out much later that the 1st Battalion, 51st ARVN Regiment, reacting to our contact, was able to engage the fleeing NVA. In a running battle over the next two days, they were able to trap them, and kill more than 200. Intense fighting would continue in the Thu Bon river drainage (Go Noi) and other coastal river basins for the next two long years!

~ LAST PATROL ~

It was August 29, 1968, in the hot part of the afternoon when everything sizzles. We assembled at the edge of the patrol base, a ragtag group of new Marines and Vietnamese ARVN already showing signs of disinterest at the prospect of a day patrol in the sweltering heat.

My world had greatly changed since arriving in Vietnam. The fear of dying would always exist, but it would no longer have as much power over me. The frightened teenage boy who had arrived here in April had changed. The sleep-walking dream voyage was now over. I had gotten accustomed to combat and had started to like it—a disturbing turn of events. I was on the brink of going "bush," a powerful, ruthless, intoxicating form of commitment, where every day in combat you are pulled closer to being numbed and resigned to not returning to the way that you were, or not returning at all, and not caring which. I fought my war as two people, one did the fighting and the other did the judging and evaluating. My fear was that soon there would be no reconciliation – that they would become one. Then there would be no escape back into my mind from the reality. No immersion into my own thoughts, no safe haven, no denial.

The reality of combat is that it is corrosive in many ways. Multiple levels of combat are fought on many fronts, not the least of which is the spiritual and emotional battlefields. This kind of fish in a barrel war created an indelible mark that can guide me back to the experience, even decades later. It has a magnetic force of its own, a pull which is inescapable. In combat, the brain gets re-jiggered and the reconstructed network of a trillion nerves gets focused on survival and killing people, an oddly fulfilling simplicity—the complete use of the brain to know only this very specific and primal universe.

My mind and senses amped up as we walked quietly through the dried crumpled leaves on our patrol – soon to be my last. Our pace was carefully calibrated and metered to be able to see, hear, feel, and smell everything. Then, suddenly, the putrefied fumes of a dead human body tickled their way up my nose. The sickening sweet smell is unmistakable, the same as the "Crispy Critter." I stopped and hand signaled danger to the patrol following behind. I dropped to one knee and looked out onto the distant sand bars and bamboo patches. Looking around to the others in the patrol, I touched my forefinger to my nose. To my astonishment, no one could confirm that a strong smell had suddenly passed this way. They dutifully shrugged their shoulders. Maybe it was just me? No! I had smelled it. The smell blotted everything else into invisibility. I stood up and resumed walking. I held up the patrol by raising a clenched fist, as I again sniffed the air, hoping for a shift in the wind. A soft breeze guided the odor of decaying human flesh back to my nose. I motioned the patrol to move forward, and I scurried from the head of the patrol to just behind the point man, who was 10 yards or so in front of all of us. I whispered to him to move out carefully and told him that we had walked into *"injun country."*

Joey, the point man hunched over and set one foot in front of the other, looking for trip wires and signs of the enemy. I followed cautiously, looking back to ensure the other members of the patrol were alert and following suit. I was confident the new Marines would imitate those of us in front, but they looked clumsy and stupidly out of place. They were way too clean—too fresh.

Joey rounded the corner of the bamboo cluster and disappeared. I could see his silhouette crouched over, moving through the shadows like a stalking cat. Suddenly he increased his pace and was moving too fast now, too direct, and purposeful. He had seen something that had captured his interest. I hurried to catch up and, as I turned the corner, I saw him standing on the edge of a clearing. The open patch of sand, with no cover, had two dead bodies rotting in the intense tropical sun. The contorted figures were swollen, bloated. They appeared to be NVA soldiers in full battle dress, their gear scattered around them – a garage sale of highly coveted stuff. At this time Marines were wearing NVA equipment as highly prized symbols of having been in combat. Getting close enough to count coup and take their stuff proved you had been there. The highest value was placed on enemy knives and knapsacks, and both were just lying there in the sandy beach-like clearing.

"Whoa. Stop," I said to Joey, in a hushed voice. "Let's figure this shit out."

I signaled to the Marines and ARVNs behind me to get down and keep their eyes open while I tried to get the attention of Joey, who was standing erect on the edge of the clearing, staring longingly at the NVA stuff.

I shouted, "Hold what you got!" Marine jargon for - stand still don't move. Nothing was right – the area was too open, too quiet. Suddenly, from a distant hill, three rapid bursts of machine gun fire raked the area. The hilltop was a known Marine position, usually occupied by mortar platoons. I looked toward the hill, searching for a reason for the machine gun fire. As I did, Joey walked into the clearing, toward the bodies.

"Jesus Christ," I thought, and took two steps forward to retrieve him. As I stopped, I looked down and spotted, not two inches from my left foot, the exposed trigger of a Bouncing Betty land mine, connected to trip wires. I looked up to yell a warning and a cold chill came over me, the Marine on the concourse at O'Hare had silently told me the truth. The vision in my dreams perfectly balanced and composed. This could not be the

work of some blind force steering my life in some chaotic, random pattern. My predestined time had come on this day. I had gotten the roller coaster "E" ticket. My heart raced and my pulse doubled up. We had walked, with me leading the patrol, into an ambush. The trap was set, the spring wound tight. Adrenaline revved my mind, and then everything suddenly slowed to a frozen calm.

Most of my boyhood had been invisible to my parents, brothers, and sister. Like most boys, I took to living a private life, an almost feral existence, in which I had risked going beyond my limits. I had relished all aspects of my Huckle Berry Finn childhood, first in the doing, second in the secrecy and third in the remembering. I grew up playing war games, mostly Cowboys and Indians full of sneaking, skulking and imaginary scenes of surviving and victory. I would say "bang, bang, you're dead," and I'd clutch my shoulder and roll to the ground. I'd lay still and surprise my hapless playmates at the time with my guile and cunning. I'd spring to my feet as they approached, "Gotcha, I was only wounded!" Then "bang, bang you're dead!" But those boyish days were over forever. The enemy was real, and "bang-bang" meant your guts were laid open in a horrific jolt by the hydraulic shock and force of a fragmenting AK-47 bullet, or the excruciatingly painful ripping of your flesh by the ominous and ever-present booby traps.

In my mind's eye, I was still the salty, lean and hungry warrior I had wanted to become. The reality was much different. I was emaciated, sun burned, and thinned to around 150 pounds by the constant patrolling and dysentery induced diarrhea. The skin of my darkly tanned forearms had been peeled away by the toxic chemistry of the mosquito repellant mixed with my own sweat. And I smelled. A stubbly beard popped out of my dirty face. My neck, front and back, were burned scarlet red from the sun. The area around my eyes and cheeks was a deep reddish brown color, wrinkled from hiding my eyes from the sun. My hands were scared, callused and cut from plowing through bamboo. My feet were diseased, swollen and rotting from walking in dank, festering pools of water and in the occasionally flooded rice paddies. The decay was progressive, but almost undetectable in the course of everyday occurrences. As my spiritual acceptance of being in combat accumulated, my physical body was gradually being worn away. It was the cruelest of contradictions. I had never been stronger, more alert or focused, yet my body was being eaten away imperceptibly.

Just as I was shouting a warning, I saw black smoke, dust, and Joey thrown into the air by a buried landmine. The NVA (or the Marine Corps) had mined the entire area around the dead bodies, using them as bait. Time began to slow again as Joey's crumpled body huffed to the ground falling into a heap between the two dead NVA—blown apart, whole to half at the speed of sound.

Seconds later, without knowing why, I felt myself being lifted off my feet and hurdled through the air. I landed face down in the sand. I could not hear or see anything. A loud ringing filled my head. The blast and shrapnel from the mine Joey had set off knocked me to the ground. As I fell backward, my foot tripped the trigger wire on yet another mine, and it bounced upward. I was face down in the sand when I regained consciousness. I rolled my tongue around in my mouth, and found holes where teeth had been only moments ago. The magnitude of what was occurring escaped me. My first thought was, *"Wow, now I'll need false teeth. Cool."*

Once, when I was six or seven, I'd run headfirst into the brick wall of a neighbor's house while playing Army. I knocked myself out with that headlong run. Now I'd done it again.

I could taste the warm liquid copper flavor of my own blood. There was so much blood in my mouth that I could not swallow without choking, so I let it slip between my shredded lips, draining it directly into the sand. I could feel tingling all over my body, but no real pain, yet. I could sense that all my extremities had been wounded. I had been disintegrated. I struggled to regain control of my body, forcing my arms and legs to move, and then I pulled my face out of the granular dust. I could only see out of my right eye. My left eye was either missing or it was being forced shut by rapid swelling. All I knew was that it didn't work, and it was too early to tell why. I could raise my right arm, but the left was numb and wouldn't function. I moved my left leg but could see that the calf on my right leg had been partially sliced off. I was astonished at the lack of authentic pain but the terrible ringing in my ears was getting louder. I could feel my head swelling and my tongue enlarging. I feared now that I would drown on my own blood or choke to death and wink out right there in the sand.

I waited, laying still. It was then I made *the second deal*: "God, if you get me out of this, I'll be a really good man, live a purposeful life and, as a bonus, I'll give up swearing."

I thought I was dying. I was on the ground, oozing into it slowly, my blood soaking into the sand. Moments later a surge of resolve swept over me. "Nope," I screamed at myself, "Not today. I'm getting out of here and I'm going to make it home."

I started to crawl, inch by inch, back to the edge of the sandy area toward the squad past the other wounded moaning Marines and ARVNs. I had mysteriously experienced a resurgence of energy. I realized I had a duty to get them and myself out of this predicament. As I crawled, sensation and feeling started to reappear – it was pain. I became angry and indignant, furious that I had been taken down. As rage poured over me, my sense of survival accelerated. As I got to the edge of the sand spit I thought to myself, *"Fuck man, that was too close."*

Then, I remembered my bargain and apologized, "Oh, sorry big guy." I think God understood, but I've minded my manners ever since then and remembered most of *the deals*.

The patrol's young, new radioman stood stupefied, staring at the turmoil. He was unable to do anything, he had seized up and was frozen by the carnage. I crawled over to him and with my one working arm, grabbed the entire radio set, which he had rested on the ground. I fumbled with the dials to change the frequency to the medevac band.

"One, this is one-dash-one. Be advised that…" I lost control of the handset and started over.

"One, this is…" Blood from the wounds in my mouth dripped into the handset, causing a gurgling sound that muffled the transmissions. I was losing blood fast, from everywhere, and was quickly running out of time. In desperation, I broke standard radio protocol and blurted into the handset, in a very unmilitary way that a patrol from Company C of 1st Battalion,

27th Marines was down with dead and wounded, and told them to send a helicopter pronto. Then I passed out, momentarily.

A reply came quickly from the patrol base, asking about our location. I responded giving the best rendition of the map coordinates I could remember. Then I heard a familiar voice. It was PJ.

"Hang on George. We're coming to get you."

I blacked out again, briefly. When I regained consciousness, I ordered the stunned Marines around me to take out their bayonets or K-bar knives, whatever they carried and crawl out to each of the bodies, probing for more mines as they went and to bring our wounded to safety. Every Marine immediately obeyed. After about fifteen minutes I heard a voice from a Marine helicopter over the radio, asking if we were experiencing incoming fire, what our location was and telling me to pop a certain color smoke grenade on his command.

Moments later, the low flying, bull-nosed UH-34 Seahorse helicopter roared overhead but heading away from us at a very high rate of speed. Worried, I clicked the handset and yelled, "Hey, you just flew over us. Turn around. I'm going to pop whatever color smoke we have."

The pilot protested the lack of military procedure, but complied. The unwounded Marines of the patrol had gathered up their comrades and laid them in a row tending to their injuries as best they could. Just then PJ and Cobb arrived, picked me up and carried me to the makeshift landing zone. PJ and Cobb had sprinted all the way from our PPB and risked their lives on this blistering hot August afternoon. Comrades-in-arms, in particular Marines, allow the borders of their self to disintegrate. Self-sacrifice becomes an impulse. Marines very often do what they do only for other Marines – for the Corps.

I was still losing blood and getting weaker all the time. I needed to lie quietly to conserve my strength. I eased down on a mound of sand, so I could partially sit up and pretend I had the facility to still be in charge. It was still my fire team, my patrol, and my men, but the vanity of command was gradually giving way to good sense. I was toast.

As I sat there, the pain building, I noticed red ants crawling all over my legs, darting stealthily in and out of the holes in my trousers. They appeared on my hands and arms, biting ants injecting formic acid into my skin. Each bite produced a stinging response from my numb body. I was resting on a fire ant mound. I swatted as many as I could, then rolled away from the ant hill and the fierce little swarming beasts, Vietnamese ants, VC's no doubt. They were resolute devils, attacking opportunistically, scurrying here and there before they could be crushed, darting in and out of torn body parts, biting quickly, decisively, and then moving away. Whenever I crushed one, another took its place. It was maddening, the little sharp stings – each bite taking a measured toll.

Finally, in desperation, I yelled for help. "Get these little pricks off me!"

A Marine came to my rescue, patting my legs and arms, ridding me of the pests. Vietnamese fire ants had probably been the scourge of all who invaded Vietnam.

As I edged back to my senses, the realization of what just occurred materialized. Three other wounded men lay around me, some of them perhaps dying. I was in the middle and alive. I had survived, intact for the most part. For me, now, the war would be over. The haunting shadows of the war would be behind me and only my bright future lay ahead. I had gotten a "million dollar wound" - a head wound - I was, in fact, going home. But the war, and what it brings with it, would set a determined stain on my life. The war would rattle around inside me and like all grunts who served in Vietnam, I would never be entirely free of its wrath. We could not come home with honor and glory or dead upon our shields. We weren't offered the choice. We got neither.

We were all piled into the stubby helicopter. I said goodbye to PJ and Cobb. PJ's last words were, "I'll write your mom and tell her. You should get the Bronze star."

I laughed to myself; I'm getting clean sheets and a shower. I'll never go camping or hunting again, I decided. I began to imagine going home a hero and being welcomed with open arms. That would not happen. The collative memories of many Marines who served in Vietnam always include the abject loneliness of returning home misunderstood - even hated. Vietnam would become an eternal and universal symbol for failed military and foreign policy.

The bumpy helicopter ride north to Da Nang lasted only 15-20 minutes. We touched down on an asphalt tarmac that served the tented, forward deployed Navy field hospital. The helicopter ride, all of us piled together, bleeding and in and out of consciousness had been very uncomfortable, Navy corpsmen rushed to the chopper with stretchers to carry the wounded inside. The pain from everywhere was starting to amplify and I had to bear down and grit my teeth to withstand the onslaught. When my turn came, the corpsmen tossed me on the litter, like an oversized ham out of the oven. As they raced toward the double swinging doors of the hospital the corpsman holding the rear of the litter tripped and I spilled out onto the asphalt landing pad. I remember thinking how different asphalt appeared. I had been in the bush too long.

"Oh, wow, sorry Marine. I slipped," he said sheepishly.

As I was carried inside the field hospital, I felt the air temperature take a dramatic drop, perhaps 40 degrees cooler than outside. It was freezing. Scissors, wielded by a skilled hand immediately cut all my clothes away, then cut the laces of my boots, which were taken off as well. I was X-Rayed naked, like a piece of basted pork roast first one side then the other. I was being rolled around by 18-20 year-old Navy enlisted personnel ("Squids") who were just as tired and absorbed into their own worlds as I was – only mine was really starting to get painful.

Finally, I was headed to the operating room (OR). There, I knew I'd get treated quickly and efficiently, be given piles of pain killers and I'd be on my way home in only minutes – Tally Ho. As my Gurney rounded the corner of the hallway I was stunned. There, in front of me lay at least 50 other Marines, many of them in much worse shape than me, all of them waiting to get into the OR. Some were screaming and others were bouncing around on their gurneys dealing with their newly acquired wounds. I received some sort of medication, intravenously, that quieted me down. Finally, after what seemed like hours, my turn came.

The Navy surgeons were as glib as they were competent – a very exclusive, particularly skilled group of people. I was wheeled into the OR with a bright surgical light shining in my swollen eyes. I heard a pleasant, deep baritone voice ask, "Well Marine, what happened to you? And what happened to that front tooth?"

The masked man was referring to my upper front tooth, which was hanging in the socket, and twisted 90 degrees from its original and rightful position. He reached in with some stainless steel pliers and twisted it back to as close to straight as he could. "There ya go, let's see if that takes. But I'm no dentist."

I answered a bunch of incomprehensible questions with either a nod or a "Yes, Sir." Those surgeons were the only naval officers I ever actually said yes sir to and meant it. The surgical team started another IV. The doctor asked me to count backwards from 100 as the narcotic started to work. Drugged, I complained to the doctor that I had lost my friends today, hoping that he would understand.

"Me too, son," the surgeon sternly replied, as if to say, *I've been here 18 hours all ready and have crammed two years of surgical training into the last three months. I've seen hundreds of Marines in here this week. 1968 has been a really bad summer!*

As someone placed the breathing respirator mask over my mouth and nose, I could feel the tears flooding my sunken eye sockets, but I didn't tilt my head to let them run free, still reluctant to reveal any outward sign of sadness or remorse. What those Navy doctors saw during their tours in Vietnam must have been ghastly and appalling. I was realizing the magnitude of what had happened that afternoon and coming to terms with the potential far-reaching consequences. The maelstrom of this war entered the lives of the Doctors and their medical teams forever, too. It probably made them compassionate, calm and extraordinarily competent doctors. It probably made them total wild men in private, as well. Their emotional landscape would be expanded across continents.

Hours later, I woke up in a post-operative area, groggy and dazed. A corpsman came by and said, "Here's a mirror and wash kit. You need to clean yourself up."

I took the stainless-steel mirror and held it to my face which was a hideous mess. Both eyes were black, and stitches held the red, swollen skin together everywhere. My lips were sown back together with long, black surgical thread along the edges and at the corners, the end of which hung down. I looked like a cheap 1940's horror movie version of Frankenstein.

As I lay there, stunned at the damage and thinking about my fate, a Korean Marine strapped down to restrain him in the bed across from me, was thrashing around and ripping the IV and breathing tubes out of his own throat. He thought he was disgraced being cooped up in a hospital and was desperate to return to his Blue Dragon Division and the war. He rocked and rattled the restraining side rails of his comfortable bed until the Navy Corpsmen and a nurse injected him with a sedative and knocked him out. I stared intently at him, speculating about his motives. Then I quietly fell asleep, not yet ready or able to return to my war.

I stayed at that hospital for a few days, until my condition was stable enough for my next move, which was closer to the Da Nang airfield, and my trip home. There, I stayed in a hospital operated by the Air Force for two or three days, waiting for my wounds to

29 Aug.

Dear Mr. & Mrs. Berg,

You don't know me, but you may have had your son tell you about me in his letters, my name is Davis but they call me P-J.

I'm writing cause I think it's me duty to tell you that George has been hurt a little, please don't worry everything is alright, you may know off this before you get my letter, but I thought it was my job to write and tell you also.

He was out on patrole with his fire team, and came across some N.V.A. boys, not knowing the field he was in was booby traped, so he was doing his job by going in to investigate, there were two marines wounded and two South Viet Nam troops, all four will be O.K. He ass me to write and tell you.

When I got to him he was talking with one off his men

she looked at me and smiled and
said P.J. I'm O.K. I said George
you'll be O.K. but the N.V.A
will pay for what they have
done, Mr & Mrs. Berg, George was
like a brother to me, we always
done things together, and I was very
sad when I was told, but when
I heard that he's going to be alright
I was very happy, you have a good
son, I wish to God a brother like
him.

Well, dear folks I guess I'll
be closing for now, please don't
be upset or worry too much, I'm
sure Berg wouldn't want
that, because he'll be O.K.

Take Care & God Bless

George's friend
Louis
(P.J.)

stabilize. The "Zoomie" (air force) hospital had an aura of slackness about it. People busy doing nothing, idling away their respective shifts, weathering the unrelenting carnage of the war in protected housing and air-conditioned bliss, or so it seemed at that time. On my second day there, an Airman First-*something or other medical person*, presented himself at the side of my bed and ordered me to shave my mustache.

"Regulations require that you remove your mustache and that all U.S. government personnel be clean shaven."

I was incredulous! My rage and indignation erupted immediately. I wasn't U.S. government personnel. I was a United States Marine. As he approached me with a razor, stainless wash bowl and towel, I unleashed, and the emotions of loss and guilt transformed into raw fury.

"If you want this shaved," I said, pointing to my mustache, "you're going to have to do it yourself, you sawed-off piece of Zoomie shit. Fuck you, you bow-legged cock sucker!"

"Well!" he exclaimed, and shuffled away to a back room. A mustache was a special emblem, signifying that you were a combat infantry Marine – a ground pounding grunt. No one but a ranking Marine could order that hair off my face. Months in the bush had made me, like most Marines, a wild creature, with little tolerance for civilized things. The time it would take to wrench the bush out and become half tame would be considerable, and I thought at the time, that my premature departure from the war was a terrible waste. Combat Marines become animals in some important and irreversible ways. It is the unsavory but necessary underside of the business of war.

~ August After-Action Narrative (USMC) ~

During this reporting period there was a drastic increase of enemy activity throughout the 1st Battalion, 27th Marines TAOR. The VC/NVA "Third General Offensive" became a reality on 22-23 August 1968 when elements of three (3) VC/NVA Battalions committed themselves to all-out ground attacks against ARVN and USMC positions with the hope of gaining a temporary foothold in Da Nang City itself. All of these attacks were stopped with light friendly casualties.

Saturation patrol activities of the areas defined as the "Rocket Belt" and "Mortar Belt" to prevent attacks by fire and enemy infiltration against Da Nang. The command received orders to begin planning initial operations for its return to the 1st Marine Brigade.

22 August: At 222115H, Company "C," squad combat patrol vicinity AT965650 made contact with five (5) VC. Resulting in two VC KIA and one USMC WIA with two (2) enemy weapons captured.

23 August: At 23030011, Company "C" PPB located AT973642 received incoming mortar fire followed by ground attack, resulting in one USMC KIA, 14 USMC WIA (minor), and three VC MA and three weapons captured.

24-25 August: Company "C," squad combat patrol made contact with large enemy force vicinity BT000662. 1st Battalion, 51st ARVN Regiment reacted to contact. Action was heavy and continuous for two days. Initial report of results are 200 VC KIA. Remainder of Battalion continued patrol activity to secure base positions.

26 August: Various elements engaged in security patrols vicinity AT969656, made sporadic light contact with NVA forces, resulting in three NVA KIA, two USMC KIA, one USMC WIA, and 6 (six) 60mm rounds captured along with 1 AK-50.

~ POST SCRIPT TO AFTER-ACTION REPORTS ~

The incident involving the land mine on August 29, 1968 was not included in the Marine Corps after action report. However, a Purple Heart was recorded in the official Navy documents was awarded in Great Lakes Naval Hospital. The wound on August 26, 1968 was not recorded at the time, but a Purple Heart was awarded later by headquarters Marine Corps. The 1st Battalion 27th Marine Regiment was relocated to Hawaii in early September, and records and documents were being transferred to new units for all Marines that had not finished their full 13-month tours.

~ 1ST BATTALION, 27TH MARINES AFTER-ACTION SUMMARY ~

In August 1968, the battalion was ordered to return to Hawaii. All Marines in the battalion who had not served their full tour of duty in Vietnam were transferred to other units. Upon its arrival in Hawaii, ceremonies were held honoring the 1st Battalion for a job well done. It is presently a part of the 1st Brigade. Although 1/27 has been active for only a few years, it has proudly and courageously served its country and the Marine Corps.

Pg 30

DEAR MOTHER,
    WELL WHAT CAN I SAY?
I'VE BEEN HIT - AND A·OK!
I DIDN'T WANT TO WRITE BUT
THEY Made Me - This is my
second heart (purple type) -
You see I CAN Still put one
over on the ol' gal. Ha.
        I'M NOT TO Bad - mine
They operated on my gord last
Night; I guess - I'm coming out
of Anesthesia (s̸)
        I got hit everywhere
I am OK! will ~~come~~ Go to japan
to convel; or Maybe to USA
    I will recover rapidly -
; Kept them Laughn to the end

I'm in one piece and still have everything Don't tell JoAnne it might distract her from studies – which are most important. tell people I'm fine – I had R&R coming up to Malasia in 4 days – damn will write more later.

Love

WESTERN UNION TELEGRAM

CLASS OF SERVICE
This is a fast message
unless its deferred char-
acter is indicated by the
proper symbol.

W. P. MARSHALL
CHAIRMAN OF THE BOARD

R. W. McFALL
PRESIDENT

SYMBOLS
DL=Day Letter
NL=Night Letter
LT=International
Letter Telegram

The filing time shown in the date line on domestic telegrams is LOCAL TIME at point of origin. Time of receipt is LOCAL TIME at point of destination

W1 2D EB369 MA1 05 SSBO 47

M CBO59 LONG GOVT NL PDB XV=WUX TDC PWS FT SHERIDAN ILL 15:

=CAROLIN BERG=

819 EAST 3 ST DIXON ILL=

=YOUR SON GEORGE PHILLIP BERG LCPL USMC 2380364 HJS ARRIVED
THIS HOSPITAL HE HAS BEEN HOSPITALIZED AS A RESULT OF
FRACTURE LEFT HAND. LEFT ULNAR NERVE INJURY, WOUNDS TO FACE,
CHEST AND LEGS AND HIS CONDITION IS CONSIDERED SATISFACTORY.
THE WARD MEDICAL OFFICER DOES NOT FEEL THAT YOUR PRESENCE
IS REQUIRED FROM THE MEDICAL STANDPOINT. YOU MAY SEE THE
PATIENT AT ANYTIME ON YOUR FIRST VISIT, AND FROM 2:00 PM
TO 4:00 PM AND FROM 7:00 PM TO 9:00 PM THEREAFTER. HE IS
ABLE TO WRITE AHTHIS TIME. HIS MAKLING ADDRESS IS NAVAL

WESTERN UNION TELEGRAM

CLASS OF SERVICE
This is a fast message
unless its deferred char-
acter is indicated by the
proper symbol.

W. P. MARSHALL
CHAIRMAN OF THE BOARD

R. W. McFALL
PRESIDENT

SYMBOLS
DL=Day Letter
NL=Night Letter
LT=International
Letter Telegram

The filing time shown in the date line on domestic telegrams is LOCAL TIME at point of origin. Time of receipt is LOCAL TIME at point of destination

HOSPITAL GREAT LAKES ILLINOIS 60088 WARD 4 EAST. YOU ARE
ASSURED THAT HE IS RECEIVING THE BEST MEDICAL CARE AND
THAT YOU WILL BE ADVISED OF ANY SIGNIFICANT CHANGE IN HIS
CONDITION=

J W ALBRITTAIN REAR ADMIRAL MC USN COMMANDING OFFICER=

= NAVHOSP GLAKES 152110Z SEPT 68=

=2380364 2:00 4:00 7:00 9:00 60088 4 152110Z 68.

WU1201(R2-65)   THE COMPANY WILL APPRECIATE SUGGESTIONS FROM ITS PATRONS CONCERNING ITS SERVICE

THE AMERICAN NATIONAL RED CROSS

Hi again Folk
    Greetings from Japan
I may stay here or come
back to the world depends
on X-Rays etc. I'm OK and
still hard as a rock
    Can't tell you about wounds
except- facial, head, all Limbs, back
chest- everywhere I'll have 3
Scares on my mug and false teeth
on the 2 bottom front and my
Lips are suctured together. IT Takes
1hr. to eat but refuse Liquid dieT.
    my chopper to a bigger
hospital is here, so must close

RéR
Tisa groove

Hospital Time

Purple Haze - Jimi Hendrix

~ Japan ~

In a very short time, I was sent to Japan for more surgeries and diagnosis. A strange pulsating and ringing in my ears persisted far longer than normal; something was wrong inside my head. I traveled on a litter in an open helicopter across Japan (I think to a different hospital) and took photographs from the open door as we were flying. My spirits were returning. I got settled into a large Army Hospital in Japan. I underwent more surgery on my face and head. The wounds on my arms and legs were doing well except I couldn't walk without crutches and spent most of my time in a wheelchair. A demented Marine Sergeant wandered around the wards, bellowing that the Marines in the hospital weren't real Marines because they hadn't died in combat. His self-incriminating rants were evidence of his apparent insanity. Japan was mostly a blur, except the day I wheeled over to the assignment board to see if I had gotten orders. Then one day Bingo! "L. CPL. Berg, G.P., USMC, CONUS, Great Lakes Naval Hospital." I was going back to the States – to "the world."

Later that week I boarded a C-130 transport plane that had stretchers piled from the top to the bottom. When the plane was loaded, the tail ramp closed, the plane turned onto the tarmac then rolled down the runway, rapidly increasing speed and then it heaved into the sky. My next stop was Anchorage, Alaska. I slept most of the way. Others were not so lucky. Many of the wounded needed constant care and treatment during the long flight. Military medics, corpsmen and nurses tended dutifully to them the entire time. I was on automatic pilot and only needed an occasional drink of water. Civilization and military female nurses seemed bizarre to me – instead of being gone for months it seemed like I had been gone a few years.

When we landed in the U.S. in Seattle, I was transferred to a plane bound for Scott Air Force Base, north of Chicago, Illinois. We arrived there late at night, I believe by design, and shuttled to the Great Lakes Naval Hospital. The war casualties were increasing at a

Sept 5

Dear Folk,
    I had my last operation yesterday now im all put back together again.

    Japan is a beautiful country, what ive seen, out of my window and from a low flying helocopter (from airforce base to Hospital). All that lies ahead is physical Thearpy. I can "walk" but slow and I get tired easy. they told me I was going to Great Lakes Naval Hospital to regroup, I should get some leave after my stay there. 26 - 30 days.

    I didn't want to come home this way. I feel defeated. I can't grunt anymore but I could be a door gunner on a chopper— if they guranteed it id go back again. I was good and getting better and "enjoyed" or at least took satisfaction is doing my job

    3 nights before, I had gotten my first "confirmed" kills. in an ambush.

the man with me, Steele died on the U.S.S. Repose. (2 ARVN's also zaped

We had contact with a Company of NVA for four days. We had taken alot of WIA and a few KIA.

By the time you see me it will look like I was never hurt I am improveing fast and try to exercise as much as possible before that Sadist PT nurse gets around to me – She's a whip.

Say Hello to everyone for me I'll have leave during October a Groovey month – Ball, football leaves etc.

Love
da' kid

I still have my stache

Sept. 11

Folk,
    Who knows? Om I coming home
or not? They said I was but I
don't believe, I think its a plot.
My face looks OK, now that its
cleaned up and the swelling has
gone down I've got a red eyeball
and black and blue but am confident
that will go away soon. My mouth
is OK also my jibs (lips) are back to normal
they were swollen and bruised aslo.
the stitches are out. I shaved my
mustache down to David Niven style
and it looks - chass HA How coarse!
but it does look cool. The marine liason
will make me shave, he's a _____
Today was my first mail it was a
groove.
        Those "chopper" boys are clubby
phfarts I had to talk them down while
passing out, and directing them, my
squad, the "ARVNS Steeles bandages, and
keeping the fire "ants out of my eyes
and they asked questions like

F-4C PHANTOM

when was the last time we took fire - when I told them we hit a mine! (although we did take fire I <u>lied</u>). They were <u>fast</u> However only because they were called fast I'll give the story later...

Steele I think is dead he had brain damage, convulsions etc. & torn to bits.

Japan swings! I wish I could get off this Army Post YOKAHAMA - to TOKYO - VIA Thain monorail type - zoom

Japan T.V. is good. and they have teen shows all the time the girls are cute! and dance good etc.

The 27th USMC reg. is Home

Love George

rapid rate by 1968, and many soldiers, sailors and Marines were coming home mangled or in coffins. By arriving late at night, we were hidden from view by the darkness, to avoid having people see the true cost of the war.

~ HOME FROM THE HOSPITAL ~

We, the hundreds of thousands of wounded from the Vietnam War, endured a long trip back to the States. Again, my journey, like many of the others, began with a flight from Vietnam to Japan, another flight up to Alaska, another down to Seattle and a fourth to Waukegan, Illinois by way of Scott Air Force Base. From that airfield we were transported to Great Lakes Naval Hospital, a venerable old hospital that had withstood World War II, Korea, the occasional brush-fire wars, and now Vietnam. The red brick structure set back from the fenced and guarded entrance to the navy base looked palatial and imposing. Like an aging retiree, sitting on the porch in a rocking chair, it gave the impression that it had been there forever and had witnessed most of what there was to see.

We finally made it to the hospital at 1:00 a.m. dazed and miserable. Medical personnel checked and recorded our vital signs and a presenting diagnosis was determined. It was September 15, 1968 and the abject lack of spirit among us was evident. It had been a long, arduous journey home. I was glad to be home, but was juggling the uncertainties of my circumstances nonetheless.

We were assigned to floors based on the type and extent of our injuries. My hospital clinical record read: *"9/15, 0100 am. This 20-year-old Cau. male was admitted via Gurney to Ward 4-E, with wounds to face, chest, and both legs. Short arm cast on left arm.* Appears to be in good spirits."

Outwardly I appeared happy, but I was secretly giving way to the guilt gnawing inside of me. I felt guilty for making it home alive, when so many others had not. The image of the Marines I had left behind was still fresh in my mind. I felt guilty for my wounds knowing they would preclude me from ever returning to combat. Mostly, I felt guilt at the thought that the catastrophe which had resulted in my wounds and the wounds of so many others that August day may have been more my fault, a result of my negligence, than I had allowed myself to recognize. These subtle, underlying pangs of

Great Lakes Naval Hospital

177

guilt and remorse filled my days as I began the treatments and physical therapy I would have to endure for many months to come. I still could not walk without help - for the time being I was a cripple.

My first visitors were my older brother, my mom and dad. They arrived right after one of my many operations. When they arrived, I was groggy from medication but still thrilled to see them, even though I was ashamed of the way I had returned home, wounded. In the midst of a post-procedure narcotic twilight, I heard my brother describing his prognosis of me.

"Damn! He'll never be the same!"

My brother's words stung. My first reaction was to surrender to his observations, yield to the medication and drift away, but in only a few minutes I came to full consciousness with a new- found determination. My fate was in my own hands. I would heal. I would become whole again. I wasn't sure how, but I was certain now that I would. I was determined to prove my brother's predictions to be a foolish guess and vowed not to die before I was dead. I would become my own salvation. In Vietnam I had other Marines. Here, there was no one outside of the hospital who could ever understand any of this.

~ WAREHOUSE OF LOSERS ~

After a surgery, moving through *"anything goes"* – a kaleidoscopic complexity of outrageousness to reality, was always entertaining and full of revelations. Under the influence of the medical narcotics many of the evaluations and distinctions I made in everyday life evaporated. The effect of drugs and the consciousness they produced usually forced a sort of calm resignation to my predicament. My mind was separated from my beat-up body and I was catapulted into my version of enlightenment and impossible ideas. My mind was like a ghost in a machine, because anything anywhere was better than being in that warehouse of losers threatened by meaninglessness every day.

But this was the surgery ("the big one") where my dad, mother and quickly exiting girlfriend were asked by staff to visit the hospital. The surgical team was going (again) up into my head to repair more vascular damage, the fountainhead of the noise we all could hear coming from my left ear and the cause of my eclectic dreams. By now I'd squarely faced the fact of my own mortality repeatedly.

But the visit by this lovely girl presented a new chance at happiness. She represented the possibility of a normal life. She had long brown hair with easy curls at the bottom that bounced when she walked. Tall, very thin and long legged; she took exaggerated strides when she walked. She set her heels down with crushing firmness. Her dad had been a Marine. She was artistic and had a style about her even at her young age. Her hands and fingers were long and masculine. If she ever had any testosterone it was located in her fingers. She had moved beyond high school pretty and become beautiful in her freshman year in college.

I recognized the sound of her footsteps as she walked through the ward toward my bed. Her perfume was the same she'd worn in high school. I never knew its name. The soft murmur of the air being wafted by her motion passed over me and awakened our history as an adolescent couple in milliseconds. Lying there with my jaws wired closed unable to really talk or move – estranged from humanity no longer and without immediately noticing, I'd been expelled from the hospital's dead pecker club.

As she grew closer, I could see (although with tears in her eyes) she was trying to be brave. She wore a brown skirt with a light brown cobra skin belt cinched around her narrow waist. Eye level, I starred at her fine leather belt knowing that I'd eaten snakes in Vietnam. My appetite was growing.

I wanted her to say: *"Welcome home Marine, I'll be waiting for you when you get out of here. I'm proud of you. In the meantime, give me a big wet kiss with those nasty shredded shards of raw meat that used to be your lips. Honest to God George, I think black and blue are your colors and I'll be damned if you don't look like you've lost some weight. Why don't we just get naked right now? I'll be Zesta Goddess of jungle love…"*

None of that would happen. After a short meeting, fatigue set in – I was sinking back into my blurred world of pain and drug induced hallucinations. The doctors and nurses said it was time for them to leave. I guess she said a sweet goodbye I don't remember. But I do know she turned slowly toward the exit of the ward, walked past a hundred other Marine casualties and out of my life forever. I didn't blame her, I understood. I just didn't like it.

~ Hospital Hero ~

By October my wounds were healing pretty well, other than I still struggled to walk. Each night, after dark, in the dimly lit stairwell I would struggle up the flight of stairs to strengthen my legs. Pain was present with each step. There were times when I felt pathetic, even hopeless, but I was determined to recapture as much of the physical ability I had before I had been blown up. I needed to avoid becoming masterfully inactive and enjoying the luxurious inertia of hospital life, doing nothing except waiting for my body to heal itself.

The days passed slowly in the hospital. At times each hour could feel like a week and the routine of the ward only adds to the boredom, for it never varies. Day in, day out, week after week, month after month it was all the same. Progress was slow, treatments and physical therapy were endless, and the tedium rarely broken. The Chicago-area Italian-American Association visited us one afternoon. They gave all of us money and a small gift of appreciation. After much physical therapy, I eventually got to the point where I could hobble around and no longer needed a wheelchair. I was surprised by the sense of freedom it gave me.

A highly decorated Marine Sergeant had been assigned to our ward, although he was rarely seen. Somehow, he was always gone. No one knew where, No one really asked, I guess, he was truly a hero. For inspections he would lay his full-size medals out on the rack (bed) and leave. He had a full house, two Silver Stars, a Bronze Star and three Purple Hearts. One morning, for some reason, he actually slept on the ward. I had gotten up early and was slowly gimping my way to the showers. The Sergeant caught up to me and we talked as we walked down the hall. I complained about the stiffness and pain of rehabilitation. He nodded a lot but didn't say anything. He just listened. When we got to the showers, I took off my bathrobe and hospital pajamas and quickly turned the old chrome knobs on the dingy tile wall, below the showerhead. As I was adjusting the temperature and pressure of the water, I noticed that the Sergeant had moved through the steam to the other side of the shower area to a wooden bench. He had not taken off his robe yet. It seemed odd to me to have a robe on near the showers.

"Hey," I yelled, "What are you doing?"

My words stuck in my throat when I looked over and saw the Sergeant unharness his artificial leg and hang it on the towel hook. He had never said a word the entire time, while I had been complaining about my comparatively mild wounds. He was a brave Marine with a missing leg and a body tattooed with shrapnel scars. I vowed to never complain about anything again. Not ever. He balanced himself on one leg, bouncing slightly, his face close to the nozzle, and washed silently.

~ Pirate and the Punch Bowl ~

On one of our platoon sized patrols, we were walking across the "beach," a long stretch of sand on Go Noi, slowly advancing to our next firefight. The engagement was large enough to have tanks leading the way. Suddenly we heard a thunderous explosion up ahead of us. One of the tanks had hit a mine, throwing parts and pieces of metal in all directions, killing or wounding several Marines. As we hunkered down waiting for everything to get sorted out, the word was passed back to us who the unfortunate casualties were. A Marine we later called Hollywood had gotten badly wounded. We had to wait for the "dust off" so Hollywood and the others to be helicoptered out of the battle zone. They had to get medevaced out before we could resume our slow plodding advance across the seemingly endless expanse of Go Noi.

Hollywood had arrived on Ward 4-E ahead of me and had taken over the place. He was a rakish, devil-may-care, live-life-on-his-own-terms wild man. His movie star good looks and brilliant, engaging smiles were now crisscrossed with butt ugly, deep red, jagged scars. He was disfigured for life, his lips, nose and cheeks all mutilated, but thankfully for him, his devilish smile somehow still remained. He had also lost an eye, but had been issued a glass prosthetic that he wore with a fixed-eye, proud stare. He was especially proud of the price of the prosthetic, $99.00. He had lost several of the glass eyes. They had become a source of recreation and entertainment for him, and he was currently wearing the last one the military would issue without a penalty. He ruled over the ward, dominating it with his humor and unflappable positive attitude.

The most pure relief from our tedious daily rituals were the darling Gray Ladies: young, teenage girls who volunteered to be in the hospital and help Marines deal with their wounds. The young girls would play string games with us – Cat's Cradle or they would just sit and talk, read to us, or otherwise just be there to help. The first book I ever read was due to one of these Gray Ladies. She would push the library cart through the ward and the only way to get her to stop, so I could smell her hair and ogle her teenage frame was to order a book. I would eventually read many of Hemingway's works just to get to see her up close. I had never read a single book cover-to-cover before being hospitalized.

One of the favorite girls on the ward pushed a cart to dispense Hawaiian Punch. She would dip out cups of the punch with a glass ladle for invalid, bedridden Marines. This day the beautiful Gray Lady pushed her small cart down the aisle of the ward, spreading joy, whether intentional or not, with her infectious, radiant smile and aura of purity. She would pour a cup of punch and walk from the center of the aisle to each bed and dutifully set it on the nightstand of a Marine who was sitting in his rack. While the girl was busy with her chores, Hollywood skulked up to her cart, reached up to his glass eye and popped it out of the socket, using his thumb and forefinger in a theatrical, exaggerated unscrewing motion. With the quickness and slight-of-hand of a magician, he dropped the glass eye into the punch, while looking around to assure that everyone nearby was watching. The eye sunk slowly, rolling down the side of the bowl end-over-oblong-end until it came to rest at the bottom of the punch bowl, dead in the center. There it lay, dully staring upward through the bobbing chucks of ice at the hospital's aging, cream colored, water-stained acoustic ceiling.

Word spread rapidly throughout the ward about what Hollywood had done, and soon all the Marines were roaring with laughter at its absurdity. The infectious laughter wouldn't stop. Instead, it got louder and more raucous. When she finally saw the glass eye, confused and embarrassed, the beautiful, innocent Gray Lady fled from the ward, hands in the air crying. We never saw or heard from her again. Shortly after the incident, Hollywood disappeared, too. Apparently, he needed more emotional and mental health help than was available on ward 4-E. His wildness finally caught up with him.

Contrary to misconceptions by the media and the self-serving orthodoxy of the liberal left; Vietnam veterans did not suffer any more emotional distress (psychiatric casualties) during or after their war than did Veterans from other wars including World War II. Along with inflated claims of emotional issues, drug use by Vietnam Veterans was also exaggerated as was the post-service suicide rate. Drug use may have been a widespread problem but only after 90% of the warriors had left Vietnam. After the initial post-service period of five years, suicides by Vietnam veterans were less than all other American wars.

Many Vietnam veterans are glad they served and were employed and as employable after the war, as the general population. Most volunteered (66%) to serve in Vietnam, particularly in the Marine Corps (although some were drafted, to their surprise, into the Corps). 70% of those killed in Vietnam were volunteers.

Another myth that's been dispelled by research, is the exploitation of Blacks. Many served with distinction (awarded 20 Medals of Honor), and they represented themselves well, 12.5% of those serving in Vietnam were Black. The young weren't exploited either, Marines and soldiers who went to Vietnam were the best educated and on average the oldest fighters (22 years old) ever fielded by the United States. Portraying Vietnam's veterans as Well-adjusted and untroubled by the war would have undermined the liberal left's anti-war agenda that lasted for decades.

My wounds were healing well. Fake teeth had been installed, a bridge to replace the lower teeth that were knocked out, the leg, arm and chest wounds were pretty much taking care of themselves. I had gone through several surgeries for my head wounds. Family and friends from Dixon had visited me in the hospital a few times and I had received a few unexpected cards and letters, all very welcome. The doctors said my progress was acceptable, except for the vascular damage done to the left side of my head and face. I was getting used to hearing "stand by Marine, this may sting a little." When the Doctors addressed you as "Marine," they were teeing you up for the pain, reminding you to maintain your bearing as they skewered you one more time. The days in the hospital ate away at me, like a tiny swarm of pesky insects.

I was occasionally allowed liberty on the weekends and had returned home to Dixon, Illinois a few times to visit friends and family. Over Thanksgiving 1968, my mom prepared a liquid diet for me by pureeing turkey, dressing, gravy and cranberry sauce, because my jaws were still wired shut. It was surprisingly good. Everything else about Thanksgiving was really pathetic. I was miserable and was growing weary of the rehabilitation routine and even wearier of the way all but close family and a few friends received returning veterans. People hesitated to even speak to a veteran, and those who did definitely did not want to discuss Vietnam. The war had become very unpopular by 1968, and the warriors who were fighting it and returning home were just as unwelcome. We were pariahs.

On one liberty from the hospital, I did get a chance to go to a Doors concert. I rocked all night with some friends from high school. I was awed by the apparent solidarity of the audience, all mindlessly endorsing Jim Morrison (the Doors lead singer) as heroic with their cheers and adoration. It was at the concert, during the song *Light My Fire*, I realized that although I loved the music, the poetry of our time, I was no longer part of my own generation. The isolation was evident. I was alone inside my experiences. I had traveled a different road than my high school friends and the others around me. We had entirely different perspectives about heroes and adoration and our frames of references were light years apart. I think I had grown up, to a degree, far more (differently, at least) than the others had.

~ 21st Birthday — Home Alone ~

It was November 1968, and I was about to turn 21 in the hospital, and would then be able to vote and drink alcohol legally. To celebrate my 21st birthday in style, I had requested liberty. Before allowing me to leave the hospital though, the doctor wanted to see me. My jaw was surgically broken to get access into my skull and my mouth was wired closed, so the doctor gave me a pair of surgical scissors to cut the wires away in case I had got too drunk and had to throw up. I don't remember my official coming of age, not one moment, no recollection, no recall, nothing, nope. My 21st birthday is not just a blur—there is no recollection of it at all. I don't remember a thing about what happened or who I was with.

In my mind, I was prepared for my coming of age. I could see it with the clarity of Gin. In that moment, when I turned 21, I'd understand how to be a man. A legal man, and with the legality I'd be endowed with the strength, wisdom, kindness, the continuum of responses necessary to govern livestock and industry. But the doctor had said that because of my very rare vascular disorder I would have to be careful of my activities, and I should consider living a sedate sedentary life or risk bursting a blood vessel in my head, which would most certainly result in my instant death. Soon after his cautionary speech, I took a weekend liberty to Madison, Wisconsin, to a large sporting goods store, and bought SCUBA gear, snow skis and mountain climbing equipment all on the same night. I was going to load test the medical procedures the doctor had performed on me. I had no intention of slowing down.

Weeks later, because I was 21, I was often nominated to sneak out at night, off the ward, out of the hospital, and off the base to buy liquor for the new arrivals. Bottles of booze were hidden all over our hospital ward and were hauled out at the slightest provocation. Any excuse would do.

I had a fistula in the blood vessels in my temporal region that produced an audible sound ("bruit") in my ear. Standing next to me you could actually hear the noise. With every heart beat it sounded like Elmer Fudd pronouncing "Woo - Woo." It was maddening, but the Navy surgeons loved it. I became a medical celebrity for a while, a dubious and fleeting distinction because each week there were more and more arrivals with "great" wounds the doctors could hone their medical surgical skills on. I enjoyed the distinction as long as it lasted.

The Doctors operated on my head several times. I remember at least three, to correct the noisy condition. It eventually diminished gradually and then finally disappeared altogether. The only remnant is a condition called Frey's Syndrome the result of confused re-attachment of facial nerves. I sweat when I eat, it stings when I chew food, and I salivate when I get hot. I have the symptoms to this day. It makes dining an adventure unto itself.

After one of my operations, while I was still in the grog of semi-consciousness, returning from the dreamless, bottomless crossover into eternity, I had a drug induced hallucination in my emergence delirium that I had been rendered a vegetable, not just any garden variety generic plant, but a turnip. Apparently, I'd laughed my way back to reality and acquired the tag "Corporal Turnip" along the way. Fortunately, the nickname only lasted a few weeks.

Marines on a hospital ward can be very empathetic, kind (at times) and giving, but only in their unique Marine Corps way. With very few exceptions, everyone was teased unmercifully about whatever ailment, wound or disfigurement they had. We were ruthless, making fun of each other. The baiting and sparring may have served the purpose of conditioning each of us to be hard as steel when we got discharged to face civilian life as "baby killing" freaks. The cajoling never let up, and we passed the time thinking up new insults to hurl at each other.

I was transferred to Ward 9-E (Ear, Nose, and Throat) because of my head injuries, and on one particular afternoon the unruliness got out of hand. The teasing and slamming evolved into drinking and taking our rat-holed medicine, usually Darvon or other painkillers, in large doses, pill after pill. In an unspoken agreement, the raucous tenants of 9-E had decided on that late afternoon they would swallow all the pills and drink all the booze they had stashed away.

The party quickly got way out of hand. Someone opened several of the old steel framed, single pane windows that pivoted in the middle. The large glass windows, when opened were parallel to the floor. Once the windows had been opened, a few artillery "commandos" started calling in targets from firebase 9-Echo.

"9 Echo this is Zulu 6, request fire support over?"

"Zulu 6, 9-Echo standing by. Over?"

"9-Echo your coordinates are 69, 69, 69. Over?"

"Zulu 6 repeat, that is 69, 69, 69. Over?"

"Roger 9-Echo, range 900 meters, elevation 1-2-0, deflection 4-5."

"Zulu 6, 9-Echo. Shot out, over?"

A single, empty liquor bottle flew out a nearby window, but fell short of the parking lot.

"9-Echo, adjust fire. Add 5-0. Fire for effect. Over."

"Roger that Zulu 6 Add 5-0."

After the last imaginary radio transmission, empty liquor bottles were thrown out the window by their necks. The bottles whirled horizontally, whistling softly like owls hooting who-who-who as they spun through the air – imaginary artillery rounds, directed at an imaginary enemy in the parking lot. The imaginary enemy, of course, was someone's real car.

The artillery barrage of empty bottles went on until the nurses, backed by Marine and Navy Shore Patrols armed with night sticks, rousted everyone into their beds. The nurses, with their armed protection, bravely bellowed "Get in your racks, God damn it, and that's an order!"

The ward eventually quieted down, and the lights were turned off. The festivities continued however, albeit more quietly throughout the night, not ending until dawn. Many of us were still stoned or were at the least suffering from epic hangovers when the nurses came through the next morning to get us out of our beds. Some of the Marines elected to ignore the Nurses' orders and without a minute's hesitation, the nurses called the Marine Military Police (MPs) and Shore Patrol once again.

~ MEDICAL HOLDING COMPANY – MARINE BARRACKS ~

Gradually the operations, physical therapy, dental work, and hospital treatment became infrequent and eventually the necessity of constant medical care was over. When that time came, I was transferred to the Medical Holding Company, which was in the old brick barracks on the other side of the base.

Medical Holding was for patients who were ambulatory, waiting for transfer to their next assignment or discharge from the Marine Corps, for whatever reason. The routine was boring and non-productive. We would get up each day, make our bunks, have head call, breakfast, and then report for one menial make-work detail or another. My job was opening the doors for visitors to the hospital and offering them a pleasant official greeting, accompanied by a crisp salute for officers. It was like an entire month of Mondays. This was now the service I was providing for my country. It was degrading. I had been a warrior. Now I was a door man.

I was gimpy and at about 145 pounds, very thin. I had a limp and was physically weak.

Dear Mandy,   Dec. 10
    About Christmas cards, - ech!
I should write Aunt Ester and Uncle
kick but - I'll go seen them when I
come home next.
        I should get unwired next monday (16th)
and Maybe come Home the 19th for 20 days
until the 1 of Jan. The Navy is playing
games again, so I may not even get home
until Christmas eve — who knows?
    Grampaw's letter was interesting. Funny
tho' he was always my hero-gordon and
Churchill and a Coach from Alabama I had
at Osborne H.S. also were my youthful ideals
    I've read MAO-TSE-TUNG till he haunts
me. I'm in the middle of "THE STRANGE TACTICS
OF EXTREMISM," OVERSTREET(s) It is about The John
Birch Society, Dan Smoot and compares-them with
communism. It has-turn'd me into "a middle of
the road," slightly listing to the RIGHT, with my
left elbow resting to the left. So again, who
KNOWS!?
    I don't feel much like writeing letters
to anyone (?) because my letters are.
supposed to be funny and I'm running

out of material - I guess I'm preoccupied*
with the future. I've decided to keep
my plans to myself and just go ahead
with them and everybody else can ——!
        So the new car is a Greave that's groovy!
the Archives (crewsdibrary) is less than
it should be. —
        I feel good, look good and (am) good.
haha!

Happy Birthday Steve,   Well See Ya as soon
where ever you are!   as possible
                                                      love,
                                                        [?]   (ret.)

    *
        preoccupied, not depressed
makeing a slection of the
billion opportunities is funnn
but I have to choose between $
and what I really want to do
and if I should include other
people (spousette)

As I was standing in a long line, waiting to get paid, I was becoming increasingly impatient with garrison life. I was becoming angry.

The method of payment was standard. You showed your identification card to a Sergeant sitting at the pay table next to a Lieutenant. The officer would look up your name on a ledger to find out what you were due in payment. You had to announce your name and rank.

"Sir, Corporal Berg." I had been promoted in December – a Christmas present by the Marine Corps. The officer would then count out the allocated pay, usually in twenty-dollar bills. After he finished counting, he would fan the money across the green blanket covering the table and we would say, "Sir, the pay is correct, sir." Then you would collect your money and leave.

I was boiling with rage at the prospect of having to serve out my time standing in endless lines, occupied by nonsense. I missed the comfort of a rifle and the smell of dirt. As I was leaning against a wall, while waiting in the pay line, I saw a flier for Tae Kwon Do classes. I needed something to challenge me and help me get back in shape, and also recover some of who I'd been. I signed up for the classes, and with my arm in a cast and bandages on my wounds, I started working out twice a week at the base gym.

The Korean instructors were "right off the boat" and were ruthless, teaching Americans like they were still in Korea. The discipline was intense and the long hard workout sessions were exhausting and invigorating at the same time. To toughen the students, the instructor would have us lay down, side by side, and he would then walk on our stomachs across the length of the classroom. I enjoyed the diversion and re-hardening of my mind and body. I felt as though I was becoming a warrior again. I earned a black belt in Tae Kwon Do years later.

In addition to those of us in the Medical Holding Company, our barracks also housed the guards for the base's military brig. These jailers were brutal martinets that only associated with one another. I witnessed these narrow-minded goons beat the hell out of a Jewish Marine in the squad bay just because of his religion. They were a foul, sinister bunch, hardened by their work in the military prison where rules associated with the real world are suspended just like in combat. The overlap was apparent, and their vocation insinuated its way into their personal lives. Years later I would help build prisons in California and I spent time learning about some of the relationships between inmates and guards. The deviance and pathology of prisoners can map over to the correctional officers, and the only difference is that the guards get to leave the facility after their shift, can go home and have sex with a more willing partner. Here, the Marine Corps bond was not the same as in combat. These were lesser Marines— they had not earned their hard-core attitudes from the bush but from treating other people poorly.

Life in the Medical Holding Company and living in the transient Marine Barracks waiting for a change in status was increasingly mind-numbing. There was really no point to it, performing busy work and trivial tasks. The superficial duties were like a counter poise to an electrical circuit that gradually took me to ground (reality) over time. Being a warrior and not being in combat was senseless. In 1969 there was rioting in the streets in almost every major city in the United States and on most major college campuses. The shelter of the hospital, away from current events and a rapid shift in cultural values, compounded the concept of being a warrior with no war. It kept us isolated. The Marine Corps had no need for warriors too injured to fight, and society at large did not seem to particularly cherish its returning Marines either.

January 1969 was very cold and bleak, so I decided to invite myself to visit my older brother in DeKalb, Illinois, a college town located about 60 miles west of Waukegan and 40 miles east or so of Dixon. A train ran there every day, so I secured weekend liberty, bought a train ticket and took off on a freelance adventure. My brother was left-leaning, very avant garde, and hung out with the "fringe:" the outer edge of society, self-proclaimed poets, artists and politically social radicals.

My older brother was painting abstractly and had read Sartre, Camus and other existentialist writers in the eighth grade. Intellectually ahead of his age, he'd also been responsible for himself since he was seventeen.

As brothers we were in many fundamental ways diametrically opposed. He was decidedly anti-war, I was anti-intellectual. I thought visiting him would resolve some of the differences. My now very ex-girlfriend was attending school at Northern Illinois University, and I had fantasies of a chance meeting with her there.

I had no civilian clothes, nor for that matter any real concept of how rapidly the world had changed while I had been gone, so I arrived at my brother's house in my Marine Corps uniform. I received a lukewarm but civil reception and watched as various eccentrics came and went from his artistic world. He seemed like the center of a strange universe of writers, hippies, poets, freaks and Students for a Democratic Society (SDS). They called themselves freaks and defined who they were by elliptical freakishness. Being really "out there" was a status symbol and most of his associates were. I was clearly behind enemy lines, doing recon on a new alien culture which had invaded the United States.

I would not become part of the civil rights movement, nor the movement to liberate women or any social movement for that matter. I would not join Vietnam Veterans against the War. None of the revolutionary changes would capture my attention. Instead, it was the sweat, blood, and tears of my war that held me. In some important ways, I'd stay locked within its boundaries for decades.

A small group of eccentrics huddled around my brother, making plans, deciding how to entertain themselves that night. I clearly was not being included or was I wanted. As I sat in a large, high-back chair, one of his friends handed me a very small off-white pill saying, "Here, take this with your beer. It'll keep you company."

Then they all left, still busy making plans as I sat alone in an old threadbare but comfortable, overstuffed chair with only a half-finished beer in one hand and the small pill in the other, to keep me company until I could catch the train back to Great Lakes the next morning. I swallowed the small, bitter pill and chased it with the rest of the warming beer. Then I got another beer from the refrigerator and sat back down to listen to my brother's stereo record player and some of the rock music that was popular at the time. I got comfortable preparing for my long night alone and resigned myself to enjoying the three-ring circus around me.

Across from me, hanging on the wall, was a coarsely woven, antique tapestry of muted grays and greens. The tongue and cheek pattern was a wide-eyed grinning cartoon-like monkey climbing a coconut tree. I closed my eyes, just listened to the music, and began drifting away. When I opened my eyes again, to finish the beer the monkey smiled and shimmed down the bending tree. The monkey smiled again and up the tree he went. I was hallucinating. The small bitter pill had been LSD, a powerful hallucinogenic popular with some in the late 1960s. I began to sweat and took off my jacket, called a blouse in the Marine Corps, and loosened my tie. I figured out what was happening and thought that no matter what occurred I could handle it.

For hours I listened to music and watched the monkey climb the tree and thought about all the possibilities that awaited me after my discharge from the Marine Corps. The rigid, ironhanded grip of the military had been loosened. That evening and into the early morning hours I began to think like a civilian, like a young man. It was as though I'd regained some faint memory from the distant past. I smiled and thought, *"I'm back!"*

The next morning I hastily gathered my gear and caught the train. The ride was uneventful. I just stared out the window watching the flat cold landscape zip by. When we stopped at Great Lakes Hospital, I realized had lost my head cover (hat) and would have to navigate my way back to the Marine barracks without bumping into an officer, who would, at minimum, severely chew my ass or worse, issue an "article" for being out of uniform.

Unfortunately, this was not a lucky weekend for me. Not 50 yards through the gates at Great Lakes and I was stopped by a Captain, who took his time deriding me about my sloppy, skuzzy, unmilitary appearance, asking, "Where in the fuck is your god damn head cover?"

"I lost it," was my simple reply. Not even bothering with the mandatory "sir." The LSD, the grueling recovery, and the lack of support for a war which was technically being won by our military and lost by civilians, was redirecting my loyalties to a new focus which was not being a Marine. I refused to even engage politics, religion or any institution, for that matter. I was becoming a nihilist.

Later that week on the Medical Holding Company bulletin board was a posted announcement indicating that any Marine unable to return to combat, that had 03 military occupations (combat arms) could receive an "early out." We, the wounded, were now officially useless to the Marine Corps. Dead Grunts were buried and out of sight, but what do you do with Grunts too wounded to return to combat? We were now just an expense, a nuisance, or maybe even an embarrassment.

A New Life Starts

I applied for an early out and within a week was discharged. I was de-enrolling from the fraternity and received a cold shoulder at every point in the discharge process which only served to reinforce my decision. My time in the United States Marine Corps was over. I'd served my country, for what it was worth. I signed the papers, gathered my sea bag and headed to the front gate to catch the train to Dixon. I began to smile, looking around me to make certain that no one would stop me over some technicality. I got closer and closer and then a Navy Shore Patrol guard at the gate asked to see my papers. Satisfied, he stepped aside and there in front of me was the 100 yards to freedom. I ran to the train station at a full gallop, laughing all the way. On the train to Dixon, I met – Julie Heaton – I had gone to high school with her. We exchanged pleasantries, but I realized then that I would have a tough time communicating with normal people.

I burst into my parents' home smiling. My mother greeted me with a hug, but before I could even set down my sea bag my celebration was interrupted with startling news: "Denny Dawson was killed on patrol in Vietnam this week."

Denny had been a friend that I did really stupid high school age stuff with. I was shaken, and it was painfully clear that the haunting specter of the war refused go away. The only way to make the pain go away after Denny's funeral, I calculated in my young mind, was a road trip to Juarez, Mexico, and an endless supply of tequila. I spent several days driving across the United States into Texas and across the border into the swirling, downward spiral of tequila and "Bullfights." After this mindless reprieve, I drove back to Carbondale, Illinois and Southern Illinois University to celebrate St. Patrick's Day with Bill Buzzard and Dennis Spangler, both from my hometown. We drank for a few days and celebrated the Irish, the moon, and being 21-years-old.

~ Sauk Valley College ~

I returned to Dixon and wandered around, trying to find my compass. Then another adventurous friend, who was home from the University of Colorado, suggested I take a summer course with him at Sauk Valley Community College, the same place I'd started classes earlier. The idea was ridiculous; I was not fit for school. I took a job as a night watchman/greens keeper at Lost Nation Golf Course. I worked at night and felt much more comfortable working in the dark, alone. Jeff was convincing however, and we enrolled in psychology 100 in the summer of 1969. In class I was rude, outspoken, blunt, opinionated, defiant and otherwise objectionable. At the end of the short summer semester the instructor stopped me after the final exam and told me that I had a future in college although I received a "C" in his class.

I decided to try college, although I was entirely unfit. I enrolled for the fall semester. It was September 1969 and the anti-war sentiment was reaching a crescendo. I wandered into the pole barn structure that was hoping to become a legitimate secondary school. It was curious. The hippie subculture had reached deep into the hinterlands of the Midwest. Long haired, bearded kids wearing flower power shirts and dirty jeans lazed about campus. The girls, "hippie chicks," all had adopted a breezy nonchalance.

I felt alone among children who were essentially my own age. I didn't belong here and felt conspicuous – in fact, I was. I was the "returning vet," the first one to come back to this college from Vietnam. I was not welcomed back by them. Between classes, I usually sat in the student center, alone. In time, more and more veterans returned home, and we gathered together at "our" tables in the student center.

There were anti-war protests, hectic gatherings of signatures for one radical social movement or another. They, the other students, were sincere and focused on their burgeoning decidedly left-leaning, political beliefs. For me, politics was an illusion. There were the rulers and the ruled; the details were insignificant and irrelevant. Religion, governments, the military and universities existed to preserve and guarantee the lifestyle of those at the top.

My war was reverberating deep within me, and it had done something profoundly weird to my mind. I did not engage those who asked me to sign petitions or otherwise get involved in their particular movement (Moratorium Days). More often than not, I would send their eyes spiraling as if they were following buzzing flies around the room, when I'd go into an inarticulate, often animated and profane tirade about "pinko-commies." The first semester passed without much confrontation, and to my astonishment, I passed all the courses, and no one from the college had asked me to leave.

I was an oddity well known among the faculty. A few of the professors were above the politics of the day and incredibly dedicated to teaching philosophy, poetry, music, English and the sciences. Many of the instructors were just out of graduate school and were at the top of their intellectual game; Max Guinnup, Ed Beatty, Lee Fredrick, Robert Matter, Maxine Peterson, Frank Rausa, George Vrhel, David Lovekin and Robert Wharton, to name only a few. They all were powerful communicators and cultivated their students in a tiny school on the Rock River that only a few years earlier had been a corn field.

The next semester, while walking down the narrow hallway to my English class, a professor, David Lovekin, stopped me at the door to his classroom and said warmly, "Good morning, Mr. Berg. Welcome." That welcome became my introduction to the world of critical thinking. My entire life would change with that casual and understated greeting. Along the way, among many other books, he suggested that I read; J. Glenn Gray's – *The Warriors: Reflections on Men in Battle*. I did. The book, the professor and that small college set a new, profoundly positive direction for my life.

EPILOGUE

THE COLD, CRISP MORNING AIR FELT CLEAN. A strange eerily thick opaque fog hung over everything. Visibility was 20-30 feet and the edges and features of the rolling landscape blended together out in the creamy undulating mist. As we lay motionless in our ambush, we heard the unmistakable snap of a twig breaking in the distance. Something was headed our way. In the darkness I looked into the eyes lying next to me and got a confirming nod. Then, we heard another sharp *snap*. By the sound, the target had moved quickly in our direction, it was closing very fast.

I looked sideways again and saw two fingers pointing to the eyes – "I see." I waited for the signal to become a closed fist – "I see target." When the signal came, I took aim and held. Out of the thick, heavy, cold mist a grey silhouette moved into view and then stopped. I adjusted my aim but unsure of the target I held. The silhouette didn't move. Then, over my right shoulder, I heard a firm, articulate, familiar voice command, "Pop a cap on his ass!"

I pulled the trigger – KABOOM! – The silhouette disappeared. The blast hurled thick smoke and bright yellow and orange sparks boiling out of the barrel of my weapon. I dropped my rifle, pulled out my .45 caliber pistol from its holster and followed the line of my shot on a run, eager to finish the kill. I ran to where I thought I'd find the body. Nothing, it soon occurred to me that, in the cold fog I must have overrun the target. I circled back slowly, looking through the brush.

"Here! He is over here," I heard my partner yell. Moving to the spot, I found my 14-year-old Daughter – "Shooter" one of my nick names for my daughter Jennifer – standing over the dying bull elk.

The elk struggled but could not get up, its heartbeat still sure and strong. But the .54 caliber rifle bullet had torn off the bottom of his heart, it beat now only out of habit. My daughter and I stood staring in awe at the courage and bravery of this grand elk. I chambered a round in my pistol, held it close to the bull's head and fired point blank. My daughter gently turned her face away and averted her eyes. I had to fire two more times before the slow meticulous dissections began.

My daughter built a sled from an old parka and pulled the hind quarters, maybe 90-100 pounds of meat, hide and bone over the rough terrain in the freezing cold. She then walked

back to the elk and carried out another load of meat in a backpack. She smiled, groaned, laughed, sweated, and strained against the load but otherwise accepted and overcame the challenge. Her feet were cold and wet, covered only in light canvas shoes. I hadn't noticed or I would have never let her out in the field without proper footwear.

What she couldn't have noticed was my spiritual absence; that during the hunt I had drifted back decades to my war. While we were hunting, I was fighting my war again, reliving the tension, experiencing the fear and excitement projected into the elk hunt.

"Nice eyes, Shooter," I told her, congratulating her on her extraordinary ability to locate animals. "Good shot, Dad," she said, then quickly followed up with, "Dad, sometimes you act like a kid."

"Yep, Honey, I do," I replied, thinking to myself that part of me will always be frozen in time, remanded to that wordless, secret space that is within each of us. It is that sacred place that contains the atoms of our souls and our humanity, that place defines us, but only rarely gets opened. Mine was opened and closed in Vietnam.

Shooter seemed to have learned at an early age to be instinctive, committed, passionate, consistent, straight forward, dedicated, and honest. What's more, she had grit, speed, and would go on to acquire four varsity letters in high school swimming, usually competing in the grueling long-distance events. She eventually graduated from law school and is a criminal defense attorney.

My other daughter has it, too. When I asked her if she needed to change from her soccer shorts into something warmer before we put the ski rack on the car in December, she replied, "Dad, if I can cross an ice-cold mountain stream, then I can do this." She is an adventurer, spending time in Napa Valley in California, the U.S. Virgin Islands, Spain, Greece, South Africa, Australia and Tahiti SCUBA diving, sailing and enjoying life.

The ice-cold stream comment was a reference to the times we camped in the high country in Colorado, where we had to cross ice cold, leg numbing snow melt streams. And of course

Return to Goi Noi Island 1999
- (Photos by R. Dennis Smith)

Mear the site of Liberty Bridge
and Cu Ban (4) in 1999

Crossisng to Goi Noi Island 1999

Goi Noi Island 1999

Goi Noi Island 1999

she did, wearing a grey sweatshirt with the word MARINES emblazoned on the front. They were both hard core, high country Colorado cowgirls and on occasions, Marines.

When I left Vietnam, I was glad to have that chapter in my life gone and closed. I was sure I could move on and put all that behind me. How wrong I was. Vietnam is a metaphor in our national collective consciousness for ill-advised, unprepared and under-supported military action. As a national policy and as an overall military strategy maybe that is true, but at the grunt level few Marines had better records nor more deserving of greater credit. What Vietnam means to the Nation is wildly different from what it means to the individual warrior who lived it.

In 1999 I visited Vietnam. Flying from Saigon to Hanoi, I was struck with the same epiphany many others have had; war, and for me this war in particular, is a horrific aspect of humanity and the cultures we create. War is in fact a terrible waste, which creates only irreparable losses, but war is one of the primary ways we churn our world and our lives. War is an inevitable consequence of our humanity. Mankind and war are inseparable. Any conflicts, armed conflicts in particular, arise because of the innate difference in which humans choose to celebrate life. It is part of the machinery of the universe.

In war we can become The Dark Ignoble, creatures, or purely Homo Furens – warriors. I've reconciled my war experiences, though I've decided they will remain ambivalent, neither bad nor good. Within that episode in my life, I saw immense kindness and gentleness expressed by barbaric men. I saw brave men reduced to tears, paralyzed by their circumstances and fear. There are some days when I'd like to celebrate surviving the war. There were days, long ago, when I would have liked to be taken in by my country and embraced as a hero, so I could trade on that glory and have an easier go of life. But that would be emotional charity. Instead, we were given the G.I. Bill, designed to provide money for a college education, help in buying a home and medical care, should it be needed.

I believe, through the Vietnam experience, I gained a depth of understanding of myself and others, but it is an insight that is unserviceable in our everyday society. Rarely is there a call for the ability to see into other people's souls, read their intentions, know what they will do before they know what they themselves will do and determine where they will aim their rifles. The brotherhood and bonds forged quickly in combat are long lasting, but serve no civilian function, other than a cause for an inexplicable, spontaneous smile, every once in a while. I appreciate other Vietnam veterans, but abhor the embellished, self-aggrandizing, and sometimes completely fabricated war stories they spin to keep the free drinks flowing, or to win elections. The real vets returned, received questionable levels of treatment for their emotional and physical wounds and went to work trying to avoid quietly going insane. The thousands of collective details of their grand adventure will be lost, mostly taken to the grave – a war preferred to be forgotten. The warriors returned to their hometowns to become masons, cops, auto mechanics, teachers, firemen, and all other occupations.

There are few things in life that rival the sheer exhilaration of a combat assault, storming off the tail ramps or jumping from the doors of a hovering helicopter. I've spent most of my adult life attempting to recapture the excitement of combat, with a variety of crazed adventures. Nothing has come close, so at times I've pretended to be in combat. My erratic search has enlivened my activities, but altered my personal relationships – I am on my third, and with any luck, final marriage.

Important people in my life have been posted on the periphery, marginalized as I searched for the excitement that could rival the exhilaration of combat. Vietnam is a part of me that sneaks up on rare, unexpected occasions and shouts "BOO!," then disappears back into the black recesses from which it came. Now it is receding - Vietnam has become a phantom limb finally going numb.

I did not finish my full tour of duty in Vietnam, it was truncated – abbreviated. There have been times when I have dropped to my knees and privately thanked God for getting me out of Vietnam when he did. The experience still produces evocative, complicated emotions. What I am grateful for is that the transition into full-fledged Warrior was fleeting, and that I have fewer issues than some, but I still struggle almost every day with the memories, reminded as I look at the scars on my arm and legs. The scars are raking, desultory mortars that can produce a deep full body anxiety and hair-trigger. I have deep guilt that the mine field where we were blown up may have been, in fact, American, and that the shots fired at us were warnings shots from Marines on the hill overlooking the valley. The mine field may have been part of the corridor being built in the "rocket and mortar belt" to protect Da Nang.

I do not like admitting to the fear that occurred in me during firefights, but it was there, nonetheless. On the other hand, I take solace in a quote from John Stuart Mills, *"War is an ugly thing, but not the ugliest of things. The ugliest is that man who thinks nothing is worth fighting and dying for and lets men better and braver than himself protect him."* Very often those men are Marines.

I had already put most of my memories of Vietnam on paper when I attended a Marine Corps Birthday Ball with my two daughters in Hawaii, where my oldest daughter was a freshman at the University of Hawaii – Hilo, studying marine science and experiencing the difficulties of being far away from home at so young an age.

During the Ball I asked my daughters to disappear into the crowd of manly, young Marine officers, all smartly dressed and crisp looking, and find authentic heroes – Navy Crosses, Silver and Bronze Stars, and Purple Hearts. They didn't understand what to look for. Instead, they looked at each other, sisters through and through, and spent their time studying the merits of the gowns worn by the women.

We flew to the big island, Hawaii, from Oahu. On the drive back to Kona from Hilo, we stopped at the town of Waimea, noted for its fine cuisine. Across the way was a monument that marked the camp where the 27th Marines trained for their invasion of Iwo Jima. Farther south, I walked out onto the white sand beach, and listened to the surf and stared across the water, while watching spinner dolphins breaching through the waves, rotating and gracefully performing their signature tail dance. I wondered about the Marines who trained there on those beaches.

Charlie Company, 1st Battalion, 27th Marine Regiment, had been my unit in Vietnam. It was the same unit that was part of the invasion of Iwo Jima, many years ago, in one of the most heralded battles of World War II, made famous and remembered by the now iconic flag-raising on Mount Suribachi. The regimental motto of the 27th Marines is *"To the sound of the guns."* Its storied history will live on forever.

The tropical heat, sand, the fighting spirit, intensity, tradition, and pride would be much the same for the Marines of the 1968 version, but our experience would remain obscure, little known, mostly forgotten, except to those of us who survived. I would thrash about in an incomprehensible fog for decades, cannibalizing my own soul, eating out my own heart, trying to awaken from the bad dream of combat and the guilt of surviving. I had been wounded twice and still felt I hadn't given enough.

For the last few years, I had been putting my memories of Vietnam onto paper, studying the experiences, dissecting my feelings, and searching for the answers of how the Vietnam War had affected me, my life, and my family. Although I may never find answers to all the questions, one thing became crystal clear: in some important ways it has shaped who I am as a father, a husband, and a man - who will always be a Marine.

~ VIETNAM: A BRIEF HISTORY ~

In November 1947, during the early days of the Franco-Viet Minh War, General Vo Ngyen Giap and his forces were engaged in a fierce, pitched battle against French paratroopers and Moroccan Colonial Infantry in the mountains north of Hanoi. During that same time, his father was being held in the prison in Hue where French soldiers were torturing him to death. Ironically, this was the same month and year I was born. Twenty years later I would become a Marine grunt, about to hump throughout Go Noi Island and areas north of Da Nang, and Vo Ngyen Giap was the Senior General and chief strategist for the Viet Minh and North Vietnamese Army in what the communists called the North-South War or *The American War*, a 10-year conflict Americans called the Vietnam War.

A myriad of experts will give equally as many reasons for why that war was fought, why it was won or lost, depending on their view and political persuasion, and who were the heroes or villains. These various rationales, however, basically fell into three categories. Some people idealized the conflict as a peasant uprising that would reunite Vietnam and free it from the decadence of Capitalism. Others fervently believed that South Vietnam, like West Berlin or South Korea, was a sentinel state, an important battle in the global war against Communism. For the third group, those of us with boots on the ground, it was just a place whose beauty was overshadowed by the all-consuming concern to survive your 13 months "in country."

Dating back to the 2nd Century B.C., the history of the area now called Vietnam has been a continuum of wars. The people and country have suffered invasions from foreign powers and have invaded others as well, they have dominated other lands and have, for a great deal of their history, been dominated by others – China several times, France, Japan, and France again.

In many ways though, the history of Vietnam is as filled with irony as it is with war. The southernmost area of Vietnam, the rich, fertile Mekong Delta is a prime example. Regarded as one of the richest rice fields in the world, this region was originally part of a kingdom known as Funan. Heavily influenced by early India, the kingdom was known for its refined art and architecture, and an elaborate system of canals used for transportation and irrigation of the wet rice agriculture. In 613 A.D., however, Funan was attacked and absorbed by Chenla, which until 550 A.D. had been one of its vassal states.

Although Funan/Chenla experienced very little influence from China, the lands to the north of them had experienced more than 2000 years of contact, influence, and battle with the Chinese before being totally conquered in 111 B.C., as a result of the Han invasion. At that time, the Chinese named all those southern territories "Annam," meaning "Pacified South," a label detested by the people of those lands. It wasn't until 939 A.D. that these lands were able to oust the Chinese, although the dreaded memory of that occupation would influence political decisions for centuries to come.

After winning independence, the area around present day Hanoi and the Gulf of Tonkin was called Tonkin, the area south of that was still called Annam, and the area around present day Da Nang was called Champa, whose people, the Chams, are ethnically not related to the people north of them, and had probably immigrated from present day Indonesia. Sometime after their independence Tonkin and Amman basically united, calling themselves Vietnamese and began a southern expansion. By 1471, Vietnamese armies of the Le Dynasty conquered the kingdom of Champa, killing 60,000 Champs and enslaving another 60,000.

By 1558 the kingdom of the Vietnamese was divided between two great families. In the north the Trinh line ruled from Hanoi, while the Nguyen family ruled in the area around Hue. In the late 17th Century, Nguyen-Anh, a Hue general, asked for French military help as he fought and eventually united the two domains into the empire of Vietnam, with himself as the first emperor. In exchange for their assistance, Nguyen-Anh, agreed to cede Da Nang and the Con Son islands to the French.

By 1858, citing mistreatment of French nationals and Vietnamese Christians, the French military began operations which eventually led to the French seizing Cochin China (Saigon and the Mekong Delta) and abolishing the name Vietnam. In 1884 Annam accepted a French protectorate and conceded to France a separate protectorate over Tonkin. In 1887 both Annam and Tonkin became part of the Union of Indochina. During World War II Indochina was occupied by Japanese forces, which set up the autonomous state of Vietnam and installed the previous emperor, Bao Dai as a puppet ruler.

It was at the end of 1941 when Vo Nguyen Giap returned to the mountains of Vietnam from China, where he had earlier fled in order to avoid persecution from the French. While in China, Giap met Ho Chi Minh at the Chingsi Conference, where the Viet Minh was formed. During World War II his orders were to begin organizational and intelligence work among the Montagnards. Teaming with a local bandit, named Chu Van Tan, Giap ran a network of 34 agents throughout the north. During World War II he also recruited and trained a military force that would number some 10,000 men, although the military competence of his command was poor, with their only successes coming in the systematic liquidation of rice landlords opposed to Communism.

Ho Chi Minh is the best known of some 50 aliases used by Nguyen Tat Thanh, who was known as the father of the new Vietnam, he was the founder of the Vietnamese Communist Party and became president of the Democratic Republic of Vietnam in 1946, serving in that capacity until his death in 1969 – there were apparently no term limits in that democratic republic.

In 1911, when he was 21-years of age, Bac Ho (Uncle Ho, as he was called by many) signed on as a cook's apprentice to a French ship. It would be 30 years before he would return to Vietnam. In those years he would master English, French, German and Mandarin Chinese. He spent several politically active years in France. In 1919 he went to the Versailles Peace Conference, where he tried to present a plan, with no luck, for the independence of Vietnam to Woodrow Wilson, and in 1920 he became a founding member of the French Communist Party. In 1923 Bac Ho traveled to Moscow for training at the Communist International, after which he was sent to Canton, where he formed the Revolutionary Youth League of Vietnam and, later, the Vietnamese Communist Party. In 1941 he returned to Vietnam and founded the Viet Minh front, the stated goal of which was independence from French rule and Chinese occupation, somewhat ironic in the fact that he had lived in those two countries for most of the previous 30 years.

The Communist Party of Vietnam fought on the side of the Allies, against Japan, throughout World War II. At the same time, they were building a new Communist National Army to resist French reoccupation of Vietnam after World War II and secure for themselves a democratic people's republic, a communist state, modeled after Stalin's Soviet Union and Mao's China. They also played host to the first Americans sent to Indochina by the Organization of Strategic Services, the OSS, which would become the CIA years later. In 1941 a young Marine lieutenant was sent to Vietnam to coordinate military activity against the Japanese, gather intelligence, and train the loosely organized army, the Viet Minh, who were later called, with bias, the Viet Cong. That Lieutenant was probably the first Marine or any type of modern U.S. military personnel to be assigned to Vietnam. Twenty-some years later, I would be just another one of the tens of thousands of U.S. Marines sent to Vietnam. Then, however, we would be fighting against the Viet Minh and the people of North Vietnam.

The Japanese, of course, were defeated in World War II. Rushing in to take advantage of the temporary vacuum of power that existed throughout much of the Far East immediately after the surrender, Bac Ho publicly declared Vietnam independent on September 2, 1945. As the allies sorted out what to do with the Southeast Asian countries of Cambodia, Laos, and Vietnam, Ho Chi Minh decided to negotiate with the French, who were tasked with the responsibility of disarming the occupying Japanese Armies, repatriate them to Japan, and restore order to Vietnam.

Although Ho's decision may seem ironic, he was more concerned at that time with the 180,000 Chinese troops still left in North Vietnam at the end of the war who were pillaging their way toward Hanoi, while supporting the Viet Minh's nationalist rivals. The North, after all, was Ho's main base of power, and he realized that he had to secure that first and foremost, so he reached agreement for the French to stay for five years in return for recognizing Vietnam as a free state within the French Union. By 1946, when France had rebuilt their colonial administration throughout Vietnam, China agreed to remove its troops. As soon as they did, the Viet Minh increased their attacks against the French in both North and South Vietnam.

The Viet Minh War, as it was called, lasted eight years. During that time, despite massive American aid, and the existence of large numbers of Vietnamese anticommunists who rallied to support Bao Dai's Associated State within the French Union, the French military was able only to control the cities and less than three months after their catastrophic defeat at Dien Bien Phu, the French signed the conventions of the Geneva Accords. These accords divided the country at the 17th parallel, along the Ben Hai River, provided for prisoner exchange, allowed 300 days of free passage of people across the parallel, and for the holding of nationwide elections on July 20, 1956.

After the signing of the Geneva Accords, Ho Chi Minh returned to Hanoi and set to the task of solidifying his power throughout the North. This included eliminating elements of the population whom he perceived as threats to his power. He also introduced a radical land reform program that resulted in the hasty arrest, prosecution, and imprisonment of more than 50,000 people, and the execution of more than 10,000 others.

In the South, Ngo Dinh Diem was also solidifying his power base. A staunch anticommunist Catholic, Diem's base was strengthened significantly as more than 900,000 refugees, many of them Catholic, took advantage of the free passage to flee the Communist North. Despite that, Diem was convinced he could not win a nationwide election, so in 1955, with the urging of the United States, Diem refused to implement the election portion of the Geneva Accord and, instead, held a referendum vote on his continued rule of the South Vietnam, which he won with 98.2% of the vote. Ignoring the obvious fact that the election had been rigged, the United States, France, Great Britain, Australia, New Zealand, Italy, Japan, Thailand and South Korea recognized Diem as President of the Republic of Vietnam. Within days the United States would close its consulate in Hanoi, and the course that would result in the deaths of 58,183 Americans was unalterably set.

The threat of a communist Asian continent was overwhelming and, as a matter of national policy, the United States was committed to stopping communism in its tracks wherever it could. No President during those years had the insight or political vision to adequately address the complicated issues they would have to face, and the histories of the United States and Vietnam would be inextricably woven together forever in time.

Battle Honors

1ST BATTALION (REIN), TWENTY SEVENTH MARINES

DA NANG

QUANG NAM

PHU BAI

ALLEN BROOK

HUE

GOI NOI IS.

ACKNOWLEDGEMENTS

I owe a debt of gratitude to the following; Mike Graff for your; writing, edits, research and patience, A.K. Thompson for your professionalism, formatting ideas, writing and helpful critiques, and John Thompson, for saving the draft manuscript when the electronic copy was lost. Lloyd Fernung for your photographs, adding key dates, your personal recollections, and encouragement, and Grady Birdsong for your encouragement, maps, corrections, support and detailed editing. Additionally, thanks to Barb (Gunner) Lazaris, Tim Rock, Tom Shaw, Jane (Crabtree) Nelson, Ashley Deen, Malcolm Berg and Elizabeth (Berg) Nagy for reading various drafts and offering your insights and suggestions. Finally, thank you Lenora M. Berg for your support and understanding for my need to reduce to writing the experiences of the (my) war. Thank you Jan and Joe McDaniel for your skills finalizing and preparing the manuscript. I may have inadvertently left out a few folks - for that I apologize.

If anyone takes offense, I apologize. Any factual errors are my own. *Letters Home* was written in part from faded memories, inaccurate notes, biased letters and bad dreams. It is a personal memoir not an official record or military history.

TO THE MARINES PAST, PRESENT AND FUTURE — SEMPER FIDELIS

For more about the 1st Battalion 27th Marine Regiment in Vietnam:

- *To The Sound of The Guns – 1st Battalion, 27th Marines from Hawaii to Vietnam 1966-1968* by Grady T. Birdsong
- *YOUNG BLOOD – A History of the 1st Battalion 27th Marines, Vietnam: February 23 – September 12, 1968* by Gary E. Jarvis, Ph.D.

www.ingramcontent.com/pod-product-compliance
Lightning Source LLC
Chambersburg PA
CBHW041137120626
46547CB00020B/3024